NEW ZEALAND

CONTENTS

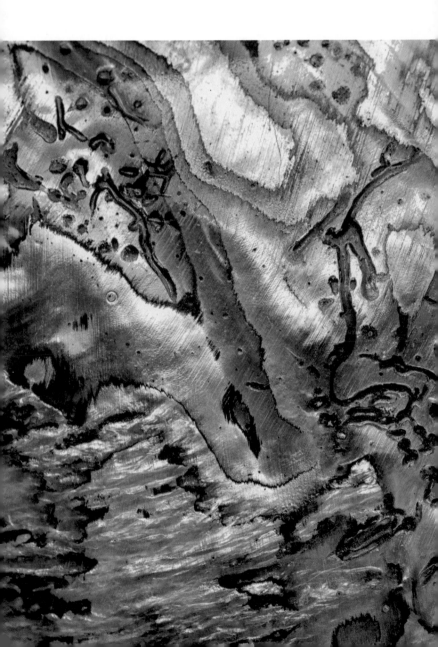

DISCOVER 6

EXPERIENCE 60

NEED TO KNOW 282

Left: Pearly interior of a pāua shell, a Māori treasure
Previous page: Mount Taranaki/Egmont, veiled in white cloud
Front cover: Sunrise over Mount Maunganui's summit track

DISCOVER

Queenstown, set on the shores of Lake Wakatipu

WELCOME TO
NEW ZEALAND

Named Aotearoa, "the land of the long white cloud", by the Māori, New Zealand is a place that seduces the senses. An explosion of dramatic scenery, this far-flung Pacific island has it all: magnificent mountains veiled in puffs of white cloud, icy-blue glacial lakes, wild unspoiled coastlines, idyllic swathes of wine country and cool, cultural cities. Whatever your dream trip to New Zealand includes, this DK Eyewitness Travel Guide is the perfect companion.

1 Auckland's skyline, with the iconic Sky Tower.

2 New Zealand's favourite coffee, the flat white.

3 A traditional Māori welcome in Rotorua.

4 A hiker walking through Mount Cook National Park.

Dominated by diverse landscapes, Aotearoa is a place of breathtaking natural beauty. On the North Island, you can stroll through subtropical kauri forests, hike past sleeping volcanoes or admire steam-gushing geysers. The South Island offers the chance to discover remote fiords, peaceful lakes and the glacier-covered Southern Alps. The country's pristine coastlines are dotted with isolated beaches, home to penguins, while inland rolling green pastures are grazed by meandering sheep. Scattered here and there are orchards bursting with seasonal fruit, farms selling wild honey and world-class vineyards offering wine tastings. Wherever you go, you're sure to be welcomed by the ever-friendly locals.

Craving the bustle of a city? You won't be disappointed. Shaped around a sparkling harbour, buzzing Auckland is New Zealand's largest city and a hub for shopping and nightlife. Further south, the compact capital Wellington has a cool café culture, creative craft beer scene and cutting-edge museums. There are plenty of other cities to explore, including cultural Christchurch and ever-adventurous Queenstown.

New Zealand can overwhelm with its sheer size and diversity. We've broken the country down into easily navigable chapters, with detailed itineraries, expert local knowledge and colourful, comprehensive maps to help you plan the perfect visit. Whether you're staying for a weekend, a week or longer, this Eyewitness guide will ensure that you see the very best New Zealand has to offer. Enjoy the book, and enjoy New Zealand.

REASONS TO LOVE
NEW ZEALAND

Dramatic landscapes, creative cities, adrenaline hotspots and tranquil vineyards: New Zealand's wonderful mix of untamed wilderness and cool culture provides endless reasons to love it. Here are some of our favourites.

1 EPIC SCENERY

Wonderfully wild, New Zealand boasts awe-inspiring scenery, whether it's dense kauri forests hemmed in by dramatic seascapes or the snow-capped summits of the Southern Alps.

WINE-TASTING AT A VINEYARD 2

Thanks to its bountiful countryside, New Zealand produces world-renowned – and truly delicious – wines. Sample them on a tastebud-tickling tour of the vineyards of Hawke's Bay *(p148)* or Wairau Valley *(p204)*.

3 MĀORI HERITAGE

Discover Māori culture beyond the haka in Rotorua *(p116)* by attending a hāngi, a traditional feast cooked underground. Or head to Waitangi *(p94)* to learn how intricate Māori meeting-houses are made.

WALKS IN THE WILDERNESS 4

There's no better way to experience New Zealand's great outdoors than on a tramp, so lace up your hiking boots and tackle one of the many trails threading the country.

RELAX IN ROTORUA 5

After a day out exploring, unwind in one of Rotorua's thermal pools *(p116)*. For utter indulgence, visit one of the city's tranquil spas for a dip followed by a reviving massage.

WONDERFUL WILDLIFE 6

Home of the famous kiwi, New Zealand is awash with wildlife. Spy penguins on the Otago Peninsula *(p254)*, whale watch at Kaikoura *(p196)* or swim with seals off Abel Tasman *(p188)*.

FREEDOM OF THE ROAD 7

New Zealand's wonderfully scenic roads, winding through its spectacular landscapes, are perfect for road trips. For the ultimate sense of freedom, hire a campervan and hit the road.

KIWI HOSPITALITY 8

A laid back bunch, Kiwis love to chat – a simple "Kia ora!" will usually get them talking. Or why not experience their chilled out approach to life at a local farmstay or B&B.

9 CITIES OF CULTURE

Each of New Zealand's cities is distinctly unique, whether it's artsy Christchurch, vibrant Auckland or down-to-earth "Welli", dubbed the capital of culture, cafés and craft beers.

10 NATURAL WONDERS

The country abounds in otherwordly wonders: picture the shimmering veils of the Southern Lights, glinting glaciers and the glowworm-lit Waitomo Caves *(p114)*.

FRESH FROM THE FARM *11*

With orchards bursting and wild herbs plentiful, New Zealand's farmers markets overflow with organic produce, including the sought-after, health-giving Mānuka honey.

EXTREME SPORTS *12*

After an adrenaline rush? New Zealand offers countless ways to get your kicks, from white-water rafting to bungy-jumping and sky diving. Head to adventure capital Queenstown to try them *(p242)*.

EXPLORE
NEW ZEALAND

This guide divides New Zealand into seven colour-coded sightseeing areas, as shown on the map below. Find out more about each area on the following pages.

Tasman Sea

AUSTRALASIA

VIETNAM PHILIPPINES
MALAYSIA
MICRONESIA
MARSHALL ISLANDS

Pacific Ocean

INDONESIA
PAPUA NEW GUINEA
SOLOMON ISLANDS
VANUATU
FIJI

Indian Ocean

AUSTRALIA
NEW CALEDONIA

NEW ZEALAND

South Island

Karamea Bight
Cape Foulwind Westport
Punakaiki Reefton
Greymouth Springs Junction

Okarito
CANTERBURY AND THE WEST COAST
p206
Franz Josef Glacier
Springfield
Mount Cook
Methven
Haast
Rolleston
Mount Aspiring National Park
Hunter
Fairlie
Geraldine
Twizel
Canterbury Bight
Lake Benmore
Temuka
Milford Sound
Wanaka
Omarama
Doubtful Sound
Fjordland National Park
Queenstown
Cromwell
Waitaki
Te Anau
Alexandra
Oamaru
Manapouri
Palmerston
OTAGO AND SOUTHLAND
p238
Waitati
Gore
Dunedin
Riverton
Otago Peninsula
Balclutha
Foveaux Strait
Invercargill
Bluff
Stewart Island
Oban

0 kilometers 100
0 miles 100

N
↑

GETTING TO KNOW
NEW ZEALAND

New Zealand comprises two islands. The North Island is most populated but predominantly rural, flourishing with prime farmland and easy-going seaside towns. The South Island is wilder, with majestic mountains, lush rainforest and ragged fiords that captivate the hearts of photographers.

PAGE 62

AUCKLAND

Perched on an isthmus, New Zealand's largest city is shaped by a meandering harbour and punctured by now-dormant volcanic peaks. Auckland's bustling centre is filled with elegant art galleries, engaging museums, vibrant quays lined with stylish restaurants and the lofy spire of the iconic Sky Tower. A little further out, fashionable seaside suburbs boast high-end boutique shops and some of the finest restaurants in New Zealand. Picturesque islands flank the east, accessible on day trips; and subtropical rainforest hems in the west side with wild sweeping spectacular beaches.

Best for
Harbourside wanderings and boutique shopping

Home to
Auckland War Memorial Museum, Auckland Art Gallery, Hauraki Gulf Islands, Sky Tower

Experience
Ascending the soaring Sky Tower for panoramic views over the city

NORTHLAND

PAGE 90

Subtropical and rural, Northland is staunchly Māori, yet has a number of historical European settlements too. The Bay of Islands, dotted with colourful seaside towns such as Kerikeri, is the region's main tourist hub: its sheltered bays are perfect for kayaking and its marine reserves are a scuba diver's paradise. The area is also home to the Waitangi Treaty Grounds, one of the country's most important historic sites. Further north lie the endless sands of Ninety Mile Beach and New Zealand's most northernly point, Cape Reinga, while its wild west is home to ancient giant kauri trees.

Best for
Stunning islands and Māori culture

Home to
Waitangi Treaty Grounds, Whangarei

Experience
Taking a low tide tour along the spectacular Ninety Mile Beach

CENTRAL NORTH ISLAND

PAGE 110

This area plays host to New Zealand's most varied landscapes. Sheep-grazed fields and fertile orchards cover great swathes of the region. The east coast – home to verdant vineyards and Art-Deco Napier – is lined by lush rainforests that stretch down to golden sands. To the north lie beautiful beaches of the Coromandel Peninsula, while Lake Taupo is set amid one of the world's most active volcanic regions, a place of steaming geysers, towering volcanoes and natural thermal spas that attract flocks of tourists.

Best for
Geothermal wonders and glowworm-filled caves

Home to
Waitomo Caves, Rotorua, Tongariro National Park, Napier

Experience
Hiking through incredible volcanic landscapes on the Tongariro Alpine Crossing

→

PAGE 150

WELLINGTON AND THE SOUTH

Tucked away in a natural harbour, laid-back Wellington is the country's cool, cultural capital. A hipster hub, this compact city is peppered with arty cafés, craft breweries and top-notch museums, and is surrounded by rolling hills criss-crossed with walking trails. Four rural retreats radiate from the city's north: Kapiti Island, home to thriving native birdlife; the verdant micro-vineyards of Wairarapa; the wilds of Wanganui National Park; and Egmont National Park, home to the towering conical peak of Mount Taranaki/Egmont.

Best for
Café culture and rural escapes

Home to
Wellington, Palmerston North, Egmont National Park, New Plymouth, Whanganui

Experience
Sipping on a flat white, the country's signature coffee, in a harbourside café

PAGE 178

MARLBOROUGH AND NELSON

Stretching to the northeast of the South Island, the rolling peninsulas of the Marlborough Sounds are scattered with hidden bays and surrounded by secluded islands. To the south, the area's expansive vineyards fuse elegant cellar doors with fine dining restaurants, and at coastal Kaikoura, steep, soaring mountains erupt from the sea, and the waters are home to whales, dolphins and seals. To the west, Abel Tasman's cobalt waters are perfect for kayaking, while Kahurangi's pristine, forested hills are a hiker's dream.

Best for
Wine tasting and whale watching

Home to
Marlborough Sounds, Nelson, Abel Tasman National Park, Kahurangi National Park

Experience
Kayaking around the stunning coastline of Abel Tasman National Park

CANTERBURY AND THE WEST COAST

The magnificent peaks of the Southern Alps dominate this region: towering snowy mountains heave with glaciers while mist-shrouded glacial lakes dot the landscape. Canterbury, with its sprawling farmland, is home to Christchurch, a charming city that boasts quirky cafés and colourful street art. The wind-swept, sparsely populated west coast is the place for solitude, its wave-sculptured coastlines backed by rugged, forested mountains and seaside settlements.

Best for
Awe-inspiring mountain scenery and cobalt-coloured lakes

Home to
Christchurch, Westland Tai Poutini National Park, Arthur's Pass National Park, Aoraki/ Mount Cook National Park

Experience
A guided hiking tour over the icy expanse of Fox Glacier

OTAGO AND SOUTHLAND

The southern part of the South Island is adorned with majestic scenery and vibrant cities. The sheer-sided peaks and tranquil waters of Fiordlands National Park dominate the west. Perched on the edge of Lake Wakatipu, and encircled by craggy mountains, Queenstown is this region's tourist hub, attracting thrill-seekers year-round. Nearby, compact Dunedin, the South Island's second largest city, revels to the tune of 20,000 university students, and nearby, tiny Oamaru has retained its charming Victorian centre.

Best for
Adrenaline-packed activities and magical fiords

Home to
Queenstown, Fiordland National Park, Otago Peninsula, Oamaru, Mount Aspiring National Park, Dunedin, Invercargill, Stewart Island

Experience
Bungy jumping in Queenstown

←

 Chilling out in
the city centre.

② The beautiful coastline
of Waiheke Island.

③ A glorious sunset from
Auckland's Skytower.

④ Mudbrick Vineyard amid
lovely gardens, Waiheke.

New Zealand's North and South Islands are packed with things to see and do, and it's relatively easy to travel around too. These itineraries will inspire you to make the most of your visit.

2 DAYS
in Auckland

▌ *Day 1*

Morning Wake to the rhythm of the City of Sails with a coffee at Caffetteria Allpress *(8 Drake St, Freemans Bay)*, before heading to the redeveloped waterfront around Viaduct Harbour *(p75)* where you'll find the excellent Maritime Museum *(p74)*. Afterwards, make for Auckland's main transport hub, Britomart *(p76)*, for a spot of pre-lunch shopping. When hunger strikes, tuck into Vietnamese street-food at trendy Café Hanoi *(Excelsior Building, cnr Galway and Commerce St)*.

Afternoon After lunch, roll yourself towards the Auckland Art Gallery Toi o Tāmaki *(p68)*, which is housed in an award-winning building on the corner of Albert Park. This gallery has a spectacular collection of local art that offers insight into Kiwi and Māori culture. Get there for the one-hour afternoon tour at 1:30pm, before a few hours exploring on your own. Break for a snack and drink at the bright café on the first floor.

Evening Watch the sun set from the sky-deck viewing platform of the iconic Skytower *(p72)*, before sampling the city's nightlife. Start your evening at nearby Depot Eatery and Oyster Bar *(p74)*, a chic local favourite with shared small plates and a fantastic wine list, before heading where the winds take you.

▌ *Day 2*

Morning While the rest of the city is still waking up, stroll downtown and catch an early ferry (sailings start at 6am) to the white-sand beaches and top-notch wineries of Waiheke Island, only 40 minutes away. The island's main town, Oneroa, is a short stroll from the wharf – explore its cafés and boutiques, but save yourself for lunch at Mudbrick Vineyard *(www.mudbrick.co.nz)*, where you can indulge in wine tastings and a delicious meal against a spectacular backdrop of Hauraki Bay views.

Afternoon After a long, decadent lunch, it's time to explore Waiheke's more rugged side on the two- to three-hour Matiatia Headland Track, which follows the clifftops, rolling hills and secret coves of the island. Make sure to stop by the i-SITE at the harbour to pick up a leaflet with information on the hike, as there are a few different routes you can take.

Evening Once you're back in the city, put on your glad rags and head to Ponsonby, Auckland's most affluent suburb. Sleek Japanese restaurant Cocoro *(56a Brown St, Ponsonby)* has an exquisite three-course tasting menu (book ahead). Follow this with a drink at late-night boozer Mea Culpa *(Unit 3, 175 Ponsonby Road)*, which mixes sensational cocktails.

←

 1 Whangarei's quayside.

2 A Māori statue at Waitangi Treaty Grounds.

3 Riding down the Te Paki Stream sand dunes.

4 Scenic Hakianga Harbour.

4 DAYS
in Northland

Day 1

Morning Start your trip by exploring the underwater worlds at Poor Knights Islands, just 23 km (14 miles) offshore of Tutukaka (p98). Dive Tutukaka (*diving.co. nz*) operate snorkelling and diving trips.

Afternoon Drive 6 km (4 miles) further north along the winding road to explore the gorgeous beach at Matapouri (p98) and walk the short coastal track to nearby Whale Bay.

Evening Stay overnight at Lodge Bordeaux (*lodgebordeaux.co.nz*) in Whangarei. Stroll down to the quayside for a dinner of Asian-fusion cuisine at No. 8 Restaurant (*8 Quayside, Town Basin*).

Day 2

Morning Rise early and follow the SH-1 an hour north to the Bay of Islands, the birthplace of modern New Zealand. The Waitangi Treaty Grounds (p94) is unmiss- able. Take in the treaty house and a Māori Cultural Performance.

Afternoon It's a half-hour walk into Paihia to lunch on the wharf at Charlotte's Kitchen (p100). Afterwards, hop on the 15-minute ferry to historic Russell (departures on the half-hour). It's a stiff walk up Flagstaff Hill, but the panoramic views are worth it.

Evening Return on the passenger ferry and request a Waitangi drop off (3pm ferry only) to reach your car. Drive on to workaday Kaitaia and book a couple of nights at Kauri Lodge motel (*kaurilodge motel.co.uk*). A good locals' favourite for dinner is Bushmans Hut (*7 Bank St*).

Day 3

Morning Make sure to reserve your full- day Cape Reinga (*harriosonscape reingatours.co.nz*) tour ahead – it starts at 9am when you're picked up from your hotel in a 4x4 bus. Walk to the iconic lighthouse overlooking the meeting of the Tasman Sea and Pacific Ocean, drive the epic Ninety Mile Beach (p106) and go tobogganing on the vast sand dunes at Te Paki Stream. Follow a picnic lunch with a swim at pretty Tapotupotu Bay.

Evening Kaitaia has a few casual diners for a bite to eat; Mussel Rock Cafe and Bar (*75 Commerce St*) is one of the best.

Day 4

Morning Journey to the charming backwater village of Rawene (p105) on the car ferry from the quaint settlement of Kohukohu. At lunchtime, pull up a chair on the deck at the bijou Boatshed Café (p103).

Afternoon Opononi (p105) and Omapere are twin towns further along the pictur- esque south bank of Hokianga Harbour and there are nearby walks to view epic sand dunes. Check in for your final night at the swish Copthorne Hotel and Resort (*millenniumhotels.com*).

Evening Get up close to the majestic kauri trees in Waipoua Forest (p106) on a guided night time walk in the forest (*footprintswaipoua.co.nz*). Greet the ancient 2,000 year-old Tane Mahuta kauri tree. If you're lucky, your trip to this part of the country will conclude with a sighting of the elusive nocturnal kiwi.

←

1 Stunning Cathedral Cove.

2 Abseiling into the network at Waitomo Caves.

3 The charming Government Garde at Rotorua.

4 The pools at Wai-O-Taupu.

10 DAYS
in the North Island

Day 1

Begin your tour of the North Island in Coromandel Town, on the beautiful Coromandel Peninsula, and hop on-board the Driving Creek Railway *(p133)* for a trip through native forests high above the town. Then it's an hour's drive across the peninsula to remarkable Hot Water Beach *(p132)*, where you can dig your own hot pool in the sand. Afterwards, cool off with a swim at picturesque Cathedral Cove. Spend the afternoon exploring the peninsula's vibrant art scene: browse galleries and artist's studios in Coromandel Town *(p133)*. Then, it's on to Thames, "Gateway to the Coromandel", where Boutique Cotswold Cottage is your home for the night *(www.cotswoldcottage.co.nz)*.

Day 2

Waitomo Caves are New Zealand's most celebrated underground wonder – take a tour combining a boat ride through the luminescent Glowworm Caves and a guided walk through vast chambers dripping with stalactite formations *(p114)*. Feeling adventurous? The brave can try black-water rafting through Ruakuri Cave, or abseil or zipline through the other caverns. Above ground, take the short but pleasant walk to Ruakuri Natural Tunnel. Suitably tired out from the days activities, overnight at charming little Abseil Breakfast Inn *(www.abseilinn. co.nz)*, which is within walking distance of the caves.

Day 3

Rise early for the two-hour drive east to the popular (and notoriously smelly) themal village of Rotorua *(p116)*. Stroll the Government Gardens and the lakeshore to St Faith's Anglican Church in the Māori village of Ohinemutu, around which Rotorua sprung). Further around the lake, take a gondola ride up to the skyline lookout on Mount Ngongotaha *(p118)* for panoramic views of Lake Rotorua. Set aside the evening for a visit to Tamaki Māori Village *(p119)*, to discover traditional Māori crafts and traditions. Dinner is an unforgettable hāngi feast, cooked in an earth oven. Splash out with two nights' stay at stylish Peppers on the Point hotel *(www.peppers.co.nz/ on-the-point)*.

Day 4

After breakfast in town, drive out to Wai-o-tapu Thermal Wonderland *(p142)*. You could set your watch by the Lady Knox geyser, which erupts at 10:15am every day. While there, marvel at the vibrantly coloured Champagne Pool, Primrose Terraces and Artist's Palette. Rotorua has plenty of adventure activities for those after an adrenalin hit. Try your hand at river jetting, rafting, canopy tours – and don't leave town without spending an hour or two soaking away your cares in the famous hot mineral waters of the Polynesian Spa *(p116)*.

$\rightarrow$

Day 5

Today, it's time to explore the country's most active volcano, White Island (p140). Head east to the Bay of Plenty and sunny Whakatāne (p140), the gateway to the island, which is located 48 km (30 miles) offshore. You can take a boat trip out to the island, or get an exhilaratingly aerial view on a helicopter tour. Most of the volcano is below the water, so once you're on the island, you'll find yourself within the volcano's crater. Make sure to pull out your camera: the almost lunar landscape, with its billowing white smoke and yellow-and-orange hues, makes for some truly astonishing photographs. Leave enough time to drive to Gisborne, where an evening of fine dining at elegant Bushmere Arms is highly recommended (Hexton, 4071).

Day 6

Rise early and head into Hawke's Bay. Here, take a tractor tour along the rugged beach and spot the colony of nesting gannets at Cape Kidnappers (p144).

Tours are dependent on the tides, so check times online and book ahead. Have lunch at a Hawke's Bay vineyard (p148) and purchase a bottle of world-class Chardonnay or Syrah before moving on to Napier, one of the world's finest Art Deco towns (p124). Continue the wine tasting into the evening at Mission Estate Winery, which has an award-winning restaurant and stylish accommodation (www.mission estate.co.nz).

Day 7

Drive to Taupo (p145), the main town on Lake Taupo, for a relaxing day by the water. The town is famous for trout-fishing, as well as a whole variety of watersports. Pick up a fishing licence (ask at the information centre) and set up with a rod on the lakeside to see what the catch of the day is. After some leisurely angling, head to the powerful Huka Falls (p142), where the lake empties down the Waikato River. There's a footbridge so you can get up close to the raging waters. Base yourself in Turangi for a couple of nights; it's the quieter alternative to Taupo.

① Nesting gannets at Cape Kidnappers.

② Canoeing on Lake Taupo.

③ Wellington's hilly and green Botanic Gardens.

④ The iconic and stunning Tongariro Alpine Trek.

⑤ A tour of Wellington's famous Weta Workshops.

Day 8

Set aside a full day for Tongariro National Park (p122), a UNESCO World Heritage site and one of the country's most epic natural environments. The best way to take in the park is by hiking the strenuous Tongariro Alpine Crossing, one of the finest day walks in the country. Its volcanic landscape and striking emerald-green lakes are unlike anywhere else in New Zealand, but if 18.5 km (11.5 miles) is more than you want to tackle, choose from the shorter walks on the slopes of the park's (occasionally active) volcanoes.

Day 9

Get an early start to arrive in Wellington, New Zealand's capital of cool, in time for a seasonal lunch at Nikau Café (p154). Set aside a couple of hours for the Museum of New Zealand Te Papa Tongarewa (p160) and its outstanding Māori exhibits. Stop for coffee at Memphis Belle Coffee House (p159), and then enjoy the views from the Wellington Cable Car on a ride up to scenic Kelburn. Meander through the lush Botanic Gardens (p159), before heading to trendy QT Wellington hotel, where you'll spend the night (qthotels andresorts.com/wellington).

Day 10

In the morning, take the Marine Drive Tour around the city's wild and windy coast, with its rocky headlands, sheltered bays and rolling farmland. If you're a Lord of the Rings buff or a fan of Thor: Ragnarok, you can't miss dropping in to the famous Weta Workshop en-route; here exhibits of props and sets will fascinate and astonish in equal measure (www.wetaworkshop.com). In the early evening, head to the eco sanctuary of Zealandia (p158), abundant with native birds, wildlife and reptiles. Grab a torch and join the night time tour to spot shy kiwi birds, glowworms and tuatara.

←

1 Lush vegetation meets golden sands on Totaranui beach, Abel Tasman.

2 Christchurch's landmark Cardboard Cathedral.

3 Rowing on the River Avon in Christchurch.

4 A majestic whale dives into the ocean, Kaikoura.

2 WEEKS
in the South Island

Day 1

Kick off your tour in the pleasant city of Christchurch *(p210)*. Cathedral Square is a poignant reminder of the earthquake that struck the city in 2011 – see the ruins of the old church and the award-winning transitional Cardboard Cathedral. At the nearby Antigua Boat Sheds *(p210)* hire a boat for a paddle on River Avon; bring a delicious hamper from the café on board. In the late afternoon, drive two hours' to Kaikoura for a night at the friendly Austin Heights B&B *(www. austinheights.nz)*.

Day 2

Rise with the sun and head out onto the water with Whale Watch Kaikoura *(p43)* for your chance of spotting all manner of marine life. Back on dry land, try some of the town's famous crayfish at Kaikoura Seafood BBQ *(p196)* before driving 5 km (3 miles) southeast of town to the Kaikoura Peninsula Walkway to explore the rugged coastline on foot. Hop back in the car and follow the coastal road north for two hours to luxurious Marlborough Lodge in Blenheim *(p200)*, pausing to spot fur seals at Ohau Point.

Day 3

Spend the morning tasting New Zealand's most famous wine variety, Marlborough Sauvignon Blanc, at Wairau River Wines, followed by lunch at the restaurant *(11 Rapaura Rd, Blenheim)*. After your meal has settled, continue to Picton *(p194)*, where you can leave the car. Catch a water-taxi to the delightful waterfront Mahana Lodge *(www.mahanalodge.co.nz)* beside the Queen Charlotte Track in Marlborough Sounds *(p182)*.

Day 4

After breakfast, take a water-taxi back to Picton and drive the winding, delightful Queen Charlotte Drive *(p194)* to laid-back Nelson *(p184)*. Check into the Trailways Hotel *(trailwayshotel.co.nz)*, before an afternoon getting to know the town. Follow the Maitai River Walkway to visit the Suter Art Gallery *(p184)*, with its paintings and ceramics. That evening, fall in love with Nelson over dinner at the iconic Boat Shed Café *(p187)*, which has panoramic sunset views over the sea.

Day 5

Plan a full day exploring the unmissable Abel Tasman National Park *(p188)* on a tour with Wilsons Abel Tasman *(abel tasman.co.nz)* who will meet you bright and early at Kaiteriteri, gateway to the park. The tour starts with a cruise, before you are dropped off for a breaktaking hike along the park's magnificent Coast Track. The day ends with a cruise back to Kaiteriteri; from here return to Nelson.

→

Day 6

For a morning coffee hit, make for Kush Coffee *(5 Church St)*, before heading to the surreal rock formations of Pancake Rocks in Paparoa National Park *(p232)*. Stop to explore and then drive to Westland Tai Poutini National Park and its unmissable glacier region *(p216)*. The best way to see Franz Josef glacier is on a heli-hike: fly over the glacier before a thrilling walk on the ice. Spend your night recounting your day at the Te Waonui Forest Retreat *(www.tewaonui.co.nz)*.

Day 7

After the adrenaline of the previous day, slow down on an ambling drive through the temperate rainforest towards the lakeside town of Wanaka *(p272)*. If you have children in tow, you will find head-scratching entertainment at Stuart Landsborough's Puzzling World *(p273)*. In the late afternoon, indulge in a wine tasting at Rippon Vineyard *(p273)*. Overnight at Edgewater Hotel, which is known for its great restaurant *(www.edgewater.co.nz)*.

Day 8

It's a scenic route to pretty Arrowtown *(p274)*, where you'll have lunch at the cute Provisions of Arrowtown *(www.provisions ofarrowtown.co.nz)*. Continue on the Lake Hayes road towards Queenstown *(p247)*, the gem of the South Island. Settle into elegant Hotel St Moritz *(www.stmoritz. co.nz)* before riding the Skyline Gondola *(p246)* up to Bob's Peak. Dine overlooking the town and Lake Wakatipu.

Day 9

Rise early, and ready yourself for adventure. Go bungy jumping, white-water rafting, jet-boating, paragliding, sky diving or heli-biking, or all of them in one day with a combo deal in summer. In winter, hit the ski fields at the Remarkables and Coronet Peak. Once you've had your fill, kick back and relax with a drink at charming Bardeaux *(Eureka Arcade)*.

Day 10

Book in a daytrip from Queenstown to visit Fiordland National Park *(p248)* and

① Westland Tai Poutini National Park.

② Queenstown's gondola.

③ Sunset at Nugget Point.

④ Jetboating in Queenstown

⑤ Dunedin Railway Station.

the dramatic Milford Sound (p250) – Intercity NZ (intercity.co.nz) do a great tour. Spend many happy hours soaking up the fiord's sheer cliffs, lush green scenery and plummeting waterfalls.

Day 11

Set out from Queenstown for the sparsely populated Catlins (p280). The winding roads and rugged landscape encourage a slower pace of life, so take your time. Call in at the petrified forest in Curio Bay, say "hi" to the cute Hector's dolphins in Porpoise Bay and snap a picture at Nugget Point's iconic lighthouse. Book a night at Breadalbane House in Kaka Point (accommodationcatlins.co.nz).

Day 12

Breakfast with an unbeatable view of the Catlins coast at your hotel before heading to Dunedin (p260). Take a short walking tour of the city before an afternoon spent exploring the Otago Peninsula (p254), home to New Zealand's only castle, Larnach Castle (p254). In the evening, watch blue penguins returning to their

burrows, before heading back to Dunedin to fall asleep at The Brothers Boutique Hotel (www.brothershotel.co.nz).

Day 13

Drive to the wonderfully preserved town of Oamaru (p256) for lunch at Riverstone Kitchen (1431 SH-1). Turn inland towards Mount Cook National Park (p222) and drop your bags at the sumptuous Hermitage hotel (hermitage.co.nz). This afternoon, trek some of the nearby Hooker Valley Track, a half-day tramp with views of high peaks, alpine streams and glaciers.

Day 14

After a lazy breakfast, hit State Highway 8 south, and then east along the water – take plenty of breaks to photograph reflections of Mount Cook. At the southwestly point of Lake Tekapo, Mount John Observatory (earthandsky. co.nz) has the spectacularly sited Astro-Cafe. After lunch, it's a gentle motor through Mackenzie Country back towards Christchurch.

NEW ZEALAND FOR
WALKERS

There's no better way to explore New Zealand than by lacing up your walking boots and heading off on a hike – or, as the Kiwis call it, a tramp. The country has an astounding variety of walking routes, from challenging hikes over volcanic moonscapes to easy ambles through ancient forests.

Short Walks

You don't need to be a hardcore hiker to discover New Zealand on foot. Gentle short walks abound: enjoy fabulous coastal views along the Coromandel Walkway or wander with giants in Waipoua Forest *(p106),* home to towering kauri trees. For something a bit more strenuous, try Avalanche Peak in Arthur's Pass National Park *(p218)* to enjoy dramatic views over glacier-gouged valleys. Most of the iconic Great Walks have short walk sections too, such as the 3-hour Routeburn Taster.

→

The Coromandel Walkway's scenic coastal views

Full-Day Hikes

New Zealand boasts a number of epic day hikes, so grab some scroggin (Kiwi slang for trail mix) and get walking. Take on the challenging Tongariro Alpine Crossing *(p123)* to traverse a landscape dotted with bright blue lakes. On the North Island, wander the slopes of Mount Taranaki/Egmont's perfectly cylindrical cone on the Pouakai Crossing *(p166)*. On the South Island, the area around Wanaka *(p272)* has some spectacular day hikes – both the well-trodden trail to Roy's Peak and the lesser-known path to Isthmus Peak offer breathtaking views over the Southern Alps.

← Hikers on the Tongariro Alpine Crossing

> **INSIDER TIP**
> **A Wild Night**
>
> For a truly Kiwi night out, hunker down in one of the country's beautifully located backcountry huts. Run by the Department of Conservation, most offer dorm-style sleeping and stunning views.

→ Traversing volcanic terrain in Tongariro

Overnight Tramps

Offering some of the country's best hiking, New Zealand's Great Walks wind through awe-inspiring landscapes, from ancient forests on the Heaphy Track *(p193)* to dramatic fjords in Milford *(p248)* to golden beaches in Abel Tasman *(p188)*. All ten trails are peppered with cosy sleeping huts to hunker down in. If you'd prefer to avoid the crowds – these routes can get very busy – there are hundreds of other backcountry trails to explore. Feeling adventurous? Walk the 3,000-km- (1,865-m-) long Te Araroa route, which stretches the whole length of New Zealand.

↑ Hikers crossing a bridge on the Heaphy Track, one of New Zealand's Great Walks

Thermal Wonders

An otherworldly landscape of popping mud pools, exploding geysers and jewel-bright thermal lakes can be found all around Rotorua. Oozing with sulphurous aromas, New Zealand's thermal heartland encompasses a dozing super volcano whose crater forms the massive Lake Taupo. Experience this raw volcanic power at one of the geothermal parks surrounding the lake – Hells Gate *(p119)*, home to a hot waterfall, and Wai-O-Tapu are two of the best.

→

A colourful thermal pool at Wai-O-Tapu

NEW ZEALAND FOR
NATURAL
WONDERS

Sky-high mountains cloaked in icy glaciers; golden beaches fringed by lush green rainforests; aquamarine lakes, isolated fiords and perfectly conical volcanoes: New Zealand is blessed with an abundance of magnificent landscapes. If you're looking for natural beauty, you're in the right place.

CHANGING LANDSCAPES

New Zealand is a geological natural wonder, one shaped in part by its location on the edge of the Australian and Pacific tectonic plates. Persistent collision between these plates has led to the creation of the Southern Alps, one of the most rapidly rising mountain ranges in the world. Volatile volcanic activity has also led to the birth of new mountains, while powerful glaciers have sculpted the landcape, carving out new valleys.

Wild Coastlines

The country's meandering coastline is incredibly diverse, ranging from the deserted sandy shores of Karekare *(p84)* to the sunken river valleys of the Marlborough Sounds *(p182)*. The country's west coast is often wild and dramatic: at Paparoa *(p232)* on the South Island you'll find limestone cliffs, caves and the bizarre Pancake Rocks, while in Northland the steep dunes of Ninety Mile Beach *(p106)*, New Zealand's most famous stretch of sand, are great for sandboarding.

→

Sunset over Karekare's beautiful sandy beach, found on the North Island

Glacial Giants

New Zealand is home to an astonishing 3,000 glaciers, with all but 20 of them blanketing the dramatic ridges of the Southern Alps. Possibly the most impressive is Franz Josef (p216) on the West Coast – climb to Alex Knob for panoramic views of its icy bulk – but it's closely followed by Fox Glacier (p276) and the Tasman's frosty expanse (p222). Get up close and personal with these frozen giants on a walking tour, or splash out on a helicopter ride over icy peaks.

A group of hikers navigating the ice fields of Fox Glacier

→

The volcanic White Island, found in the Bay of Plenty

TOP 5 PICTURESQUE SPOTS

Cathedral Cove, Coromandel
This sandy beach is framed by an elegant natural rock arch (p132).

Moke Lake, Queenstown
Fringed by wildflowers, this lake reflects the Southern Alps (p242).

McLean Falls, The Catlins
A single large cascade splits into a parade of terraced falls (p280).

Milford Sound, Fiordland
An awe-inspiring fiord encircled by steep-sided mountains (p250).

Mount Taranaki/ Egmont
This perfectly pointed volcano dominates its surrounds (p166).

Vaporous Volcanoes

Straddling the Pacific "Ring of Fire", New Zealand is dotted with active volcanoes. Admire three of the most impressive in Tongariro National Park (p122), including soaring Mount Ruapehu, the North Island's highest peak. Or head to White Island (p140), the world's most accessible marine volcano, to scuba dive among caverns with steaming vents.

Fly Like A Bird

If you've a head for heights and a taste for adventure, take to the skies for adrenaline-pumping thrills above stunning scenery. Take a helicopter for a spin over Fox Glacier *(p217)*, fly over Lake Wanaka *(p272)* or zip line through lush forest canopy in Rotorua *(p116)*. The home of bungy and paragliding, Queenstown promises aerial adventures aplenty. Dive off the ledge amid stunning mountain scenery *(www.bungy.co.nz)* or, for the ultimate airborne experience, take a leap of faith and skydive.

$\rightarrow$

Soaring through the skies on a tandem skydive

NEW ZEALAND FOR
THRILLSEEKERS

Whether it's luging down Queenstown's mountains, bungy-jumping off Kawarau Bridge or abseiling down Waitomo's underground caves, New Zealand promises endless possibilities for thrillseekers. Here we round up some of the best activites this adrenaline-packed hotspot has to offer.

Wheelie Breezie

Seeking an action-packed trip on two-wheels? New Zealand Cycle Trail operates 22 scenic routes around the country *(www.nzcycletrail.com)*. Bike rugged mountain trails in Tongariro *(p122)*, peddle through the thermal wonderland of Rotorua or wheel beside serene Marlborough Sounds *(p194)* where there are overnight lodges along the way. For leisurely wine-tours by bicycle, there are paths crisscrossing Hawkes Bay and Wairarapa vineyards.

$\leftarrow$

Riding mountain tracks, with Kapiti Island in the distance

INSIDER TIP
Adventure Tours

Want to enjoy all the activities without the hassle of organizing? Try Haka Plus Tours, who promise adventurous trips led by passionate Kiwi guides *(www.hakatours.com)*. Tours take travellers around the whole of the country, and can include heli-hiking, bungy-jumping, kayaking and horse-riding. Flying Kiwi offers explorer tours with cycling and camping along the way *(www.flyingkiwi.com)*.

Did You Know?

At 134 m (440 ft) high, Nevis in Queenstown is New Zealand's highest bungy jump.

Make a Splash

In early spring, mountain snow meltwaters swell the rivers, allowing plenty of opportunities for white-water rafting. Jet boating is big business year round: speed through narrow gorges and the thundering rapids of the Shotover River and Haka Falls *(www.shotoverjet.co.nz)* or skim the shallow waters of Dart River, which winds through Mount Aspiring National Park *(p258)*. For jet-skiing and water-skiing head to the seaside town of Tauranga *(p138)*.

→

Rushing over the rapids of Shotover River, Queenstown

Going Underground

For subterranean adventures, Waitomo Cave system is hard to beat. Here, astonishing rock formations materialize from the gloom and glowworm grottos pulsate with the eerie light of these biolumi-nescent creatures *(p114)*. Abseil down a 100 m (330 ft) chute to reach the caves, clamber through rocky tunnels and black water raft along labyrinthine waterways.

←

Climbing limestone rock formations in Waitomo Caves

Surfing and Diving

Hoping to catch the perfect wave? New Zealand's beaches are the best place to try. Experts should head to New Plymouth *(p168)* and laid back Raglan *(p128)* where rollers crash against the shore, while novices will find a good selection of surf schools at stunning Piha beach *(p84)*. If you'd rather dive beneath the waves, Poor Knights Marine Reserve is a scuba paradise *(p98)*, with volcanic coast-lines sheltering myriad marine species.

→

Catching a wave on Raglan's Manu Bay, a surfer's haven

NEW ZEALAND
ON THE WATER

With a coastline stretching 18,200 km (11,300 miles) and almost 4,000 lakes dotting its interior, New Zealand is renowned for its regattas, surfing life and cruises. From catching a wave on Piha beach to sailing majestic Doubtful Sound, these are the best ways to get out on the water.

Cruise the Sounds

Drifting through the astonishing fiords of New Zealand's Fiordland National Park is an unmissable experience *(p248)*. Take a guided cruise into striking Doubtful Sound: tours promise spectacular scenery, and even a glimpse of the elusive bottlenose dolphins that inhabit the sounds *(www.puresalt. co.nz)*. Scenic trips around Marlborough Sounds are equally popular, taking in the epic scenery and native wildlife *(p184)*.

A cruise ship voyaging ↑ through Milford Sound, Fiordland National Park

Get Hooked

This island nation is a land of lakes, many brimming with hefty trout and salmon. Some of the best angling and fly-fishing spots are in the waterways and streams between Taupo and Rotorua, a region known as a mecca for trout fishing (p144). Specialist guides in this region are so confident you'll get hooked that some offer a "no-fish no-pay" guarantee. For the best deep-sea fishing, anglers should make for the North Island's east coast, beyond the Bay of Plenty (p140); for marlin fishing, the Bay of Islands is hard to beat (p98).

← Casting for trout in the waterways surrounding Lake Taupo

PADDLE WHANGANUI RIVER WILDERNESS

Within the stunning Whanganui National Park, Whanganui River winds through deep gorges, past sheer cliffs and over 239 listed rapids (doc.govt.nz). Explore this 145-km- (90-mile-) long river on a 5-day canoe or kayak journey, overnighting in Department of Conservation backcountry huts along the way. Set out on a guided trip with Canoe Safaris (www.canoesafaris. co.nz) or rent your own vessel and enjoy a self guided tour down the river (www.canoe whanganuiriver.com).

INSIDER TIP
Take a City Ferry

One of the nicest (and least expensive) ways to cruise around Auckland Harbour is to hop on a local ferry (at. govt.nz). The 15-minute trip from the Central Business District out to the pleasant suburb of Devonport affords stunning coastal views, and costs just $7.

Sailing Phenomenon

One look at the yachts bobbing around Auckland Harbour (p74) and it's little wonder that New Zealand is such a successful sailing nation and winner of the prestigious America's Cup. Head to Auckland to watch regattas, and to the Hauraki Gulf for skippered sailing trips around the islands (p70).

→ Sailing in the calm waters around Auckland Harbour

TOP
4 MĀORI ART GALLERIES

Te Papa Tongarewa
A large collection of Māori treasures and a meeting house (p160).

Museum of Waitangi
This historic site was the location for the treaty signing (p94).

Auckland Art Gallery
Over a thousand arti-facts on display (p68).

Tawhiti Museum
Dedicated to showing early Māori life, including models of settlements (p177).

→
A group performing at the annual ASB Polyfest schools competition

NEW ZEALAND FOR
MĀORI HERITAGE

From feasts cooked in earth ovens in traditional villages to the moving site commemorating the treaty between the Māori people and the British, New Zealand abounds with places to explore the country's proud indigenous heritage and experience its culture, crafts and traditions.

Craft Culture

From stone-carving distinctive pounamu greenstone to plaiting and weaving using swamp flax, reeds or bird feathers, Māori traditional crafts are experiencing a resurgence in popular culture. Pick up a souvenir from a living Māori village such as Te Puia or Whakarewarewa - the Living Māori Village (p120) or try your hand at traditional flax weaving in an informal and hands-on workshop (www.tepuia.com).

→
Carving a pounamu greenstone, a trad-itional Māori craft

Traditional Dance

The beloved New Zealand rugby team, the All-Blacks, famously perform the haka as a challenge before every game. But in Māori culture, dancing is about more than just sport - rhythm and movement are used to convey everything from ancient stories to love. Experience a dance at Te Puia *(p120)* or watch the spectacular ASB Polyfest school competition *(asbpolyfest.co.nz)*.

← Energetic performers at ASB Polyfest celebrations

TĀ MOKO

A traditional Māori tattoo, tā moko features incised lines that are deeply personal and reveal the wearer's heritage and character. These are often hidden, but full facial tattoos are becoming more common. Moko kauae is a striking and sacred traditional tattoo worn by women, which typically covers the chin and lower lip.

Sacred Sites

Keep your eye out for traditional Māori sites all over the country - among the most remarkable are the marae, which are traditional meeting grounds. This collection of buildings is a sacred spot where a tribe comes together - while you can look at these often intricately carved structures from the outside, you can only visit a tribe's marae if you've been formally welcomed. Take a walking tour with an elder at Waimarama, south of Hastings *(waimara mamaori.co.nz)*. Other landmarks include the nine giant statues on Mount Hikurangi in East Cape, which honour the Māori god Maui and his family.

↑ Statues celebrating the Māori god Maui, Mount Hikurangi

A pod of dusky dolphins leaping through the waters off Kaikoura ↑

NEW ZEALAND FOR
WILDLIFE

With one of the lowest population densities in the world, is it any wonder that these islands are a haven for a colourful cast of animals? But don't expect to find many land mammals here – instead you'll encounter balletic cetaceans and meet some unique species of flightless birds, including the iconic kiwi.

Life in the Colonies

Watch chunky little blue penguins waddle to and from the sea at the Oamaru Blue Penguin Colony *(p256)*. The best time to visit is at dusk when the birds return with their daily catch – you might spot yellow-eyed penguins too. Join a guided Bushy Beach Tour for a good chance of seeing the famously shy birds land *(penguin. net.nz)*. Penguins are far more graceful in the water, so join them on a sea kayak tour of the Tonga Island Marine Reserve, off Abel Tasman National Park *(p188)*, with Abel Tasman Kayaks *(p191)*.

→

Two elusive yellow-eyed penguins on an Oamaru beach

Over-whale-ming Sights

According to Māori mythology, whales are the descendants of Tangaroa, the god of the oceans, and were often deemed to be sacred guides. Nowadays, roles have reversed and the Ngai Tahu tribe take visitors to sperm whale haunts off the Kaikoura coast *(www.whalewatch.co.nz)*. Here, spot dusky dolphins leaping through the waters and fur seals lolloping across beaches. On an eco "Dolphin Encounter" tour, you can even bob alongside these creatures *(www.dolphinencounter.co.nz)*.

← New Zealand fur seals lazing on the rocks near Kaikoura

NEW ZEALAND'S FAVOURITE BIRD

Over 10 million kiwi birds could once be found in New Zealand, but today it is thought that only 90,000 of the country's national bird remain. There are actually five different species of the bird, but all are nocturnal and hard to spot in the wild; Kapiti Island Nature Reserve *(p172)* and Stewart Island *(p270)* are your best bets. To improve your chances, head to a controlled natural environment like Pukaha Mount Bruce National Wildlife Centre *(p174)* or the vast Zealandia *(p158)* for night tours.

HIDDEN GEM
Penguin Pad

Spend the night with some feathered friends with Pohatu Penguins *(www.pohatu.co.nz)*. As a guest, you'll catch the penguins' sunrise and sunset marches from the lodge's hides.

Australasian gannets at Cape Kidnappers ↑

Watch the Birdie

Home to over 250 native bird species, New Zealand is a haven for twitchers. And even the most casual of bird-watchers will delight in encounters with some of the country's funniest species, such as the friendly fantail, cheeky kea and clumsy kakapo parrot. Away from the forests, New Zealand is the seabird capital of the world. Hop on a vintage tractor to see the sea of yellow-headed Australasian gannets at Cape Kidnappers *(p144)* with Gannet Beach Adventures *(www.gannets.com)*.

Wild Workshops

Some of the visual effects behind the biggest movies in the world were made at Weta Workshop in Wellington. Take the Weta Cave Workshop Tour to go behind the scenes of films like the *Chronicles of Narnia*, *District 9* and *Lord of the Rings* or try to make some movie magic yourself in a creative workshop, where you can craft fake blood or attempt to mould a sculpture *(wetaworkshop. com)*. Wellington is the movie capital of New Zealand: combine a Weta Workshop tour with a trip to film locations around the city with Wellington Movie Tours *(www. movietours.co.nz)*.

→

A troll looms out from the undergrowth on a Weta Workshop tour

NEW ZEALAND
ON SCREEN

Full of blockbuster natural scenery, New Zealand has been immortalized on screen, from *Lord of the Rings* to *Hunt for the Wilderpeople*. Tramp through epic mountain scenery like Frodo and friends or head out into the wilderness and experience the magic for yourself.

Made in New Zealand

Before Taika Waititi directed a god in *Thor: Ragnarok*, he cut his teeth making low-budget comedy-dramas, often featuring Māori characters, such as *Boy*. Other film classics depicting the varied Māori experience include *Once Were Warriors*. You can watch locally made movies for free at the Ngā Taonga Sound and Vision archives in Wellington *(ngataonga.co.nz)*.

←

Considered a classic, *Once Were Warriors*, a brutal film set in Auckland

↑ New Zealand, once again standing in for Middle Earth in *The Hobbit* trilogy

Fellowship of Film Sets

There's one film location to rule them all in New Zealand – and that's Hobbiton at Waikato, the iconic location from Peter Jackson's *Lord of the Rings* and *the Hobbit* trilogies. The unmissable tour around the 12-acre set of "The Shire" includes the Green Dragon Inn, where you can stop for an elevenses or luncheon of pie and ale. For those who want to follow Frodo's journey through Middle Earth, take a 4WD tour from Queenstown to explore the locations of Isengard and Lothlorien with Nomad Safaris *(nomadsafaris.co.nz)*.

TOP 4 BEAUTIFUL FILM LOCATIONS

The Piano
Desolate Karekare Beach in Auckland *(p84)* was where Holly Hunter played her piano, an escape from life on the frontier.

Chronicles of Narnia – Prince Caspian
Stunning Cathedral Cove on the Coromandel Peninsula is the setting for the ruins of Cair Paravel castle *(p132)*.

The World's Fastest Indian
Shot on Invercargill's Oreti Beach, where Burt Munro attempted to break the land-speed record *(p268)*.

Hunt for the Wilderpeople
This heartwarming comedy was filmed at the Waitakere Ranges wilderness *(p84)*.

Kiwi Comedy

Hits like bloodthirsty vampire spoof *What We Do in the Shadows* and friendship love-fest *The Breaker-Upperers* prove that Kiwi comedy is serious business. Catch some budding stars before they make it to the big screen at Auckland's Classic Comedy Club *(www.comedy.co.nz)*.

→

Vampiric horror meets comedy in *What We Do in the Shadows*

Welli Café Culture

The Kiwi coffee scene is well established: in the capital city of Wellington, budding baristas flock to trendy Mojo to learn their trade *(www.mojo.coffee)*. Cafés spill out onto the streets, Mediterranean style, with the most vibrant between Courtenay Place and Cuba Street. Meanwhile, hip haunts like Flight Coffee Hangar *(p159)* and Nikau Café *(p154)* serve up delicious brews alongside fresh seasonal cuisine.

 INSIDER TIP
The Foodie Trail

Bon viveurs should take a foodie walking tour of Auckland to see behind-the-scenes at the city's fish market, visit artisan bakeries and breweries, and sample tasty treats along the way *(www.thebigfoody.com)*.

$\rightarrow$
Modern interior of Wellington cafe, Flight Coffee Hanger

NEW ZEALAND FOR
FOODIES

With its abundance of fresh fish, seafood and lush vegetables, it's little wonder that New Zealand is a firm foodie favourite. The culinary scene is diverse, from traditional Māori hāngi, through french-inspired fine dining and fusion cuisine, to sweet oysters eaten fresh from the ocean.

↑ Delicious dishes at the Wild Foods Cooking School, Treetops Lodge

Māori Cuisine

Experience an essential part of Māori heritage and partake in a traditional hāngi feast. To lay the hāngi, large stones are heated on a fire and an oven pit, or umu, is dug for the food. Earth is piled over the top and the food is left to slow-bake for hours. The result is succulent, tender meat and smoky, savoury vegetables. The tastiest hāngi can be found at local festivals like Hamilton's Kawhia Kai in February. To forage for traditional native foods, make for the Wild Food Cooking School at Rotorua's Treetops Lodge. Here you can also take a fascinating cooking lesson with talented Māori chefs *(www.treetops.co.nz)*.

To Market, to Market!

Kiwi produce is showcased at a vast array of bustling farmers markets. Browse organic veggies at Wellington's Underground and Harbourside markets *(p157)*, and north of Auckland get insider tips on a chef's tour around Makatana Village Farmers' Market *(thelocalfoodkitchen.co.nz)*.

→

Makatana Village Farmers' Market, a small but popular spot for brunch and browsing

Hooked and Cooked

Across the country, you'll be spoilt for choice with delicious seafood *(kaimouana)*. Head to Bluff for oysters *(p279)*, Havelock for green-lipped mussels *(p194)* and Whitianga for scallops *(p133)* – all have annual festivals to celebrate their prized produce. Make sure to taste the Kiwi speciality of battered Southland blue cod and chips, too!

→

Tempting fish and chips, best eaten beside the seaside

Wine from the Vine

New Zealand's 700 wineries produce some of the world's finest and most intensely flavoured fruity wines. Herbaceous Sauvignon Blanc is the country's biggest hitter, while wonderfully light Pinot Noir is the most widely planted red variety. Most wineries offer tours and tastings – and, with many vineyards within easy reach of each other, it's easy to visit several in a day. Why not take a tour of the Wairau Valley *(p204)* or Hawke's Bay *(p148)* for stunning scenery and world-class wines?

$\rightarrow$

Vistors enjoying lunch at a Wairau Valley vineyard

NEW ZEALAND
RAISE A GLASS

Producing an abundance of award-winning wines, New Zealand's vineyards are firmly on the bucket list of most connoisseurs. These same sunny orchards are now infusing fantastically fruity ciders, while the country's creative craft breweries are dreaming up ever-more delicious beers.

Fluid Festivals

Kiwis love a party, with boozy drinks festivals perenially popular. Fans of a pint should head to the rowdy Beervana in Wellington (August) or to Christchurch's lively Great Kiwi Beer Festival (January). A more intimate craft beer festival is MarchFest (March), while those with sweeter tastes can head to Cider Festival (November), both in Nelson. Wine-lovers can enjoy a glass with live music at Toast Martinborough (November) or the Marlborough Food & Wine Festival (February).

A crowd enjoying live music at wine festival Toast Martinborough

TOP 3 VINEYARD TOURS

Mission Estate
Boasting the country's oldest vineyard, this Hawkes Bay estate *(p148)* offers classical wines and tours of its buildings *(www.missionestate.co.nz)*.

Cable Bay
With vineyards from both Marlborough and Waikere, this winery produces a broad selection of wines making it a great sampling starter *(www.cablebay.nz)*.

FROMM
This organic winery in Marlborough bucks the region's Sauvignon Blanc trend, producing Syrah, Riesling and Pinot Gris from single variety vineyards *(www.frommwinery.com)*.

→
The bar at the iconic Speights Brewery in Dunedin

INSIDER TIP
Sip and Cycle

A great way to taste some of New Zealand's lesser-known wines is by cycling around the micro-vineyards surrounding the quaint town of Martinborough *(p174)*. Most of the vineyards are a short distance away from each other along flat country roads, making rolling from boutique winery to boutique winery wonderfully easy.

Crafty Brews

Across the country, there are over 150 small craft breweries producing everything from fruity bitters to malty ales. Wellington, the craft beer capital, has a fantastic walking trail featuring nine craft breweries *(www.craftbeercapital.com)*, while Speights, one of the oldest breweries, has excellent guided tours of its stalwart buildings in Dunedin *(www.speights.co.nz)*. Cider lovers should tour McCashins Brewery in Nelson, the home of Rochdale Cider *(www.rochdalecider.com)*.

NEW ZEALAND FOR
WELLNESS AND RELAXATION

Geothermal pools, rejuvenating crisp mountain air, relaxing tranquil landscapes: New Zealand is the perfect place to slow down and unwind. From secluded yoga retreats to luxurious day spas, here are the best ways to get a bit of Kiwi chill on your trip.

FARMSTAYS

For a real taste of the rural Kiwi lifestyle, get your hands dirty at one of the country's many farmstays. From rounding up a flock of sheep and mending fences to foraging for your dinner at a perma-culture farmstay, you'll get to experience a slice of farm life, alongside a dollop of true Kiwi hospitality from your lovely hosts. If mucking in isn't your thing, there are more opulent options too, often including relaxing spa treatments.

↑ One of the relaxing treatments offered at Auckland's Spa Ayurda

Day Spas in Auckland

Auckland is sprinkled with indulgent day spas, and a treatment at one is the perfect way to chill out after a busy day of sight-seeing. The reputed Spa Ayurda *(www.spaayurda.co.nz)* in leafy Ponsonby creates a synergy between body, mind and spirit, while Salt Cave Halotherapy *(www. saltcavenz.co.nz)* gives treatments in its cave crafted from Himalayan rock salt.

Back to Nature Lodges

Wake to the chatter of birds in one of the country's wilderness lodges, the perfect place to unwind. These eco-friendly lodges offer everything from yoga to tours of New Zealand's diverse flora and fauna. Nestled in lush native bush, Golden Bay Anahata Retreat *(www.anahata-retreat.org.nz)* in Abel Tasman provides an authentic yogic lifestyle, while Resurgence Luxury Eco Lodge *(www.resur gence.co.nz)* in Abel Tasman is completely engulfed in forest. To really embrace nature, try camping on the wildlife sanctuary of Kapiti Island *(www.kapiti island.com)*.

←

Group meditation session and forest-shrouded accommodation *(inset)* at the Resurgence Luxury Eco Lodge

TOP 3 NEW ZEALAND WELLNESS EXPERIENCES

Aro Ha
Combining nature and personal wellbeing, this state-of-the-art, zen-inspired luxury spa retreat in Glenorchy has a stunning subalpine setting *(www.aro-ha.com)*.

Te Moata
Spiritually focused group programmes are on offer at this meditation retreat on the Coromandel Peninsula; book in to one of the charming forest huts *(www.temoata.org)*.

Tiaho Mirimiri
A Rotorua day spa offering authentic Māori treatments with hot stones and therapeutic deep tissue massage *(www.wikitoriamaori healing.co.nz)*.

Natural Geothermal Spas

New Zealand is blessed with health-giving hot springs, with the most energizing thermal spas found around Rotorua: the Polynesian Spa *(p116)*, the area's largest, has 28 natural outdoor baths whose waters range from relieving acidic to nourishing alkaline. On the South Island, the mineral-rich waters of Canterbury's Hanmer Springs *(p228)* beckons purists.

←

One of the many thermal pools at Rotorua's relaxing Polynesian Spa

Team Spirit

Swaying with chants and erupting in cheers, the crowd at Auckland's Eden Park ardently supports its local teams. Catch the Blues playing rugby union at home or a cricket match featuring the Auckland Aces to experience the frenetic atmosphere. From February to June, rugby fans delight in the Rugby Super 15, which features teams from Auckland, Hamilton, Dunedin, Wellington and Christchurch. If you can't get your hands on a ticket to a game, why not head to a sports bar? The atmosphere is always electric.

$\rightarrow$

The All Blacks rugby team performing the haka at Eden Park

NEW ZEALAND FOR
SPORTS FANS

Despite its small size, New Zealand consistently proves its mettle on the international sporting stage, especially when the All Blacks are playing. But Kiwis aren't just spectators. Join the locals and make the most of the country's great outdoors.

Horsing Around

The wide open spaces of the Kiwi countryside promise fantastic horse riding and pony trekking. Meander through forests and gallop along high country trails on an expedition with Adventure Horse Trekking, which operates tours in the stunning wilderness surrounding Queenstown (*adventurehorsetrekking. co.nz*). For the real rural experience, overnight in a restored muster hut where farm hands once slept when gathering their animals.

$\leftarrow$

A group horse riding through dramatic scenery in Glenorchy

Hit the Slopes

The South Island is a skiers' paradise, offering slopes for everyone from beginners to boarders. Craigieburn, near Arthur's Pass, offers off-piste adventures and reliable powder, while Coronet Peak in the Remarkables Ski Area has rolling trails and unparalleled après-ski *(p242)*.

A snowboarder blasting a heel-side turn on Coronet Peak in the Remarkables Ski Area

Above Par

At stunning coastal Cape Kidnappers Golf Course it's all too easy to spend time looking at the horizon, rather than the hole *(www.robertsonlodges. com)*. A more unusual place to tee off is the Arikikapakapa Golf Club in Rotorua, where the thermal pools and vapours waft around the course *(www. rotoruagolfclub.co.nz)*.

↑ Aerial view of Cape Kidnappers Golf Course

A YEAR IN
NEW ZEALAND

JANUARY

Bread and Circus (*late Jan*). Christchurch's lively ten-day festival of entertainment features street busking, circus performances and comedy acts.

△ **New Zealand 7s** (*late Jan*). The Rugby Sevens World Series hits New Zealand for a weekend of fast-paced action in Hamilton.

FEBRUARY

△ **Waitangi Day** (*6 Feb*). Ceremonies at the Waitangi National Trust commemorate the signing of the Treaty of Waitangi.

Marlborough Food and Wine Festival (*second Sat*). Blenheim's Brancott Vineyard hosts international food stalls and tastings of world-class wines.

MAY

International Comedy Festival (*May*). A month-long calendar of comedy at lively venues across Auckland and Wellington.

△ **Bluff Oyster and Food Festival** (*late May*). Enjoy fresh oysters, wild foods and wine at this winter fête in the southern seaside town.

JUNE

Pacific Dance Festival (*early–late Jun*). Auckland's three-week celebration of contemporary Pacific dance performances, plus costume exhibitions.

△ **Queenstown Winter Festival** (*mid–late Jun*). This four-day winter festival includes music-filled street parties, jazz and comedy performances, spectacular night skiing and firework displays.

SEPTEMBER

Alexandra Blossom Festival (*mid-late Sep*). This small-town carnival has a long and proud history, celebrating its community and ushering in spring.

△ **World of Wearable Art** (*late Sep or early Oct*). A choreographed fashion competition in Wellington where designers dazzle audiences with their ingenious costumes.

OCTOBER

△ **Rotorua Tagged Trout Competition** (*1–14 Oct*). Rotorua's premier fishing competition has a $10,000 trout waiting to be hooked.

Akaroa Frenchfest (*mid-Oct*). This small seaside town celebrates its French connections with parades and cabarets, as well as a re-enactment of the first French landing.

MARCH

New Zealand Festival *(late Feb to mid-Mar, even years)*. From opera to sculpture, Wellington's renowned arts festival is a feast for the senses.

△ **Pasifika Festival Auckland** *(mid-Mar)*. Western Springs Park hosts a weekend of cultural events by Pacific Islanders.

Turangawaewae Regatta *(late Mar)*. Electrifying Māori canoe races on the Waikato River in Ngaruawahia, north of Hamilton.

APRIL

Hop 'N' Vine *(early Apr)*. The world's southernmost craft beer festival showcases the finest Kiwi brews.

△ **Warbirds over Wanaka** *(mid-Apr)*. Classic vintage and veteran warplanes take to the skies in this world-class event in Wanaka.

Royal Easter Show *(second week)*. A five-day celebration of Kiwi heritage in Auckland's ABS Showgrounds, with livestock competitions, craft stalls and the country's largest equestrian shows.

JULY

△ **The Food Show** *(late Jul)*. This event showcases the country's diverse regional cuisines, with food stalls and cooking demos in Christchurch, Wellington and Auckland.

Christchurch Arts Festival *(late Jul–mid-Aug, odd years)*. A biennial mid-winter festival of music, theatre, dance and film celebrating Canterbury's creativity.

AUGUST

Bay of Islands Jazz and Blues Festival *(mid-Aug)*. Pahia's popular three-day jazz event sees local and global bands get together to jam.

△ **New Zealand Fashion Week, Auckland** *(late Aug–mid-Sep)*. The country's top fashion designers showcase their latest collections to local and international buyers, media and guests.

NOVEMBER

△ **Taranaki Garden Festival** *(first 10 days)*. Taranaki locals open their gardens to the public and host events like markets, lunches, guided walks and even a quilt exhibition.

Toast Martinborough *(3rd Sunday)*. Martinborough showcases its fine wine and regional food in Wairarapa to the soundtrack of music by local artists.

DECEMBER

Kapiti Food Fair *(early Dec)*. Sample the best foods from around the country at this fair.

△ **TSB Festival of Lights** *(Christmas to late Jan)*. New Plymouth's streets and Pukekura Park are transformed with festive illuminations, while music and dance performances are held each evening.

Rhythm and Vines *(28–31 Dec)*. Ring in the New Year at this three-day music festival where revellers party to international dance music at the Waiohika Estate.

A BRIEF
HISTORY

Cast adrift from the ancient supercontinent of Gondwana, New Zealand was the world's last significant landmass to be settled by people. Today the country's diminutive size belies its global influence, with its diverse cultures carving out a confident and independent identity as a Pacific nation.

Arrival of Māori Ancestors

Until about 800 years ago, New Zealand was uninhabited. Māori legend recounts that Aotearoa was first discovered in AD 950 by Polynesian fisherman Kupe. Three centuries later, a fleet of seven canoes departed Tahiti to reach the islands' shores: archaeologists date this arrival to around AD 1250. These Polynesian seafarers came in vessels laden with plants and animals like taro and kumara, and their Māori descendents spread out across the North Island, establishing tribal settlements of *pa* (fortified villages) inland and on hilltops.

1 Early map showing the North Island.

2 Dutch explorer Abel Tasman and his family.

3 The arrival of Captain Cook's ship, *Endeavour*.

4 The signing of the Treaty of Waitangi.

Timeline of events

c 1250
Polynesian inhabitants arrive in Northland and form coastal settlements.

1791
Whaling ships arrive at Doubtless Bay; whaling trade begins in earnest.

1815
First Christian mission is established in the Bay of Islands.

1642
Dutch explorer Abel Tasman sights New Zealand.

1769
Captain Cook becomes the first European to set foot on New Zealand.

Early European Exploration

In 1642, the Dutch East India Company sent explorer Abel Tasman south from Indonesia. Tasman spotted land off the coast of Hokitia, and sent rowboats out in search of fresh water. Māori war canoes ambushed the boats, and four of Tasman's men were killed. There was no further European contact until 1769, when Captain James Cook made landfall during a scientific expedition of the South Pacific, claiming the land for England.

The New Zealand Wars

By the early 1800s, a steady flow of Europeans arrived, seeking work as farmers, whalers and timber traders. This had a grave impact on Māori: outbreaks of disease caused many deaths, and the availability of guns precipitated the devastating inter-tribal Musket Wars. With increasing concerns about lawlessness and the purchasing of Māori land, leading chiefs asked Queen Victoria to provide a legal framework: in 1840, the Treaty of Waitangi was signed. However, tensions resurfaced with the New Zealand Wars: at the height of the hostilities in the 1860s nearly 20,000 government forces battled 5,000 Māori warriors.

THE 1840 TREATY OF WAITANGI

The country's founding document entrusted sovereignty to Britain and granted Māori equal rights and privileges. The initial treaty was signed at Waitangi *(p94)* by 40 chiefs, but misunderstandings arose as there were two different versions of the treaty (Māori and English). Today the treaty is displayed at the National Library in Wellington *(p154)*.

1818
Musket Wars begin between rival Māori tribes – thousands are killed over a 15-year period.

1835
Declaration of Independence asserts status of Māori lands.

1840
British sovereignty proclaimed, with the Treaty of Waitangi signed by 40 chiefs.

1858
Pōtatau Te Wherowhero is proclaimed the first Māori king.

1865
The capital moves from Auckland to Wellington.

Expansion as a Colony

With the discovery of gold in the South Island and large-scale government borrowing, the 19th century saw great economic expansion, and rail networks and telegraph lines were established. This was also a time of social innovation: in 1893, New Zealand became the first country in the world to grant the right to vote to all women. In 1907, the country's status changed from that of a colony of Great Britain to a self-governing dominion.

The War Years

World War I saw the formation of the Australian and New Zealand Army Corps (ANZAC) in 1915, and its profound involvement in the Gallipoli campaign fighting the Turkish during which thousands of New Zealand soldiers were killed. At home, the country was gripped by the Great Depression, and in 1931, an earthquake destroyed much of Napier. In 1939, New Zealand joined Britain by declaring war with Germany and its troops fought globally alongside the Allies. Military ties with the US and its South Pacific neighbours were formalized in 1951 with the signing of the ANZUS military pact.

1 Suffragists memorial in Christchurch. ↑

2 The 1931 Napier Earthquake

3 Commemorating the ANZAC soldiers who fought at Gallipoli.

4 Auckland Harbour.

Did You Know?

The first Haka performance by a New Zealand rugby team was in 1888.

Timeline of events

1869

New Zealand Wars end with Māori disunity.

1887

Tongariro National Park, the first in New Zealand, is established

1915

New Zealand troops suffer heavy losses in Gallipoli.

1939

New Zealand declares war against Germany alongside Allied forces.

1975

Waitangi Tribunal is established.

4

A Move Away From Britain

In 1947 New Zealand accepted the UK's Statue of Westminster act, which granted complete autonomy to the country. Despite this severing of political links, its economy remained wedded to Britain, with over half of the country's exports landing there as late as 1960. But the boom times came to an end when Britain joined the European Union, and trade declined sharply. New Zealand's government sought trade instead in the Asia-Pacific region and with the United States.

New Zealand Today

With its population nearing five million, New Zealand has become an increasingly multicultural landscape, with Auckland as the largest Polynesian city in the world. Agriculture remains the economy's largest sector, closely followed by a flourishing tourism industry. New Zealand still awaits its first Māori prime minister, although current leader, Jacinda Ardern, is a strong activist for reviving Māori language, along with tackling climate change, making the arts more accessible and encouraging the nation to become a front-runner for gender equality.

↑ Prime Minister Jacinda Ardern receives a Māori hongi

1986

New Zealand is suspended from ANZUS after making its waters a nuclear-free zone.

1987

Māori becomes an official language alongside English.

2011

An earthquake ravages Christchurch, killing 185 people.

2019

Major terrorist attacks take place at mosques in Christchurch.

EXPERIENCE

Watching the sunset, Mahia Peninsula

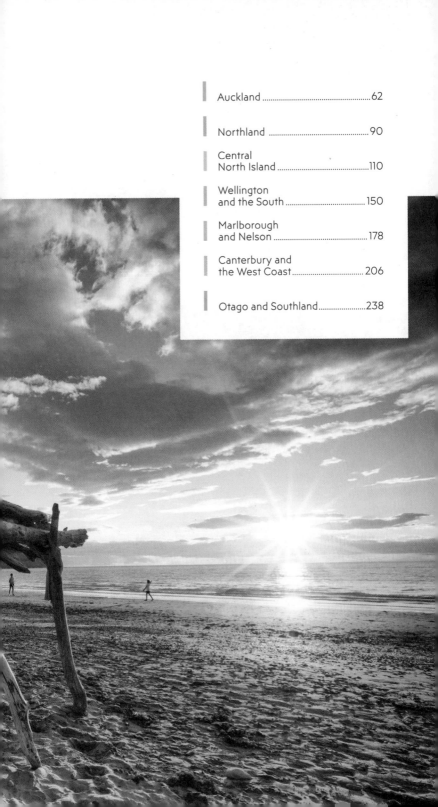

AUCKLAND

Māori settled in Tamaki Makau Rau (Auckland) as early as AD 1350, reaping the rewards of surrounding fertile volcanic soils, and the abundant seafood from the east and west coasts. But inter-tribal wars and epidemics of disease brought about the destruction of their *pā* (hill forts), leaving the area all but deserted when European settlers arrived in the 19th century. After the signing of the Treaty of Waitangi in 1840, Auckland was chosen as New Zealand's new capital, replacing Russell in the north. However, in 1865, the young nation's economic balance forced the capital to move south to Wellington. In the late 19th century, Auckland's economy was boosted by a gold rush in the Coromandel region and increased agricultural production, enabling the city to prosper once more.

As rural populations gravitated towards New Zealand's cities during the early 20th century, Auckland grew rapidly, and during the 1960s and 70s its buoyant labour market attracted workers from across the globe. Today, Auckland is New Zealand's largest city, and its economic powerhouse. A thriving cosmopolitan hub, the city centre encompasses trendy harbourside cafés and up-market restaurants and shops, but within an hour's drive, quiet beaches and bush tracks await.

AUCKLAND

Must Sees

1. Auckland War Memorial Museum
2. Auckland Art Gallery
3. Hauraki Gulf Islands
4. Sky Tower

Experience More

5. SKYCITY Auckland
6. Westhaven Marina
7. Auckland Harbour Bridge
8. New Zealand Maritime Museum
9. Viaduct Harbour
10. Waitemata Harbour
11. Ferry Building
12. Old Customhouse
13. Britomart Transport Centre
14. Auckland Town Hall
15. Aotea Square and Aotea Centre at Auckland Live
16. Old Government House
17. Old Arts Building and Clock Tower
18. Auckland Domain and Winter Gardens
19. Auckland Zoo
20. Museum of Transport and Technology
21. Kelly Tarlton's Sea Life Aquarium
22. Michael Joseph Savage Memorial
23. One Tree Hill
24. Highwic House
25. Auckland Regional Botanic Gardens
26. Rainbow's End
27. Titirangi
28. Piha
29. Orewa
30. Kumeu
31. Devonport
32. Henderson

Eat

1. Depot Eatery and Oyster Bar
2. Ebisu
3. Sidart
4. The Grove

Drink

5. Dr Rudi's Rooftop Brewing Co
6. Brothers Beer
7. The Jefferson
8. Xuxu Dumpling Bar

Stay

9. Hotel DeBrett
10. The Great Ponsonby Arthotel
11. The Boatshed

Shop

12. Shortland Street Night Market
13. La Cigale
14. Grey Lynn Farmers' Market

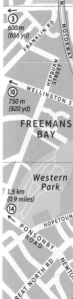

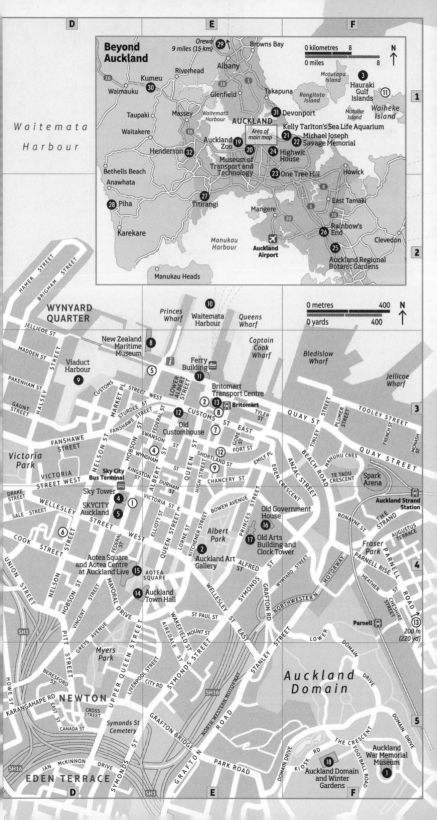

MUSEUM GUIDE

The museum's collections are housed across three levels. The ground level is dedicated to the people of New Zealand and their place in the Pacific region. There is also a special playroom for children. On the first floor, natural history galleries trace New Zealand's ancient origins from the great lost continent of Gondwana, while the top floor tells the compelling story of its emergence as a nation through suffering of war, in the World War II Hall of Memories. There is a shop in the foyer and a café in the atrium.

AUCKLAND WAR MEMORIAL MUSEUM

⬢F5 ⬛The Domain, Parnell ⏰10am–5pm daily 🚌Explorer bus or Link bus
🌐aucklandmuseum.com

More than 30,000 New Zealanders gave their lives in World War I and World War II; many of them were buried or lost very far from home. Auckland's War Memorial Museum remembers and honours every one of the province's fallen servicemen and women, in extraordinary and moving detail.

Built in 1929 to commemorate the end of World War I, the museum's design is Neo-Classical, evoking the Greek temples that many servicemen saw from the decks of warships in the Mediterranean. Serene columns grace the exterior and the entrance lobby, above which is the World War II Hall of Memories, lit by a commemorative stained-glass ceiling window. The "Scars of War" exhibit, commemorating all conflicts in which New Zealanders died, links this to the World War II Hall of Memories. The museum also provides visitors with an introduction to New Zealand's history, people and landscape, with an emphasis on accessibility for families and children, and contains one of the world's greatest collection of Māori *taonga* (treasures). There are daily Māori cultural performances.

↑ The museum's Cenotaph, mirroring the Lutyens monument in London

1

2

① The Māori galleries hold treasured artifacts including a war canoe and a carved meeting house.

② An intricately carved figure among the Māori *taonga* collection.

③ A fighter pilot on one of several windows by noted New Zealand stained glass artist Roy Miller.

3

2 ⊗ ⊠ ⊡ ⬛

AUCKLAND ART GALLERY

📍 E4 🏠 Cnr Wellesley & Kitchener sts ⏰ 10am–5pm daily
🚫 Good Fri, 25 Dec 🌐 aucklandartgallery.com

Nearly a decade ago this gallery was remodelled at a cost of NZ$121 million and has since gone from strength to strength. It houses the world's leading collection of New Zealand art, together with notable international works.

Winning the prestigious World Building of the Year award in 2013, the contemporary refit of the Auckland Art Gallery incorporated the original 1887 French Renaissance style building and later Mackelvie Gallery. The entrance, with its three vast columns and timber canopy, blends neatly with the adjacent Albert Park, which was the site of a Māori *pā* (fortified village). In deference to Māori beliefs, no trees were felled to create the canopy; only naturally fallen timber was used.

The ground floor displays artworks from the gallery's New Zealand collection – look out for work by New Zealand artists such as Ralph Hotere, Frances Hodgkins and Colin McCahon. The mezzanine level exhibits international historic art and it's here that you will often see Frank Bramley's *For of such is the Kingdom of Heaven* (1891). Levels 1 and 2 present rotating exhibits of historic, modern and contemporary art from New Zealand and abroad, and usually include an outstanding series of late 19th-century portraits by immigrant artist Gottfried Lindauer.

Gallery tours run daily at 11:30am and 1:30pm and are well worth taking to get a general overview, before roaming the building to explore independently.

Did You Know?

The museum's official name Auckland Art Gallery Toi o Tāmaki recognizes New Zealand's twin cultures.

Rock Drop by Judy Millar, a dynamic installation with seismic resonances ↑

1 Works of contemporary Māori sculpture on display in an exhibit entitled *Radical Beginnings*.

2 The gallery exterior, topped by a geometrically patterned "forest canopy" roof of kauri wood.

3 Marté Szirmay's *Splitting Egg* sculpture (1986), exhibited among the museum's collection of striking modern art.

TOP 5 WORKS OF ART

Gottfried Lindauer's Māori Portraits
Oil paintings in sharp-focused detail.

For of Such is the Kingdom of Heaven
Victorian artist Frank Bramley's poignant portrayal of grief.

Le Pont Japonais
The gallery's first Monet on long-term loan.

Te Waka Toi o Tāmaki
Māori artist Fred Graham's stone relief at the gallery entrance.

Lonnie Hutchinson Carvings
Delicate works by this female contemporary Māori artist mark the thresholds on each of the gallery's four levels.

Did You Know?

Before the Europeans came, Waiheke was called Motu Wai Heke, "island of trickling waters".

3

HAURAKI GULF ISLANDS

🅰 E2 🚌 ✈ ℹ 137 Quay St, Auckland; www.doc.govt.nz

This expansive archipelago is among the most beautiful in the world. Here, 65 stunning islands draw visitors seeking relaxation, recreational activities and access to unspoiled natural landscapes within easy reach of Auckland. Waiheke Island, only 40 minutes from the city, is among the most popular.

The Hauraki Gulf Islands offer diverse attractions. Waiheke Island, the most well known, has a reputation as a hub of "alternative" lifestyles, and offers white sand beaches, vineyards and excellent hiking trails. The proximity to Auckland has led to the island being popular with commuters. Those seeking a slower pace of life head to Great Barrier and Kawau. Great Barrier, the furthermost island in the Hauraki Gulf, is not connected to the electricity grid and drinking water comes from rainwater tanks on roofs, whereas Kawau Island is best known for the variety of animals imported by former New Zealand governor and prime minister Sir George Grey in the 19th century, including the parma wallaby.

The dramatic extinct volcano of Rangitoto is great for hiking, with 260-m- (850-ft-) high lava slopes covered in trees and shrubs including ferns, mangroves, manuka and rewa. At Rakino, a hotchpotch of houses sit perched on striking ridges. Its beaches are suitable for swimming and it is a favourite stop for yachts. Little Barrier Island, a wildlife sanctuary, has 30 native and 19 introduced species of birds, whereas the sheltered channel between Goat Island Marine Reserve and the main-land provides an opportunity to see all manner of fish life.

← The endangered North Island kokako

← Golden sands and clear waters of Korotiti Bay, Great Barrier Island

↑ Catching the ferry to Kawau Island from Sandspit Wharf near Warkworth

↑ Vineyards covering the rolling hills of Waiheke Island, popular with Auckland commuters

MARINE SAFARI

The Hauraki Gulf Marine Park protects around 50 islands and the surrounding waters, which are home to myriad wildlife. Remarkably, the park is visited by one-third of all marine life on earth including a number of endangered species. An eco-safari tour run by Red Balloon *(www.redballoon.co.nz)* guarantees that you will spot whales, dolphins and seabirds. A tour normally runs for around three hours, and there is a marine scientist on board to answer questions about research and conservation in the park.

Did You Know

The Sky Tower can withstand winds gusting to 200 km/h (125 mph) and earthquakes.

→ The unmistakable Sky Tower set against the Auckland skyline at sunset

④ 🖼 🍴 🖥 🛍

SKY TOWER

📍 D4 🏠 Cnr Victoria & Federal sts
🕐 8:30am till late daily 🌐 skytower.co.nz

An even more spectacular landmark when illuminated at night, the Sky Tower is a splendid entertainment and broadcasting facility.

Opened in August 1997 and standing at 328 m (1,076 ft), Sky Tower is the tallest freestanding structure in the southern hemisphere. Part of SKYCITY Auckland, the tower is visited by around 500,000 people per year. Its three observation levels offer expansive views while the tower's SkyJump – a 192 m (630 ft) cable controlled base jump – and 360° SkyWalk provide the ultimate in adrenaline adventure. On the main observation level, diagrams help you find Auckland's key spots and glass floor panels test your nerves. Entry to Sky Tower's lift is through an underground gallery.

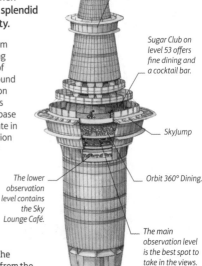

The 92 m- (302 ft-) high spire weighs 170 tonnes.

The Sky Deck is the country's highest public viewing area.

Sugar Club on level 53 offers fine dining and a cocktail bar.

SkyJump

Orbit 360° Dining.

The lower observation level contains the Sky Lounge Café.

The main observation level is the best spot to take in the views.

← Visitors enjoy the fantastic view from the tower's observation deck

EXPERIENCE MORE

⑤ 🍴 🖥 🛍
SKYCITY Auckland

📍D4 🏛Cnr Victoria & Federal sts ⏰24 hrs daily 🌐skycityauckland. co.nz

Set beside the southern hemisphere's tallest structure is SKYCITY Auckland, a luxurious entertainment and accommodation complex. Here, facilities include two hotels: the four-star SKYCITY Hotel, with 306 rooms and 38 suites, and the five-star Grand Hotel, which has 316 guest rooms and a spa. In addition, there are bars, cafés, restaurants, conference facilities, and an impressive state-of-the-art 700-seat theatre.

Lucky punters can win luxury cars at SKYCITY Auckland, New Zealand's biggest casino. Open 24 hours a day, seven days a week, the complex offers a wide variety of entertainment and leisure options. More than 1,600 gaming machines feature all the latest stepper reel, video reel, poker and keno games offering cash prizes. The complex has four casinos and over 100 gaming tables with traditional games such as Caribbean stud poker, craps, blackjack, baccarat and roulette. Chinese favourites include tai sai, played with three dice in a clear glass dome, and pai gow, played with 32 domino pieces.

⑥
Westhaven Marina

📍B2 🏛Westhaven Drive

Westhaven Marina reflects Aucklanders' passion for yachting. Founded in the 1940s, today the marina accommodates more than 2,000 vessels. Among the facilities are Pier Z (the home of several major charter boat companies), launching ramps and a mast gantry. The premises of prominent yacht clubs are on the northern side.

> **Founded in the 1940s, today the marina accommodates more than 2,000 vessels.**

EAT

Orbit 360° Dining
This is New Zealand's only revolving restaurant, rotating once per hour. Diners get free entry to viewing platforms.

📍D4 🏛Level 52, Sky Tower 🌐skycity auckland.co.nz

$$$$$⑤

Sugar Club
At this iconic restaurant, chef Peter Gordon expertly combines Asian and European cuisine.

📍D4 🏛Level 53, Sky Tower 🌐skycity auckland.co.nz

$$$$$$

↑ A forest of masts at Westhaven Marina with volcanic Rangitoto Island in the background

EAT

Depot Eatery and Oyster Bar

This lively spot attracts a cool crowd, with fine dining in an informal setting. Generous sharing dishes are cooked over sizzling charcoal.

⑨ D4 Ⓐ 86 Federal St
Ⓦ eatatdepot.co.nz

$$⑤

Ebisu

Housed in the Old Union Fish building, this elegant eatery offers exquisite Japanese cuisine, from delicate homemade pickles to sumptuous fillets of Wagyu beef.

⑨ E3 Ⓐ 116-118 Quay St
Ⓦ ebisu.co.nz

$$⑤

Sidart

Innovative Indian cuisine delights diners at this celebrated gourmet restaurant. Expect fresh flavours and seasonal produce.

⑨ C4 Ⓐ 283 Ponsonby Rd Ⓒ Sun & Mon
Ⓦ sidart.co.nz

$$$

The Grove

Vegetarians are well catered for at this upmarket haunt, where the menu riffs on contemporary New Zealand cooking with a French twist.

⑨ E3 Ⓐ St Patrick's Sq, Wyndham St
Ⓒ Sun Ⓦ thegrove restaurant.co.nz

$$$

⑦ Auckland Harbour Bridge

⑨ B1 Ⓐ State Hwy 1

Constructed in 1959, this steel structure stretches 1,017 m (3,337 ft) across Waitemata Harbour, rising high above the water to allow ships to pass beneath. Sometimes referred to as the "coat hanger" for its open, lattice-like structure, the bridge opened up transport routes from urban central Auckland to the more rural North Shore – prior to the bridge's construction, the main route to the north was by ferry.

Today the bridge is one of Auckland's most iconic sights, and it affords astonishing views of the city's skyline and sparkling Waitemata harbour. The more adventurous can admire the views from an even higher vantage point, with bridge climb tours and bungy jumps by **A J Hackett** taking visitors up to the 67-m- (200-ft-) high summit.

A J Hackett
Ⓐ 105 Curran St, Westhaven Ⓦ bungy.co.nz

⑧ New Zealand Maritime Museum

⑨ E3 Ⓐ Cnr Quay & Hobson sts Ⓒ 10am-5pm daily
Ⓦ maritime museum.co.nz

Boats have played a pivotal role in New Zealand's history, from those of the early Polynesian navigators who steered their canoes towards the country, to the whaling boats and the whalers who made Russell (p99) the centre of the whaling industry in the 1840s, to the vessels that brought thousands of immigrants to the islands in the 19th and 20th centuries.

Aspects of the country's maritime past are highlighted in the museum's exhibition galleries, which are often imaginatively laid out – one room is fitted out as a ship's interior, complete with a gently swaying floor and appropriate creaking noises.

The museum's gifted Māori name is Te Huiteananui-a-Tangaroa, which translates as "the legendary house belonging to Tangaroa", god of the sea.

← Cafés and apartments lining the boardwalk at Viaduct Harbour

INSIDER TIP
Harbour Sailing

Sail Waitemata Harbour on a traditional ketch-rigged deck scow from yesteryear, manned by sailors from the nearby Maritime Museum. Trips depart at 11:30am and 1:30pm (Tuesday to Sunday) and tickets include admission to the museum.

mooring facilities for 150 yachts. The harbour is part of an extensive redevelopment of Auckland's waterfront, following the trend in cities such as Sydney, London and San Francisco, and the precinct has a vibrant atmosphere and a variety of restaurants. The Viaduct Events Centre is the focus for large conventions and trade shows, such as New Zealand Fashion Week.

⑩ Waitemata Harbour

📍 E2

This sparkling harbour, which looks out over the green volcanic cone of Rangitoto Island, is one of Auckland's most cherished sights. The scenic harbour forms a natural barrier between the central business district and the populous North Shore. Ferries, cruise boats and commercial ships use the harbour daily.

⑨ Viaduct Harbour

📍 D3 🏠 Cnr Halsey St & Viaduct Harbour

Largely a legacy from the 1999–2000 America's Cup, the harbour's up-market apartments, shops and rest-aurants overlook a marina with

Ferry Building

📍 E3 🏠 99 Quay St 🚆

Set proudly on Auckland's waterfront, this attractive Edwardian Baroque building was completed in 1912, and today is the focal point for commuter ferries. Ferry rides and boats depart from here to nearby Devonport and Waiheke Island (p70). Designed by Alex Wiseman, the ornate brick and sand-stone building is registered with the Historic Places Trust.

Not just a transport centre, the terminal is also home to a number of cafés and restaurants with stunning har-bour views.

The grand Ferry Building, gateway to the harbour ↑

12

Old Customhouse

◉ E3 ⌂ Cnr Albert & Customs sts 🕑 9am–5pm daily

An Auckland landmark, and one of the oldest commercial buildings in the city, the Old Customhouse replaced a structure that burned down in the 1880s. Designed by Thomas Mahoney, the 1889 French Renaissance-style building is said to have been modelled on the present Selfridge's department store on Oxford Street, London. It features intricate plaster-work and kauri joinery.

Once home to the Customs Department, Audit Inspector, Sheep Inspector and Native Land Court, the building survived the threat of demolition in the 1970s thanks to campaigners, and today houses the city's largest duty-free shop.

↓ Britomart Transport Centre's shops and *(inset)* its train services

Did You Know?

Auckland Town Hall's pipe organ is the largest, most powerful musical instrument in the country.

13

Britomart Transport Centre

◉ E3 ⌂ 8–10 Queen St

What became the Britomart Transport Centre was originally Auckland's grand Post Office, designed in an Imperial Baroque style. Today, it brings together Auckland's train, bus and ferry services in a single complex. The centre was the focus of an urban renewal project in 2009, construction for parts of which is still ongoing, which included the redevelopment of surrounding streets, creating public spaces and Takutai Plaza, a precinct of shops and restaurants.

14

Auckland Town Hall

◉ E4 ⌂ 301–317 Queen St ☏ (09) 309 2677

The wedge-shaped Edwardian Town Hall, built in 1911, is Auckland's prime historic building. It has been used extensively as a political and administrative centre, as well as a cultural venue. During work to restore it to its original design, the building was gutted (non-original materials were removed) and strengthened structurally.

The Concert Chamber, Council Chamber and main street foyer were meticulously restored, a process which included using vintage glass to reconstruct windows that had disappeared over the years.

↑ Locals relaxing in Aotea Square, with the town hall behind

The Great Hall, an excellent concert facility, is a replica of the Neues Gewandhaus in Leipzig, Germany, which was destroyed by Allied bombing during World War II.

 15

Aotea Square and Aotea Centre at Auckland Live

📍D4 🏛Aotea Sq (upper Queen St) 🌐auckland live.co.nz

In the late 1980s, several New Zealand souvenir shops began stocking a postcard that was entirely black except for a small heading, "Night Life in New Zealand". Fortunately, things have changed since. Built in 1990, the Aotea Centre was designed by New Zealand architect Ewen Wainscott and is a hub of vibrant nightlife. On its opening night, the centre featured New Zealand-born Dame Kiri Te Kanawa, the world-renowned opera singer. It is a venue for dance, opera,

classical music, theatre and shows, along with festivals like the Aotearoa Hip Hop Summit.

Aotea Square, in front of the centre, houses a market as well as festivals. The wooden *waharoa* (gateway) at its entrance was created by Māori artist Selwyn Muru. The square is flanked on one side by the Metro Centre, which has an

IMAX cinema, a games centre, cafés, food court and shops. Auckland Town Hall is on the other side of the square.

Collectively, all these locations – Aotea Centre, Aotea Square, Town Hall, The Civic, Bruce Mason Centre and stadiums – are known as Auckland Live and promote performing arts and culture.

DRINK

Dr Rudi's Rooftop Brewing Co
Head up for good views of the harbour and tasty beer brewed on site.

📍E3 🏛Level 2, 204 Quay St 🌐drrudis.co.nz

Brothers Beer
Enjoy hand-crafted beers on comfy sofas from grandma's day, surrounded by old classic toys.

📍D4 🏛City Works Depot Shed 3D, 90 Wellesley St West 🌐brothers beer.co.nz

The Jefferson
This cosy speakeasy-style hangout has a staggering array of whiskeys behind the bar and tasty snacks too.

📍E3 🏛7 Fort Ln 🌐thejefferson.co.nz

Xuxu Dumpling Bar
A tiny, atmospheric bamboo bar in bustling Britomart offering Asian-inspired cocktails.

📍E3 🏛Cnr of Galway & Commerce sts, Britomart 🕐Sun 🌐xuxu.co.nz

The octagonal Clock Tower, part of Auckland University, overlooking Albert Park

⑯ Old Government House

📍E4 🏠Cnr Waterloo Quadrant & Princes St 🚪To the public

Built in Classical style, the Old Government House was the seat of government until 1865 when the capital was moved to Wellington. It was also the residence of New Zealand's governor-general until 1969. Royalty used to stay here, and Queen Elizabeth II broadcast her Christmas speech from upstairs in 1953. It is now a part of the University of Auckland, housing the staff common room and apartments for visiting academics.

Located within walking distance of the central business district, Old Government House, designed by William Mason and completed in 1856, appears from a distance to be made of stone. Like its British prefabricated predecessor, however, it is built from wood. A big coral tree and a Norfolk pine at the southern edge of the lawn are said to have been planted by Sir George Grey during his second term as governor from 1861 to 1867.

---

⑰ Old Arts Building and Clock Tower

📍E4 🏠Princes St 🚪To the public

Part of the university buildings, the Old Arts Building and Clock Tower face Albert Park, a summer gathering place for students. Designed by Chicago-trained architect R A Lippincott, it was completed in 1926. The clock tower that crowns the building was inspired by the Tom Tower of Christ Church in Oxford, England, and has come to symbolize the university. The building's octagonal interior is galleried and vaulted with a mosaic floor and piers. A major reconstruction was undertaken between 1985 and 1988, which won an Institute of Architects award.

From the rear of the Old Arts Building, the Barracks Wall runs for 85 m (280 ft) to the back of the Old Choral Hall. Built in 1847, it is the only remnant of the wall which enclosed an area, including Albert Park, where British troops were stationed until 1870. The basalt stone wall was quarried from the slope of Mount Eden, now known as Eden Garden.

Auckland Domain and Winter Gardens

F5 🏠 20 Park Rd, Grafton 📞 (09) 301 0101 🕐 Auckland Domain: 7am–dusk daily; Winter Gardens: 9am–5pm daily

Central Auckland has been built around a number of extinct volcanoes, including 14 volcanic cones, many of which are now parks. The oldest park is the Auckland Domain, situated within walking distance of both the city centre and the Parnell area. Tuff rings created by volcanic activity thousands of years ago can still be seen in its contours.

Land for the city's 1.35 sq km (half a sq mile) park was set aside in 1840, in the early years of European settlement. In 1940, a carved Māori memorial palisade was installed around a totara tree on Pukekaroa knoll. This enclosure commemorates Māori leader Potatu Te Wherowhero, who made peace with the neighbouring tribes on the site a hundred years earlier.

Nearby is a sports field where the tuff rings form a natural amphitheatre. The field is used for free outdoor concerts over the summer that attract large crowds.

The large, shady Auckland Domain is also a popular place with walkers and picnickers. Several of the large trees in the park were seedlings that came from a nursery set up in 1841 to grow and distribute European plants and trees. The formal gardens feature many sculptures, the best known of which are the three bronze sculptures standing in the free-form pond. The central, male figure represents Auckland and the two females represent wisdom and fertility of the soil.

The Winter Gardens, a legacy from the Auckland Exhibition of 1913, consist of two glasshouses joined by a courtyard that contains a large water lily and lotus pool. The dome-roofed areas contain a wide variety of plants. The scoria quarry behind the Winter Gardens

Did You Know?

The Winter Gardens are home to a *titan arum*, or corpse flower, the first to bloom in New Zealand.

has been converted into a fernery. Ferns are a dominant feature of the New Zealand landscape and there are more than 100 varieties here.

The **Wintergarden Café** is set beside the duck pond and surrounded by lush greenery, making for a pleasant spot to enjoy tea and a snack after wandering the grounds. Nearby is the domain's best-known structure, the Auckland War Memorial Museum and Cenotaph (*p66*).

Wintergarden Café
🕐 8am–4pm daily 🌐 winter gardenpavilion.co.nz

↓ Admiring tropical displays in the Winter Gardens' glasshouses

↑ Full-scale exhibits of early aircraft at the Museum of Transport and Technology

19 🛡️🍴🖥️🛍️

Auckland Zoo

📍E1 🏠Motions Rd, Western Springs
🚌Customs St, 45
🕐9:30am–5:30pm daily
🌐aucklandzoo.co.nz

New Zealand's isolated geographical position means that its fauna has developed differently from that of most countries. A lack of predators, for example, has resulted in many flightless birds. With the exception of bats, there are no native mammals. The best place to learn about the country's varied and unusual wildlife is at Auckland Zoo. Established as a small private menagerie in 1912, the zoo opened in its current spot in 1922. It houses more than 700 animals covering 117 species, including birds like saddlebacks, tui and kaka, besides the nocturnal kiwi. The zoo's population, which is not limited to native animals, is presented in natural settings. Primates such as squirrel monkeys and macaques can be seen at close range in a rainforest. Zebras and giraffes roam on an African savanna with Zulu huts and interconnected habitats. A wetlands environment features baboons as well as hippopotamuses.

Did You Know?

Auckland Zoo hosts the world's most varied display of native flora and fauna in its Te Wao Nui exhibit.

↑ An elephant statue marking the entrance to the Pridelands experience at Auckland Zoo

20 🛡️🖥️

Museum of Transport and Technology

📍E1 🏠Great North Rd, Western Springs
🚌Customs St, 45 🕐10am–5pm daily (last adm: 4:30pm) 🌐motat.org.nz

The Museum of Transport and Technology (MOTAT) has a collection of about 300,000 items, some of which can be seen in various buildings on two sites within walking distance of Auckland Zoo. The museum is run largely by volunteers. Exhibits vary from 19th-century everyday innovations, such as dental equipment, to a working miniature model railway of the North Island's main trunk line. An interactive gallery for under-fives, Motot's, offers kids the chance to play with pulleys, levers, wheelbarrows and diggers.

The focal point is a collection of 30 rare and historic aircraft. These include a replica of a homemade plane by New Zealander Richard Pearse, believed by many to have preceded the Wright brothers in being the first person to fly. Also of interest is the Solent flying boat ZK-AMO *Aranui*, a luxurious aircraft, the only one in the world of its kind, that flew around the South Pacific from 1949 until 1960. An electric tram runs about every 20 minutes from the entrance of MOTAT to the zoo gates.

21

Kelly Tarlton's Sea Life Aquarium

F1 **23 Tamaki Drive** **757, 767, 769; free shuttle from Quay Station every hour from 9:30am-3:30pm daily** **9:30-5pm daily** **kellytarltons.co.nz**

Tamaki Drive's best-known tourist attraction is Kelly Tarlton's Sea Life Aquarium. Visitors ride on a moving walkway through an acrylic tunnel inside a tank, with fish swimming around the sides. The tunnel winds past two marine aquariums, one devoted to reef fish and the other to sharks and stingrays.

Don't miss feeding time at the penguin enclosure, where King and Gentoo penguins scudder across the ice and zip through the icy waters. Throughout the day, there are also behind-the-scenes tours of the fascinating aquarium complex, creative workshops for kids and educational talks about the aquarium's conservation activities.

→
Obelisk and reflective pool at the Michael Joseph Savage Memorial

22

Michael Joseph Savage Memorial

F1 **9-15 Hapimana St, Orakei** **7am-dusk**

Located off Tamaki Drive, this park was named after New Zealand's first Labour prime minister, Michael Joseph Savage (1871–1940). The formal gardens include a sunken pool, presided over by a tall memorial column, and contain concrete fortifications that date from World War II.

The memorial park sits within an area called Bastion point, which was originally a historic Māori *pa* (village) known as Tokapurewha (or "mussel rocks"), its shoreline renowned for a plentiful supply of mussels. The area is perhaps best known for a Māori protest staged in 1977 after the government had razed a local Māori village to develop Bastion Point as a prime residential zone. A 506-day

 GREAT VIEW
Tamaki Drive

Tamaki Drive, located to the east of the city, shows Auckland at its best. The road crosses Hobson Bay and follows the water's edge past Okahu Bay, Mission Bay and St Heliers Bay. The views across Waitemata Harbour towards Rangitoto Island and Devonport are stunning and an experience that should not be missed.

occupation was organized to protest against the appropriation of the site, followed by ten years of litigation. In 1990, the land was finally returned to the Ngati Whatua tribe. The 900-sq-m (9,690-sq-ft) Orakei Marae is the tribe's meeting house nearby. Smaller ones can be found around the Kaipara Harbour and at Helensville, at the southern extremity of the harbour.

23

One Tree Hill

E1 Manukau Rd

One Tree Hill (Maungakiekie), a dormant volcanic cone and once the site of the largest prehistoric Māori settlement in the region, was named after the solitary tree that was planted on its summit in 1640. Since then, a succession of single trees have stood there. The last, a Monterey pine, was removed in October 2001 by city council workers as it was unstable (a grove of native trees has now been planted, with a plan to thin them out to one). Its most famous predecessor was a native totara tree, cut down in 1852 by workmen angry at the non-arrival of rations.

Surrounding the hill is Cornwall Park, named for the Duke and Duchess of Cornwall, and donated to the city by Sir John Logan Campbell during their royal tour in 1901.

Acacia Cottage, Auckland's oldest surviving wooden building, was built in 1841 by Sir John Logan Campbell. It was relocated in 1920 from Shortland Street to Cornwall Park, where he once had a farm.

↑ Highwic House, built in 1862 in the Carpenter Gothic Revival style

Near the entrance to the park, is the **Stardome Observatory and Planetarium**. It has two telescopes for viewing the stars, and entertaining shows on the aspects of space and astronomy are shown on a giant domed screen at the planetarium (check the website for show times).

Acacia Cottage

Cornwall Park 302, 304, 305 10am-4pm daily Public hols cornwallpark.co.nz

← One Tree Hill, formerly the site of a large Māori fort

Stardome Observatory and Planetarium

One Tree Hill Domain (best accessed from Mortimer Pass) 10am-11pm daily Public hols stardome.org.nz

24

Highwic House

E1 40 Gillies Ave, Epsom (09) 524 5729 Link bus 10:30am-4:30pm Wed-Sun Good Fri, 25 Dec

Built in 1862, Highwic was the home of Alfred Buckland, a stock and station owner. The house was built in stages, with the front part showing more

detail than the rest. The house, with its elaborate decoration and diamond pane windows, is an example of Carpenter Gothic Revival architecture. The extensive landscaped gardens are also worth a visit.

plants, and an extensive collection of ornamental plants. Surrounded by lush South Pacific vegetation and sweeping views, the Visitor Centre offers interpretative and themed plant displays.

Auckland Regional Botanic Gardens

F2 **Hill Rd, Manukau City** **8am–dusk daily** **aucklandbotanic gardens.co.nz**

These gardens contain more than 10,000 species of New Zealand native and introduced

Rainbow's End

F2 **Cnr Great South & Wiri Station rds, Manukau City** **Central Auckland, 471, 472** **10am–4pm Mon–Fri, to 5pm Sat & Sun** **rainbowsend.co.nz**

Lots of thrilling rides and entertainment are available at

GREAT VIEW
Mount Eden

Less than a mile (1.6 km) from Highwic House is Mount Eden – Auckland's highest point and one of 48 volcanic cones, it was once a fortified Māori *pa*. Today, there are exotic gardens with waterfalls, and grassy expanses. Tour the Māori ruins, and gaze out over the sparkling cityscape below.

this amusement park, which is New Zealand's largest. The most popular attraction is a roller coaster that takes you up more than 30 m (98 ft) in the air, hurls you down through a complete loop, round a corner and through a double corkscrew. Other attractions include the Motion Master Virtual Theatre, featuring dinosaurs, an enchanted forest ride, family go-karts, Stratofear and The Invader rides, water rides and the Goldrush, which takes you on a thrilling ride through an abandoned gold mine in a runaway mining cart. Kidz Kingdom provides indoor amusements and rides suitable for small children, where they can pilot their own space shuttle or twist and turn aboard the Choco Express.

SIR JOHN LOGAN CAMPBELL

Sir John Logan Campbell (1817–1912) was one of New Zealand's pioneering entrepreneurs. On 21 December 1840, he set up a tent on Shortland Street that served as Auckland's first shop. The prominent businessman was also a member of New Zealand's parliament. Today, "the father of Auckland" is perhaps best remembered for donating his farm, Cornwall Park, to the city.

27

Titirangi

📍 E2

To the west of Auckland city, the small settlement of Titirangi offers superb views of the Waitakere Ranges and the 390-sq-km (150-sq-mile) Manukau Harbour to the south. The village, which is home to a number of artists and writers, has a reputation for being trendy. Its main street is lined with cafés and restaurants. The main landmark is the Spanish-style Lopdell House, opened in 1930, which has a small theatre and restaurant with Te Uru Waitakere Contemporary Gallery next door. The square in front of the library is transformed into an art and crafts market on the last Sunday of the month (9am to noon).

Titirangi is the gateway to the Waitakere Ranges Regional Park. Formed by volcanic activity about 1.7 million years ago, the park has about 250 km (155 miles) of trails suitable for people of all levels of fitness. It attracts over two million visitors a year.

The **Arataki Visitors Centre**, 6 km (4 miles) beyond Titirangi, has well-organized displays on the area's logging history and attractions, and also stocks books, posters and detailed maps of the ranges. Large timber decks around the building offer good views of the harbour. Across the road from the centre is the Arataki Nature Trail, a self-guided walk, which provides a good introduction to native plants and wildlife.

Arataki Visitors Centre

🏠 300 Scenic Drive, Oratia, Waitakere 📞 (09) 817 0077 🕐 9am–5pm daily

---

28

Piha

📍 D2

Prized by locals but not well known to tourists, Auckland's rugged, windswept west coast beaches are within easy reach of the city and are well worth visiting. Because they are exposed to the Tasman Sea, however, swimmers and

 GREAT VIEW
Lion Rock

Climb Piha's iconic rock and be king of all you survey. Lion Rock is a volcanic leftover and old Māori fortification. Wooden stairs lead to the halfway viewing point, which has spectacular ocean vistas.

surfers need to exercise care as the currents can be treacherous and conditions often change rapidly. Piha, the most popular beach, is know for its heavy surf. Refreshment here is provided at the **Piha Surf Life Saving Club** restaurant, along with pleasant **Piha Cafe** and **Piha Store**.

The bleakest, yet perhaps grandest, stretch of coast is at Whatipu, south of Piha at the entrance to the Manukau Harbour. A sand bar visible from the beach partly blocks the harbour. It was here that the HMS *Orpheus* was shipwrecked on 7 February 1863. Just south of Piha, Karekare has several idyllic picnic spots and a swimming hole at the base of a waterfall.

North of Piha is Bethells Beach, inhabited by Māori for

↑ The pub at Puhoi, a living museum dedicated to this former Bohemian village

several centuries; some 75 sites have been recorded here by archaeologists. Ihumoana Island, just off the beach, is the area's best-preserved island *pa*.

Though not as spectacular as Cape Kidnappers (*p144*), a headland at Muriwai Beach, beyond Bethells, is home to a colony of around 2,000 Australasian gannets. Barriers and viewing platforms allow visitors to observe the birds without disturbing them.

Piha Surf Life Saving Club

🏠 23 Marine Parade S, Piha 🌐 pihaslsc.com

Piha Cafe

🏠 20 Seaview Rd, Piha 📞 (09) 812 8808

Piha Store

🏠 26 Seaview Rd, New Lynn, Piha 📞 (09) 812 8844

←

Surfers at Piha beach preparing to take on the west coast of Auckland

㉙
Orewa

📍 E1 🚌 ℹ️ 1A Baxter St, Warkworth; www.orewa beach.co.nz

Beach houses and motels line the main road through this small seaside town, 30 minutes' drive north of Auckland. Orewa's main attraction is its beach, a 3-km- (2-mile-) long stretch of sand. The beach is suitable for swimming, surfing and boating. Easterly winds from the sea also attract windsurfers.

Just north of Orewa, a small road off State Highway 1 leads to Puhoi, New Zealand's earliest Bohemian settlement. A tiny calvary shrine beside the road leading to the settlement is a reminder of the settlers' background. Pleasant local **Puhoi Pub** also doubles as a museum of the pioneers of the area.

About 48 km (30 miles) north of Auckland, Waiwera is best known for its thermal resort, **Waiwera Thermal Resort**. The complex has nine

STAY

Hotel Debrett
Luxury Art Deco hotel where each of the 25 rooms has unique styling and carpets in hand-woven New Zealand wool.

📍 E3 🏠 2 High St
🌐 hoteldebrett.com

$$$

The Great Ponsonby Arthotel
A historic villa crammed with New Zealand and Pacific art. Friendly staff and a trendy atmosphere.

📍 C4 🏠 30 Ponsonby Ter 🌐 greatpons.co.nz

$$$

The Boatshed
Chic, luxury accommodation in a sun-drenched bay just 35 minutes by ferry from Auckland. Private setting with panoramic ocean views.

📍 F1 🏠 Cnr Tawa and Huia sts, Little Oneroa, Waiheke Island, 1840
🌐 boatshed.co.nz

$$$

indoor and outdoor pools, spas, water slides, beauty therapies and picnic areas. The natural springs deliver up to 1 million litres (0.2 million gallons) of water per day.

Puhoi Pub

🏠 5 Saleyards Rd, Puhoi 0951 🌐 puhoipub.com

Waiwera Thermal Resort

♨️ 🚗 😊 👶 🏠 21 Waiwera Rd ⏰ 10am–9pm daily 🌐 waiwera.co.nz

Red skies reflecting on the water at sunrise over Devonport harbour ↑

Kumeu

 E1

A popular weekend pursuit of many Aucklanders is lunch at a vineyard restaurant followed by shopping for fresh fruit and vegetables from a roadside stall on the way home. At Kumeu, a sleepy suburb of Auckland and notable wine and fruit growing district, visitors are spoilt for choice. Award-winning vineyards abound here, many offering free tastings and tours.

Kumeu River Wines should be included in every wine safari. This lovely vineyard specializes in regionally grown grapes – its crisp Chardonnay has made the top 100 Wines of the World list of the

> At Kumeu, a sleepy suburb of Auckland and notable wine and fruit growing district, visitors are spoilt for choice.

United States *Wine Spectator* magazine five times. Meanwhile Soljans Estate Winery (p87) features a picnic area and offers visitors tours. Its premium varieties include Chardonnay. Those looking for a pint rather than a glass of wine should make for nearby Riverhead's longstanding **Riverhead Tavern**, a pleasant pub in the upper Waitematā overlooking the water.

Kumeu River Wines
550 State Highway 16
kumeuriver.co.nz

Riverhead Tavern
62 Queen St, Riverhead
theriverhead.co.nz

Devonport

E1 w visit devonport.co.nz

In comparison to Auckland's less affluent southern and western (except Titirangi) quadrants, the eastern and northern quadrants are seen to be prosperous. Although over-simplified, this view is not a completely inaccurate one. The North Shore, the suburban area north of the Harbour Bridge, is relatively wealthy and blessed with a string of beaches that also function as launching pads for sailing boats and dinghies.

Devonport is a 10-minute ferry ride from Auckland's Ferry Building (p73). It is the only North Shore suburb with a distinctly historical flavour. With many of its villas found along the waterfront, a stroll along King Edward Parade provides an impression of

←

Tasting wine from barrels in the cellar of West Brook Wines, Kumeu

the suburb's pretty Victorian architecture, as well as views of Auckland's central business district across Waitemata Harbour. From Victoria Wharf, where the ferries arrive, it is a five-minute walk to the cafés, restaurants and bookshops of Victoria Road. Mount Victoria and North Head, both extinct volcanoes, are accessible by car or by walking and offer good views.

Devonport has a long and illustrious military history. Its association with the Royal New Zealand Navy dates back to 1941 and there are still approximately 2,200 staff currently stationed at the local base. Devonport's naval heritage can be viewed at the **Torpedo Bay Navy Museum** which houses a collection of photographs, uniforms, weapons and other related memorabilia. Most revealing are the sailors's letters home, diaries, journals and scrapbooks, and personal effects.

Further north, Takapuna has its own popular beach. Restaurants, cafés and shops are found along Hurstmere Road and The Strand.

Torpedo Bay Navy Museum

⊛ ⊛ ⊙ ⌂64 King Edward Parade ⊙10am–5pm daily ⍵navymuseum.co.nz

32
Henderson

⚲E1

The vineyards at Henderson, many dating back to the early 1900s, are just half an hour's drive from Auckland city. They have become a popular weekend destination for Aucklanders and visitors alike. Many of the wineries sell food, ranging from a snack to a complete meal, and offer free wine tastings.

Family-owned Babich Wines, founded in 1916, has a picnic and *pétanque* area overlooking its vineyards. The winery has a reputation for award-winning vintages, such as Babich Patriarch, but also produces inexpensive wines.

Henderson's **Corban Estate Arts Centre** is another popular destination, an art centre set amid the verdant grounds of the former Corban Winery, which was established by Lebanese immigrants in 1902. The centre has a lively programme of exhibitions, workshops and events, and is home to artists' studios and a lovely café.

Corban Estate Arts Centre

⌂2 Mt Lebanon Lane ⊙10am–4:30pm daily ⍵ceac.org.nz

EAT & DRINK

Coopers Creek Vineyard

Just outside Kumeu, this home estate is very welcoming, with playgrounds for kids and jazz music on Sundays.

⚲E1 ⌂601 SH 16, Huapai, Kumeu ⍵cooperscreek.co.nz

Soljans Estate Winery

A short drive from Kumeu, Soljans is notable for its port wine and set-menu lunches, which include options for children and all-day champagne breakfasts.

⚲E1 ⌂366 State Highway 16, Kumeu ⍵soljans.co.nz

Babich Wines

Established for over a century, Babich is the oldest family vineyard in New Zealand. It offers eight recent vintages for tastings.

⚲E1 ⌂15 Babich Rd, Henderson Valley ⊙Sun ⍵babichwines.com

A SHORT WALK
THE WATERFRONT

Distance 2 km (1 mile) **Nearest bus stop**
Quay St/Lower Albert St **Time** 30 minutes

Excellent shops, historic buildings and numerous trendy restaurants and bars – Auckland's waterfront has something for everyone. Yet only 20 years ago, this area was of little interest to residents and visitors, and the inner city, traditionally reserved for offices, was almost deserted after dark. After extensive redevelopment and investment, downtown Auckland is now a hive of activity. Luxury apartments, many set on the water's edge, along with stunning ocean views and attractive gardens, make the waterfront a prime living and entertainment area, and the perfect place for a leisurely stroll.

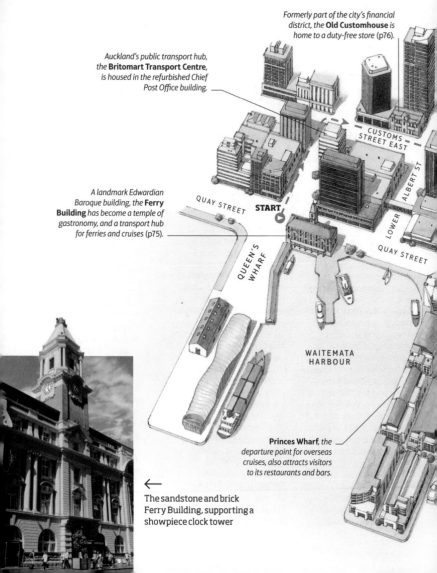

Formerly part of the city's financial district, the **Old Customhouse** *is home to a duty-free store (p76).*

Auckland's public transport hub, the **Britomart Transport Centre**, *is housed in the refurbished Chief Post Office building.*

CUSTOMS STREET EAST

ALBERT ST

LOWER

QUAY STREET

QUAY STREET

START

A landmark Edwardian Baroque building, the **Ferry Building** *has become a temple of gastronomy, and a transport hub for ferries and cruises (p75).*

QUEEN'S WHARF

WAITEMATA HARBOUR

Princes Wharf, *the departure point for overseas cruises, also attracts visitors to its restaurants and bars.*

← The sandstone and brick Ferry Building, supporting a showpiece clock tower

Locator Map
For more detail see p64

The Waterfront

AUCKLAND

← Lift bridge crossing between Viaduct Harbour and the Wynyard Quarter

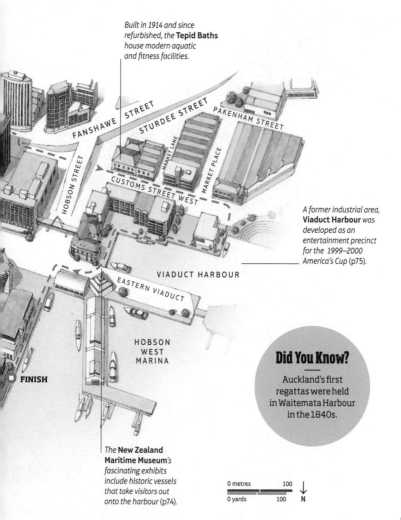

Built in 1914 and since refurbished, the **Tepid Baths** house modern aquatic and fitness facilities.

FANSHAWE STREET

STURDEE STREET

PAKENHAM STREET

HOBSON STREET

MARKET LANE

MARKET PLACE

CUSTOMS STREET WEST

A former industrial area, **Viaduct Harbour** was developed as an entertainment precinct for the 1999–2000 America's Cup (p75).

VIADUCT HARBOUR

EASTERN VIADUCT

HOBSON WEST MARINA

■ FINISH

Did You Know?

Auckland's first regattas were held in Waitemata Harbour in the 1840s.

The **New Zealand Maritime Museum**'s fascinating exhibits include historic vessels that take visitors out onto the harbour (p74).

0 metres	100
0 yards	100

↓ N

NORTHLAND

Te Tai Tokerau (Northland) is the cradle of modern New Zealand; between 700 and 800 years ago, the first Polynesian voyagers reached its northern shores. A long history of Māori occupation is evident in the region's hillside *pa* and abundant shellfishing grounds, and sites of great cultural significance punctuate the coastline. On the northern cusp of the Aupouri Peninsula is Cape Reinga – according to Māori mythology this is where spirits of the dead depart for their ancestral homeland of Hawaiki.

In the early 19th century, the first European settlers began to visit the Bay of Islands. Traders from the young Australian colonies came to swap nails and tobacco for flax and timber, and soon, whalers arrived, turning lawless settlement Russell into the "Hell-hole of the Pacific", a centre of prostitution, drinking and gun trading. Commencing with the battle of Moremonui in 1807, Northland was propelled into the intertribal Musket Wars, which devastated Māori populations, with fighting continuing into the 1830s. In 1833 the "British Resident in New Zealand" James Busby arrived, and helped to lay the groundwork of the Treaty of Waitangi, New Zealand's founding document. In 1840, the treaty was signed in the Bay of Islands before being despatched for signatures around the rest of Aotearoa.

CAPE REINGA **11**

North Cape

Te Paki Te Hapua

Parengarenga Harbour

Great Exhibition Bay

Te Kao

Ngataki **17** *Henderson Bay*

NINETY MILE BEACH

Houhora *Cape Karikari*

Pukenui *Rangaunu Bay* *Karikari Peninsula*

Mohutangi

Waiharara **1**

DOUBLESS BAY **16** Hihi

Waipapakuri Mangonui

Ahipara Bay Awanui

KAITAIA **12** Peria

Ahipara Pukepoto Mangamuka

Tauroa Point Broadwood

Tasman Sea Herekino Umawera **1**

Pawarenga RAWENE **14**

Mitimiti Taheke

Hokianga Harbour Waima

OPONONI **15**

Omapere

WAIPOUA FOREST **19**

12

Aranga

TAHAROA DOMAIN **20**

Omamari

NORTHLAND

Must Sees
- **1** Waitangi Treaty Grounds
- **2** Whangarei

Experience More
- **3** Tutukaka
- **4** Matapouri
- **5** Poor Knights Islands
- **6** Russell
- **7** Paihia
- **8** Waimate North
- **9** Whangaroa
- **10** Kerikeri
- **11** Cape Reinga
- **12** Kaitaia
- **13** Kaikohe
- **14** Rawene
- **15** Opononi
- **16** Doubtless Bay
- **17** Ninety Mile Beach
- **18** Dargaville
- **19** Waipoua Forest
- **20** Taharoa Domain
- **21** Kauri Museum

0 kilometres 20
0 miles 20

N

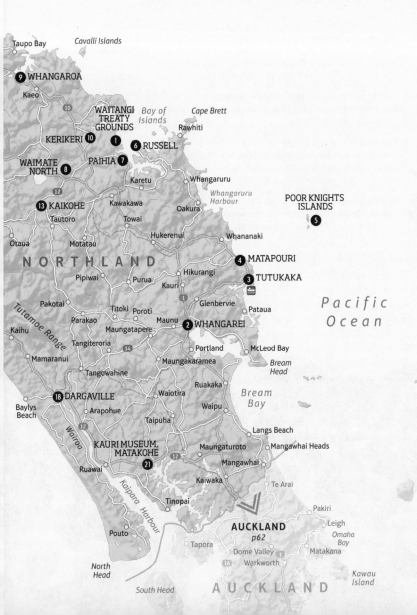

NORTHLAND

Taupo Bay
Cavalli Islands

9 WHANGAROA
Kaeo

WAITANGI
TREATY
GROUNDS
Bay of
Islands
Cape Brett
Rawhiti

KERIKERI **10** **1** **6** RUSSELL
PAIHIA **7**
Karetu

WAIMATE
NORTH **8**

13 KAIKOHE
Tautoro
Kawakawa
Towai
Whangaruru

Otaua
Motatau
Oakura
Whangaruru
Harbour
POOR KNIGHTS
ISLANDS
5

N O R T H L A N D
Pipiwai
Purua
Hukerenui
Whananaki

Pakotai
Hikurangi
Kauri
4 MATAPOURI
3 TUTUKAKA

Kaihu
Titoki
Poroti
Glenbervie
Pataua
Maunu
P a c i f i c

Parakao
Maungatapere
2 WHANGAREI
O c e a n

Mamaranui
Tangiteroria
Portland
McLeod Bay

Tangowahine
Maungakaramea
*Bream
Head*

18 DARGAVILLE
Ruakaka
*Bream
Bay*

Baylys
Beach
Waiotira
Waipu

Arapohue
Taipuha
Langs Beach
Mangawhai Heads

KAURI MUSEUM,
MATAKOHE
Maungaturoto
Mangawhai

Ruawai
21
Kaiwaka
Te Arai

Tinopai
Pakiri

AUCKLAND
p62
Leigh
*Omaha
Bay*

*North
Head*
Tapora
Dome Valley
Matakana

South Head
Warkworth
*Kawau
Island*

A U C K L A N D

WAITANGI TREATY GROUNDS

🅰E1 🏠1 Tau Henare Drive, Waitangi ⏲9am–5pm daily
🚌From Kerikeri 🌐waitangi.org.nz

Just across the Bay of Islands from Russell, New Zealand's first permanent European settlement and seaport, lies Waitangi, one of the most historically significant localities in the country.

Waitangi earned its pivotal place in New Zealand's history on 6 February 1840 when the Treaty of Waitangi *(p56)* was signed in front of the house of James Busby (1800–71), the first British Resident. The Residency, renamed the Treaty House, became a national memorial in 1932. Today Waitangi's visitor centre and museum hosts exhibits and presentations exploring the signing of the Treaty. The Treaty House itself has been restored in period style, and the Māori Meeting House, opened on 6 February 1940, contains Māori wall carvings.

In the grounds is the largest Māori war canoe in the world: 35 m (114 ft) long and carved from three kauri trees, it can carry 120 warriors. It is named Ngātokimatawhaorua, after the *waka* (canoe) in which, according to Maori mythology, the Polynesian fisherman Kupe first discovered New Zealand in AD 900. On Waitangi Day (6 February), entry to the grounds is free, there's a solemn ceremony and music, and the great *waka* is launched.

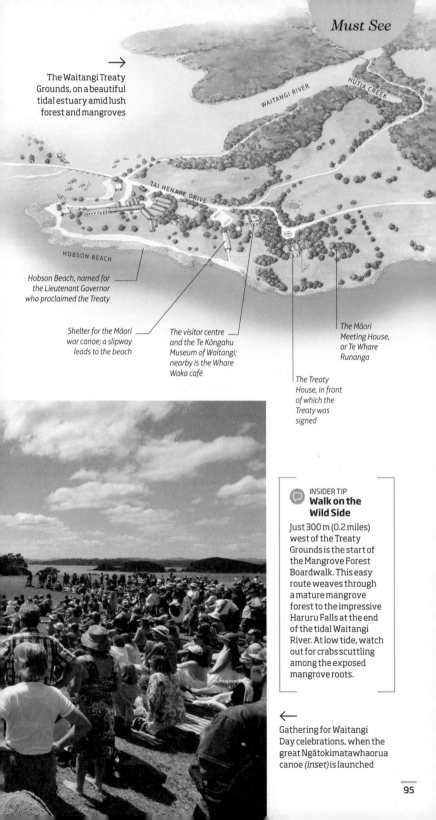

→ The Waitangi Treaty Grounds, on a beautiful tidal estuary amid lush forest and mangroves

WAITANGI RIVER

HŪTIA CREEK

TAI HENARE DRIVE

HOBSON BEACH

Hobson Beach, named for the Lieutenant Governor who proclaimed the Treaty

Shelter for the Māori war canoe; a slipway leads to the beach

The visitor centre and the Te Kōngahu Museum of Waitangi; nearby is the Whare Waka café

The Treaty House, in front of which the Treaty was signed

The Māori Meeting House, or Te Whare Rūnanga

💬 INSIDER TIP
Walk on the Wild Side

Just 300 m (0.2 miles) west of the Treaty Grounds is the start of the Mangrove Forest Boardwalk. This easy route weaves through a mature mangrove forest to the impressive Haruru Falls at the end of the tidal Waitangi River. At low tide, watch out for crabs scuttling among the exposed mangrove roots.

← Gathering for Waitangi Day celebrations, when the great Ngātokimatawhaorua canoe *(inset)* is launched

↑ Whangarei Town Basin's quayside, filled with visiting yachts

WHANGAREI

🅰E1 ✈6 km (4 miles) from Whangarei town centre 🚇 🚌
ℹTarewa Park, 92 Otaika Rd; www.whangareinz.com

Nestled between forested hills and a deep harbour, Northland's regional capital city of Whangarei is a two-hour drive from Auckland. Here, a combination of fertile soil and temperate climate is reflected in the city's lush gardens and the flourishing surrounding farmland.

Town Basin

🄰Reyburn House Ln

In the heart of the city, Whangarei's historic Town Basin has been redeveloped in a colonial theme. Its cafés, restaurants, art galleries, museums and speciality shops make it a popular gathering place. It is also a go-to destination for yatchies sailing the world, who come here to avoid cyclonic storms common in the South Pacific over the summer.

GREAT VIEW
Parihaka Lookout

For superb panoramas of Whangarei, head to the war memorial at the summit of Parihaka Mountain, reached by Memorial Drive, or along tracks from Mair Park or Dundas Road.

Claphams Clock Museum

🄰Town Basin, Dent St
🕐9am-5pm daily
🌐claphamsclocks.com

A giant sundial marks the location of the Town Basin's Claphams Clock Museum, which houses more than 1,400 items, of which 400 were donated by A Clapham, who made many of the clocks himself. The eclectic collection includes Biedermeier wall clocks, grandfather and Black Forest clocks, and a staartklok (literally a "tail clock" after the shape of its winding mechanism) from Friesland in the Netherlands.

Quarry Arts Centre

🄰21 Selwyn Ave
🕐9:30am-4:30pm Mon-Sat
🌐quarryarts.org

To the west of Whangarei is the Quarry Arts Centre, which offers local arts and crafts for sale. Set in a bush-clad quarry the centre is home to a number of artists who live on-site, some in adobe-style dwellings.

Kiwi North

🄰500 State Hwy
🕐10am-4pm daily
🌐kiwinorth.co.nz

Just outside Whangarei's town centre, Kiwi North is home to the Whangarei Museum, Kiwi House and Heritage Park. The museum's displays include fine Māori artifacts and an 1885 homestead. At Kiwi

House visitors can view the treasured and endangered kiwi bird.

gum-digging workings on all the walks, and a trail leads to a historic Māori *pa* nearby.

⑤
Parihaka Scenic Reserve

📍 **5km (3 miles from Whangarei centre)**

For those looking for more challenging activities, there are many hiking opportunities around Whangarei. The pleasant Parahika Scenic Reserve, on the eastern side of the city, has good bush walks. There are Māori pits and old

⑥
Whangarei Falls

📍 **6 Ngunguru Rd**

The most photogenic waterfalls in New Zealand lie northeast of the Parihaka Scenic Reserve in the suburb of Tikipunga, 5 km (3 miles) north of the town centre. The 26-m- (86-ft-) high waterfall drops over basalt cliffs. There are natural pools, picnic spots and two viewing platforms.

EAT

Serenity Cafe
Family-friendly sandwiches and simple meals done right.

📍 **45 Quayside**
🌐 serenitycafe.co.nz

⑤⑤⑤

Split Bar and Restaurant

Cosy cocktail and quay-fresh Croatian-style seafood served alfresco.

📍 **15 Rathbone St** 🕐 Sun
🌐 splitrestaurant.co.nz

⑤⑤⑤

Butter Factory
Signature burgers and stand-out vegan fare in a characterful former buttery.

📍 **8 Butter Factory Ln**
🕐 Sun & Mon 🌐 the butterfactory.co.nz

⑤⑤⑤

↑ Spectacular Whangarei falls, surrounded by lush native bush

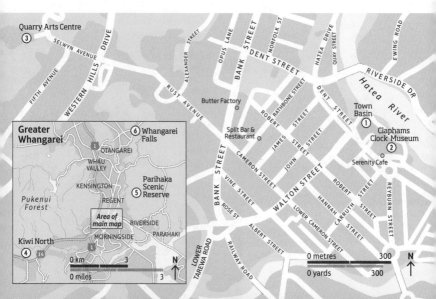

EXPERIENCE MORE

❸ Tutukaka

🅰 E1 🚇 🆆 tutukaka coastnz.com

A safe haven to mariners since Polynesian navigator Kupe first cruised past, the Tutukaka Marina lies at the head of a beautiful natural harbour. On the coastal loop road, a short distance from Whangarei, today Tutukaka is a well-known base for diving trips to the Poor Knights Islands and for big game and deep-sea fishing. Of the many diving companies that operate in this area, the biggest is **Dive! Tutukaka**. Surfing and kayaking are also popular, and the sheltered harbour is alive with yachts and fishing boats. A pathway along the waterfront leads to a small sandy beach. One of the busiest dive sites between Tutukaka and Matapouri is an artificial reef created by the sinking of two former naval ships, the *Tui* and the *Waikato*.

Dive! Tutukaka
🅰 Rona Pl, Tutukaka
🆆 diving.co.nz

❹ Matapouri

🅰 E1 🆆 whangareinz.com

Located a short distance north of Tutukaka on the coastal loop road, Matapouri has one of Northland's most beautiful beaches. Tucked between headlands and dotted with islets, Matapouri's calm waters and white sands make it a popular place for swimming and snorkelling.

A walking track connects the beach with Whale Bay, 2 km (1.2 miles) north. Lookout points on the track offer magnificent views of the coastline and ocean.

❺ Poor Knights Islands

🅰 E1 🛈 Tarewa Park, 92 Otaika Rd, Whangarei; www.whangareinz.com

About 24 km (15 miles) from the coast at Tutukaka are the Poor Knights Islands. Once a favourite spot for fishermen, the area around these two

↑ Red Pig Fish found in the waters around Poor Knights Islands

islands was established as a marine reserve in 1981. Although landing on the islands is prohibited without a special permit from the Department of Conservation, the surrounding waters are accessible to divers. Well-known mariner Jacques Cousteau considered the reserve one of the world's top five diving sites because of its exceptional water clarity and the variety of its sea life. The area benefits from a subtropical current that makes it warmer than the surrounding coastal waters, and promotes a profusion of

→ Aerial view over Tutukaka and the entrance to its sheltered natural harbour

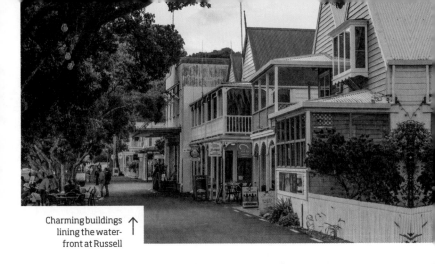

Charming buildings lining the water-front at Russell ↑

tropical and temperate marine life. Eroded volcanic rock has created a seascape of tunnels, arches and caves where divers can view fish and sponges. Scuba diving in this haven can be enjoyed all year round. Boats leave daily from Tutukaka Marina.

Reptiles such as geckos and tuataras can be found on both islands, which are thought to be the world's only nesting spot for Buller's shearwaters.

Russell

E1 ▨▨ *i* www.bay ofislandsinformation.co.nz

Originally known by its Māori name of Kororareka, Russell was the first European settlement and seaport in New Zealand. It was renamed Russell in 1844 in honour of the British colonial secretary of the day. Today, the quiet and historic town is primarily

involved in tourism, fishing, oyster farming and several cottage industries.

Formerly known as the Captain Cook Memorial Museum, the fascinating **Russell Museum** features a working model of Captain Cook's *Endeavour* and memorabilia from American author Zane Grey, who helped establish the Bay of Islands as a game fishing centre in the late 1920s. There is also a collection of early settlers' relics.

Christ Church, built in 1836, is the country's oldest surviving church. One of the contributors to the church was Charles Darwin, author of *The Origin of Species*, who visited New Zealand in 1835.

Stately **Pompallier Mission** was built on the waterfront between 1841 and 1842 to house the Marist mission's Gaveaux printing press. The building later became much neglected, until it was passed to the New Zealand Historic Places Trust in 1968 and was restored to its original state in 1993. The country's oldest standing industrial building, it now houses a printing and bookbinding exhibition, which includes the original printing press on display.

Flagstaff Hill serves as a reminder of Russell's turbulent past. It was here that Hone Heke (1810–50) cut down the British shipping

signal flagpole in 1844. The waterfront below is lined with chic cafés alongside art galleries, and the town is still a favoured spot for boaties who seek safe anchorage.

Russell Museum

◈ 🏛 🚪 2 York St ⏰ 10am–4pm daily 🌐 russell museum.org.nz

Pompallier Mission

◈ 🎭 🏛 🚪 The Strand 📞 (09) 403 9015 ⏰ 10am–4pm daily; guided tour mandatory

---

The sun setting over Russell Bay

Kayaking at the Haruru Falls on the Waitangi River at Paihia

7

Paihia

🅰E1 ⏹⏹ 🛈 Marsden Rd;
www.paihia.co.nz

Starting life as a mission post in 1823, Paihia now joins places such as Russell and Tutukaka as a base for deep-sea game fishing.

To the north of Paihia, on the road to Kerikeri is the **Lily Pond Farm Park**, a working farm that will appeal to families with small children. The park gives visitors the chance to interact with a whole range of farm animals including sheep, pigs and goats. There are also more exotic species of animal, such as eels, alpaca and emus.

Located 3 km (2 miles) from Paihia, on the Waitangi River, are the **Haruru Falls**. The small settlement close to the waterfalls is said to be the first such in New Zealand. Nearby mangroves are home to herons and nesting native cormorants. An alternative approach to the falls is by kayak along the river. You can hire kayaks from **Coastal Kayakers**, or join a group of kayakers on one of their guided tours.

Lily Pond Farm Park
 🏠RD1 Puketona Rd
📞(09) 402 6099 🕙10am–4pm daily

Haruru Falls
🚻🚻 🏠Near Waitangi Treaty Grounds 📞(09) 402 7437

Coastal Kayakers
🚻 🏠Te Karuwha Pde, Waitangi 🌐coastal kayakers.co.nz

8

Waimate North

🅰E1

Near Kerikeri is Waimate North, a missionary community in the 1830s. It was also the site of New Zealand's first large English-style farm. It is now best known for **Te Waimate Mission**, New Zealand's second-oldest house. The sole survivor of three mission houses built in 1832, it is furnished with missionary period furniture and early tools.

Te Waimate Mission
🚻 🏠Te Ahu Ahu Rd
📞(09) 405 9734 🕙10am–4pm daily; Nov-Apr: to 5pm Fri-Tue

9

Whangaroa

🅰E1 🚇 🌐whangaroa.co.nz

A small, scenic settlement with a lovely harbour, Whangaroa is best appreciated from the summit of St Paul, a rock formation that dominates the town. The surrounding hills were once covered in huge kauri trees, which have long since been turned into ship masts and timber. Croatians worked the Matauri Bay gum-fields in the late 19th century, extracting resin.

DRINK

Pipi Patch Paihia
Simple, laid-back backpacker's bar, with generous cocktails and heaps of helpful tourist advice. Modest prices and poolside service.

🅰E1 🏠18 Kings Rd, Paihia 🌐stayat base.com

Charlotte's Kitchen
Slap bang in the middle of the wharf, this place offers the best ocean views in Paihia. Enjoy the delicious cocktails, and an ecclectic menu of seafood and pizza.

🅰E1 🏠69 Marsden Rd, Paihia 🌐charlottes kitchen.co.nz

Today, Whangaroa Harbour has become well known for its big-game fishing, cruises, diving and snorkelling.

Kerikeri

E1 🚌🚲 **W** kerikeri.co.nz

The pretty town of Kerikeri is noted for its subtropical climate, citrus and kiwifruit orchards, historic buildings, and an art and craft trail.

The Kerikeri Basin is home to **Kerikeri Mission Station**, one of New Zealand's earliest settlements. It was set up in New Zealand, in 1819, under the protection of Māori chief Hongi Hika. The mission station includes Kerikeri Mission House (tours only). Constructed in 1821, the building belonged to the Kemp family in 1832 and was left to the New Zealand Historic Places Trust in 1974. Restored, it looks much as it did in the 1840s. The mission station also encompasses New Zealand's oldest surviving stone building, the Stone Store, built in 1835 as part of the mission house. Intended as a storehouse, it gradually turned into a general store and, from the 1960s, a souvenir shop, selling hand-forged nails

HUNDERTWASSER IN KAWAKAWA

South of Paihia is Kawakawa, home to the world's most visited toilet block, a public convenience and a work of art by Friedensreich Hundertwasser receiving 350,000 visitors each year. The undulating, brightly coloured structure was Hundertwasser's last work. The Austrian-born artist is perhaps most famous for urban social housing in his hometown of Vienna, but spent much of his life in New Zealand and was a Kawakawa local.

and other products in keeping with its history. On the slope behind the mission house is St James Church, constructed in 1878 of native timbers such as kauri and puriri.

Above the Basin are the remnants of Kororipo Pa, a Māori fortification. The strategic base of Hongi Hika, the *pa* is best known as an assembly point for war parties in the 1820s. Across the river from the *pa* is **Rewa's Village**, a reconstructed pre-European Māori fishing village built from native materials; those used

before the missionaries came. It provides an introduction to traditional buildings such as *marae* (gathering place) and *pataka* (communal raised storehouse). There are two ancient canoes at the village.

Kerikeri Mission Station
♿🚻🅿️ 🏠 246 Kerikeri Rd
📞 (09) 407 9236 🕐 10am–4pm daily

Rewa's Village
♿🚻🅿️ 🏠 1 Landing Rd
🕐 10am–4pm daily 🚫 Good Fri, 25 Dec **W** rewasvillage.co.nz

→
Nestled in a delightful garden, St James Church at Kerikeri

11

Cape Reinga

🅰 E1 🌐 northlandnz.com

Reinga, meaning "underworld", refers to the Māori belief that this is where the spirits of the dead leave for the journey to Hawaiki. The roots of an old pohutukawa tree at the tip of the cape are said to be the departure point for these spirits. Looking out from Cape Reinga over the Columbia Bank, visitors can see the Tasman Sea converge with the Pacific Ocean. An isolated lighthouse stands on the tip. The cape is not the very end of the country; the northernmost point is on North Cape.

> **Did You Know?**
>
> Cape Reinga's was the last manned lighthouse in New Zealand; its final keeper left in 1987.

12

Kaitaia

🅰 E1   🛈 Cnr Matthews Ave & South Rd; www. kaitaia.com

The largest town in the Far North, Kaitaia is a good base for day trips in the area. It is home to the **Te Ahu Centre**, which has the earliest authenticated European artifact left in New Zealand – a 1,500-kg (3,300-lb) wrought-iron anchor, lost in a storm in Doubtless Bay in 1769 by J F M de Surville, the French explorer.

Te Ahu Centre

🌐🌐🌐 🄰 Cnr Matthews Ave & South Rd 🕐 9am–4pm Mon–Fri 🄲 Good Fri, 25 Dec 🌐 kaitaianz.co.nz

13

Kaikohe

🅰 E1   🌐 kaikohe.co.nz

Kaikohe is best known for its natural hot springs, many of which are used to generate energy, but are also enjoyed as therapeutic spas, like the pleasant (if rather basic) **Waiariki Hot Springs**. While such complexes have been turned into major tourist attractions in places such as Rotorua (p116), they are mainly a local feature in Kaikohe, where the majority of visitors and the attendant are on first-name terms. Outsiders are welcome to enjoy the hot spring waters with temperatures between 32 and 42°C (90 and 108°F).

Kaikohe's **Pioneer Village** is an educational indoor and outdoor museum, which presents a collection of houses and artifacts related to the district's early Māori and European history. A conducted tour takes visitors to attractions from the 1862 Old Courthouse to Maioha Cottage (1875), Utakura Settlers Hall and School (1891)

$\rightarrow$

Statue of Opo, the friendly dolphin that became famous in Opononi

← The 1941 lighthouse perched on the tip of Cape Reinga

and Alexander's Sawmill (1913). Also on display are vintage vehicles (some still in working order), a fire station, a bush railway and a small railway station.

From a hillside monument dedicated to Chief Hone Heke (grand-nephew of the old chief), there are fine views of both the east and west coasts.

Waiariki Hot Springs
⊗ 🏠 Ngawha Springs Rd 🕒 9am-9pm daily 🌐 ngawhasprings.co.nz

Pioneer Village
⊗⊗📷 🏠 1a Recreation Rd 🕒 May-Oct: 10am-4pm Mon-Fri; Nov-Apr: 10am-4pm Mon-Sat 🌐 pioneervillage.org.nz

14 Rawene

🏠 E1 🚌 ℹ️ Boatshed Café and Gallery, Clendon Esplanade; www.rawene.nz

This quaint village, which has shops jutting out over the water, was home to James Reddy Clendon (1800–72), the first US Consul in New Zealand. He would later became Hokianga's Resident Magistrate. **Clendon House**, now owned by the New Zealand Historic Places Trust, was probably built after 1866.

The ferry across Hokianga Harbour links with an alternative route to Kaitaia, via Broadwood and Herekino.

Clendon House
⊗ 🏠 Clendon Esplanade 🕒 Nov-Apr: 10am-4pm Sat & Sun; May-Oct: 10am-4pm Sat 🌐 clendonhouse.co.nz

15 Opononi

🏠 E1 🚌 🍴

In the minds of many New Zealanders, the small beach town of Opononi is forever linked to that of its most famous visitor, Opo. This dolphin became a national celebrity when it spent the

summer of 1955 playing with children and performing tricks with beach balls. Sadly, it was killed by unknown dynamite fishers. Outside Opononi's pub a bronze replica of the original stone sculpture by artist Russell Clark marks the dolphin's grave. Diagonally across the road from the pub is the wharf, which is the starting point for a short boat trip to see the giant sand dunes on the far side of Hokianga Harbour.

STAY

Kauri Cliffs
In an exceptional setting, this luxury hotel has 22 suites, a spa and golf course. There is also a private cottage for true exclusivity.

🏠 E1 🏠 139 Tepene Tablelands Rd, Matauri Bay 🌐 robertsonlodges.com

⑤⑤⑤

Scenic Hotel
Set amid subtropical gardens, this resort-style hotel has spacious rooms and island-influenced architecture.

🏠 E1 🏠 Cnr MacMurray & Seaview rds, Bay of Islands, Paihia 🌐 scenichotels.co.nz

⑤⑤⑤

The Treehouse
Cabins are set in subtropical gardens overlooking Hokianga Harbour. Shared kitchen/bathroom.

🏠 E1 🏠 168 West Coast Rd, RD1, Hokianga, Kohukohu Town 🌐 treehouse.co.nz

⑤⑤⑤

16

Doubtless Bay

 E1 | | **w** doubtless bay.co.nz

Said to be the first landfall for the explorer Kupe, Doubtless Bay was an important base for whalers in the early days of European settlement. The bay encompasses a wide crescent of golden beaches, including Cable Bay and Cooper's Beach, popular with swimmers and snorkellers. The fishing village of Mangonui, situated on the bay's estuary, has many historic buildings.

 17

Ninety Mile Beach

E1 | **w** northlandnz.com

A misnomer, Ninety Mile Beach is, in fact, only 96 km (60 miles) long, but is still the longest beach in the country. This area is almost like a desert, with sand dunes that can reach 143 m (470 ft) high fringing the beach. It was once a forested region, but the kauri trees were destroyed by inundations of water during successive ice ages. Pine trees have been planted to stabilize the dunes. Surf fishing and digging for shellfish are popular activities. Rental cars are not allowed to be driven on the beach.

18

Dargaville

E2 | | **i** 4 Murdoch St; www.dargaville.co.nz

Dargaville is the nation's *kumara* capital and many roadside stalls with honesty boxes offer the opportunity to buy these sweet potatoes.

The **Dargaville Museum** is not just of interest to sailors. Apart from Māori canoes, ship models and other nautical items, the displays range from old photos of the local Croatian Social Club to memorabilia from the Northern Wairoa Scottish Society and a pig skull from New Mexico.

 INSIDER TIP
Ride the Rails

Disused railway lines out of Dargaville go to Tangowahine on a two-hour golf cart route ideal for families. Rails skirt the river passing through farmland. Make sure to book ahead at *www.port dargavillecruises.co.nz*.

Dargaville Museum

32 Mt Wesley Coast Rd, Harding Park
9am–4pm daily **w** darga villemuseum.co.nz

19

Waipoua Forest

E2 | **w** waipoua-forest.co.nz

Waipoua Forest is well worth a visit because of its kauri trees.

> Dargaville is the nation's *kumara* capital and many roadside stalls with honesty boxes offer the opportunity to buy these sweet potatoes.

→ Strolling the desert-like sand dunes sweeping across Ninety Mile Beach

↑ Admiring Tane Mahuta, New Zealand's largest kauri tree, in Waipoua Forest

history, with indoor exhibits and interactive displays along with outdoor reconstructions of traditional buildings made from kauri.

Within the main museum there is kauri furniture and timber panels as well as a collection of kauri gum, featuring carvings made from the amber-like fossilized resin of the trees.

Outside are a number of vintage buildings built using the precious wood, including a steam sawmill showing how the logs were milled, a kauri post office from 1909, a six-room fully furnished early 20th-century home and an 1867 pioneer church.

With New Zealand's kauri forests under threat from the fatal kauri dieback pathogen, exhibitions here showing the tree's role in the nation's history gain added poignancy.

Being in the presence of a tree that has entered its third millennium is a memorable experience – photos seldom capture the grandeur of these trees. Local Māori have christened the country's largest living kauri Tane Mahuta, "Lord of the Forest". Reached by an easy five-minute walk from the road through the park, the tree is 51 m (168 ft) high, has a girth of 14 m (46 ft) and a volume of 244.5 cu m (8,635 cu ft). Department of Conservation experts estimate the tree to be 2,000 years old. Four other known giant trees in the forest are at least 1,000 years old.

camping areas and signposted footpaths through forest to the coast of the Tasman Sea. The three Taharoa freshwater lakes – Taharoa, Kai Iwi and Waikere – with their white-sand beaches and phenomenal clear blue waters, delight swimmers, water-skiers, fishermen, picnickers and campers alike. Kai Iwi, the largest and most popular of the lakes, is remarkable for its vast stretches of very shallow turquoise water, warmed by the sun, leading to chilly dark blue depths.

Taharoa Domain

 E1 Kai Iwi Lakes Rd, Omamari ⓦ kai-iwi-lakes. co.nz

Just a 30-minute drive north of Dargaville, this extensive nature and recreation reserve encompasses three deep-water lakes, with serviced

21 ⊗ ⓜ

Kauri Museum

Ⓐ E2 Ⓐ Church Rd, Matakohe Ⓒ 9am–5pm daily ⓦ kau.nz

Located 45 km (28 miles) south of Dargaville, the Kauri Museum in Matakohe gives visitors an insight into the significance of the kauri tree. The museum illustrates the role these mammoth trees played in New Zealand's pioneering

North Cape

Bowling Bay

Spirits Bay *is the starting point for the 28-km (17-mile) walk to Cape Reinga.*

Hooper Point

Kapowairau

Waikuku Beach

Cape Reinga

Cape Reinga Lighthouse

Spirits Bay

Te Werahi Beach

Motuopao Island

Cape Maria van Diemen

CAPE REINGA ROAD

Te Paki

Te Hapua

Parengarenga Harbour

Ohao Point

Paua

Rarawa Beach

The solitary **Cape Reinga Lighthouse** *is New Zealand's northernmost lighthouse.*

Scott Point

Pukekarea 120 m (393 ft) △

Te Paki Reserve

Te Paki Dunes

Karatia

Apouri Forest

Te Kao Bay

Great Exhibition Bay

Tangoake

Lake Wahakari

Te Kao

FAR NORTH ROAD

Tobogganing off the massive sand dunes is the main attraction at **Te Paki Reserve**.

← The impressive sand dunes at Te Paki Reserve on Ninety Mile Beach

N i n e t y   M i l e   B e a c h

Ngataki

FINISH

End this drive on **Ninety Mile Beach**, *where hard sands make it the perfect place for biking and coach tours.*

A DRIVING TOUR
AUPORI PENINSULA

Length 96 km (60 miles) **Stopping-off points** Pukenui, Te Kao, Cape Reinga **Terrain** Largely flat, some unpaved roads

Called "The Tail of The Fish" by Māori, Aupori Peninsula is a thin strip of land no more than 12 km (7 miles) wide between Ninety Mile Beach on the west coast and a number of beaches and bays along the east coast. The unspoiled beaches and coastline, together with high year-round temperatures, make this region a pleasant driving destination, with plenty of stops along the route for swimming, walking, sand tobogganing and fishing.

↑ Sweeping views of the rugged peninsula from Cape Reinga Coastal Walkway in Te Paki Reserve

Locator Map
For more detail see p92

Aupori Peninsula

NORTHLAND

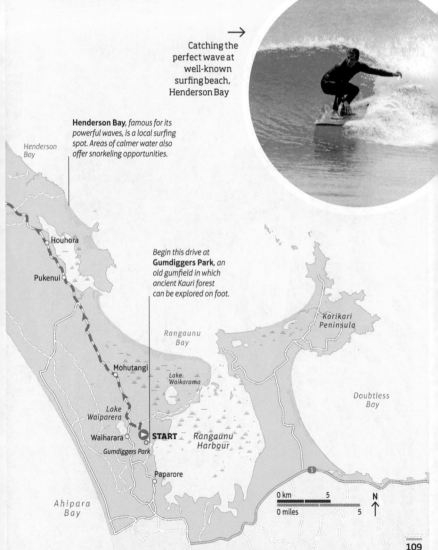

→ Catching the perfect wave at well-known surfing beach, Henderson Bay

Henderson Bay, *famous for its powerful waves, is a local surfing spot. Areas of calmer water also offer snorkeling opportunities.*

Henderson Bay

Houhora

Pukenui

Begin this drive at **Gumdiggers Park,** *an old gumfield in which ancient Kauri forest can be explored on foot.*

Karikari Peninsula

Rangaunu Bay

Mohutangi

Lake Waikarama

Doubtless Bay

Lake Waiparera

Waiharara ● **START** *Rangaunu Harbour*

Gumdiggers Park

Paparore

Ahipara Bay

0 km · · · 5
0 miles · · · 5

N ↑

109

CENTRAL NORTH ISLAND

Stretching from Auckland down to Taranaki, Manawatu and Hawkes Bay, the Central North Island includes a great variety of natural sights, and is rich in Māori history. The Waikato-based Māori King Movement began here in 1858, shortly before battles waged between the government and Māori over land. Te Arawa Māori around Rotorua famously sided with the Crown, so it is perhaps unsurprising that it is Rotorua that has become the main centre for experiencing Māori culture.

Today, the region's sparse towns mostly exist to support farming: in the west, the dairy farmers of the Waikato, the King Country and the Bay of Plenty compete with horticulturists for the best land, while sheep, cattle and deer roam larger paddocks on hills clear-felled in the early 20th century. Along the North Island's eastern coastal strip, rugged mountain ranges cast a rain-shadow which make Poverty Bay and Hawkes Bay ideal wine-growing regions. Between lies the Volcanic Plateau, centring on a trio of active volcanoes in Tongariro National Park. Mount Ruapehu forms the southern limit of the Taupo Volcanic Zone, whose steaming heart pulses strongest at Rotorua, with its geysers, bubbling mud pools, multi-coloured silica terraces, steaming lakes and mineral pools.

CENTRAL NORTH ISLAND

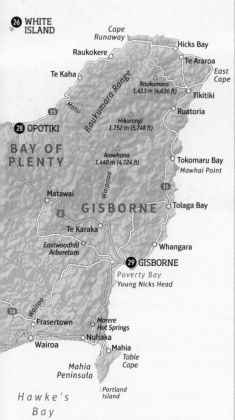

WAITOMO CAVES

E3 ☖ **21 Waitomo Caves Rd** ⏲ **8:45am–5pm daily** 🚌 **From Hamilton, Auckland and Rotorua** 🖥 **waitomocaves.com**

With underground tours ranging from eminently accessible walks to adrenalin-fuelled thrills, a trip to the Waitomo Caves is a great adventure, and one that's suited to all ages and abilities.

The area known as Waitomo consists of a 45 km (28 mile) network of underground limestone caves and grottoes linked to the Waitomo Stream; the simple action of dripping water rich in dissolved limestone has, over eons of time, created all the marvels to be seen here. There are three major caves here: Waitomo Glowworm Caves, Ruakuri Cave and Aranui Cave. A chamber of the Waitomo Glowworm Caves was first explored in 1887, and a tranquil boat trip through this luminous wonderland is a highlight of the caves. More glowworm grottoes and fantastic limestone formations of towering stalagmites and looming stalactites can be seen on relatively easy guided walks through Ruakuri and Aranui caves. For the more active and intrepid visitor unafraid of tight squeezes, there's a fine range of cave-based adventure activities, including abseiling into a limestone shaft and cave system, and black-water rafting, an adventure sport unique to New Zealand.

The level of organization and attention to safety here is first-class and the guides highly capable and well-informed. The caves have superb lighting, good paths and handrails. Admission is by guided tour only; wear non-slip comfortable shoes and loose, warm clothing; any specialist equipment and clothing (such as wet- and drysuits) can be provided.

💬 INSIDER TIP
Beat the Crowds

Masses of tour buses bring visitors to the Waitomo Caves; most don't arrive before 10:30am and usually depart from 3:30pm onwards, so if you can, arrange your visit outside this window. The caves' website has lots of suggestions for overnight stays, some basic, some quirky: at the Woodlyn Park motel, you can sleep in Hobbit holes, on a boat or a train, or even in the cockpit of a Bristol Freighter aircraft.

←

The magical Glowworm Grottoes, one of the chief attractions at the caves

① The spiral ramp down to the wheelchair- and pushchair-accessible Ruakuri caves and their amazing stalactites.

② "Lost World" tours start with a 100-m (330-ft) abseil down a huge limestone shaft followed by some exciting caving.

③ Black-water rafting adventures on tyre inner tubes; these "wet" tours end with welcome hot showers and drinks.

↑ Pohutu Geyser, the largest active geyser found in the southern hemisphere

❷

ROTORUA

🅰 E3 ℹ 1167 Fenton St; www.rotorua.com

Set on the southern shore of a lake of the same name, Rotorua is the North Island's most popular tourist destination. The city is renowned for its hot and steamy thermal activity (evident from countless bores, geysers and bubbling mud pools) and healing mineral water. Rotorua is also known as the heartland of Māori culture and offers the chance to experience Māori art, architecture and cultural performances.

①
Government Gardens

🔲 Queens Drive

The formal Government Gardens are laid out in front of the stately Tudor-style Rotorua Museum (closed).

They comprise a series of trimmed croquet and bowling greens and formal flower gardens dotted with steaming thermal pools. This site is of historical importance to local Māori people, for here significant battles have taken place.

The 1927 Arawa Soldiers' Memorial, which stands a short distance north of the museum, symbolizes the history of contact between Pakeha and local tribes. At its base is the Arawa migration canoe, from which Rotorua's Te Arawa people trace their descent.

 ← Maori designs displayed on a fence in the Government Gardens

❷
The Blue Baths

🔲 Queens Drive ⏰ 10am–6pm daily 🚫 25 Dec 🌐 bluebaths.co.nz

These heated pools were built in the 1930s and offered the then-novel attraction of mixed bathing. Housed in a Spanish mission-style building, they were once a symbol of New Zealand's ambitions to become the premier spa of the British Empire. A museum here documents the social history associated with the construction and use of the baths.

❸
Polynesian Spa

🔲 Hinemoa St ⏰ 8am–11pm daily 🌐 polynesianspa.co.nz

People from around the world visit the Polynesian Spa's mineral waters, which range from 33 °C (92 °F) to 42 °C (107 °F). Radium and Priest waters, both acidic and cloudy, are sourced from an underground spring while alkaline Rachel water is piped to the spa from nearby. Adults have access to a mineral pool overlooking a large, heated, freshwater pool, with a shallow end for toddlers. Users can regulate the temperature in the spa's private pools. Aix massage (under jets of water) and other therapies are available in the luxury spa area.

Flying Column, a guerilla unit of local Māori who fought for the British army in the New Zealand wars.

④ St Faith's Anglican Church

🏛 Ohinemutu ⏰ Daily

Built in 1910, the Tudor-style St Faith's is the second church built at Ohinemutu, a Māori village on the shores of the lake around which Rotorua grew. An etched-glass window in the chapel at the far end of the church depicts Christ dressed in a *korowai* (chief's cloak) and appearing to walk on the waters of Lake Rotorua. The interior is richly embellished with Māori carvings, woven wall panels and painted scrollwork.

There are a few graves of interest next to the church, including that of Seymour Mills Spencer (1810–98) who preached to the Arawa for 50 years, and Captain Gilbert Mair (1843–1923) of the Arawa

⑤ Tamatekapua

🏛 Ohinemutu

The magnificent Tamatekapua meeting house, built in 1873, is the main gathering place of the Arawa tribe. Opposite St Faith's, it was named for an earlier house that stood on Mokoia Island and the captain of the Arawa, one of the canoes that brought the ancestors of Māori to New Zealand. The figure at the base of the centre post is Ngatoroirangi, the canoe's navigator, whom mythology credits with bringing thermal activity to the region.

⑥ Kuirau Park

🏛 Kuirau Rd ☎ (07) 348 4199

Within Kuirau Park there are a number of boiling mud pools, steam vents and small geysers. Free thermal foot pools, picnic

SPA CITY

Rotorua is renowned for its mineral rich waters. Two mineral waters were used in a succession of 19th-century and early 20th-century spas, the largest being the Bath House, opened in 1908. The waters were considered "stimulating and tonic in reaction". Today, on the shores of Lake Rotorua, QE Health uses hot mineral waters to relieve pain, relax muscles and stimulate joint movement.

areas, well-kept gardens, a children's playground, a small warm lake and a scented garden are other attractions within the domain.

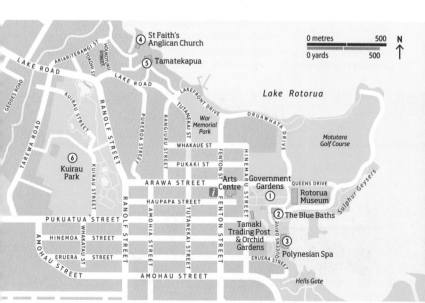

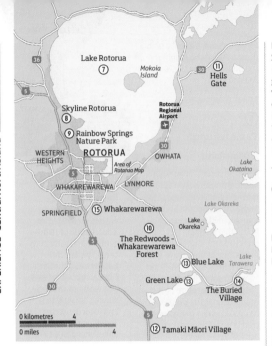

Lake Rotorua
Mokoia Island
⑦
⑪ Hells Gate
⑧ Skyline Rotorua
⑨ Rainbow Springs Nature Park
WESTERN HEIGHTS
ROTORUA
Rotorua Regional Airport
Area of Rotorua Map
OWHATA
Lake Okataina
WHAKAREWAREWA
LYNMORE
SPRINGFIELD
⑮ Whakarewarewa
Lake Okareka
⑩ The Redwoods – Whakarewarewa Forest
Lake Okareka
Lake Tarawera
⑬ Blue Lake
Green Lake ⑬
⑭ The Buried Village
0 kilometres 4
0 miles 4
⑫ Tamaki Māori Village

Mount Ngongotaha, the Skyline lookout, at 487 m (1,598 ft), can be reached by gondola, and gives stunning views. At the top, you can also explore 10.5-km (6.5-miles) of biking trails. An exciting way to descend the mountain, by day or night, is by luge (a short, raised toboggan on wheels).

Rainbow Springs Nature Park

🏠 Fairy Springs Rd
🕗 8:30am-5:30pm daily
🌐 rainbowsprings.co.nz

Visitors can feed some of the thousands of rainbow, brown, brook and tiger trout in the crystal-clear freshwater streams and fern-fringed pools here. Rainbow Springs is also home to the National Kiwi Hatchery Aotearoa, which explains national efforts to protect wild kiwi.

The Redwoods – Whakarewarewa Forest

🏠 Long Mile Rd 🕗 8:30am-dusk daily 🌐 redwoods.co.nz

This 40 sq km (15 sq mile) forest, which adjoins the

AROUND ROTORUA

⑦
Lake Rotorua

This nearly circular lake can be enjoyed by paddle steamer, kayak, jetboat or water scooter. Mokoia Island, in the centre of the lake, is famous for the love story of Hinemoa, who defied her family's wishes and swam at night to the island to be with the chief Tutanekai, who played his flute to guide her.

The island offers 4 km (2.5 miles) of walking tracks as well as Hinemoa's thermal pool.

Skyline Rotorua

🏠 185 Fairy Springs Rd
🕗 Daily 🌐 skyline.co.nz

Located halfway up the 778-m- (2,552-ft-) high

↑ A platform jutting out over the calm waters of Lake Rotorua

↑ Walking beneath the towering redwoods in Whakarewarewa Forest

Whakarewarewa thermal area (*p120*), contains majestic groves of redwoods, firs and other plantation trees. The Redwoods Treewalk within the main Redwood Grove features a series of 28 suspension bridges traversing the gaps between the enormous 117-year-old Redwood trees, allowing visitors to admire these giants at close quarters.

Hells Gate

🏠 State Hwy 33 🕐 8:30am–10pm daily 💻 hellsgate.co.nz

Sixteen kilometres (10 miles) from Rotorua, at Tikitere, Hells Gate is famous for its ferocious volcanic activity. Drifting, wraith-like mists part to reveal a fierce and spectacular thermal valley that includes the Kakahi Falls, the largest hot waterfall in the southern hemisphere, and New Zealand's largest boiling whirlpool. Another cauldron of water, the Sulphur Bath, is purported to heal septic cuts, bites and other skin ailments.

The area is well signposted, with good pathways and barriers. Traditional Māori massage can be enjoyed at the Wai Ora Spa.

Tamaki Māori Village

🏠 State Hwy 5 🕐 Daily 💻 tamakimaorivillage.co.nz

Visitors are introduced to Māori customs and traditions at this replica of a Māori village. Sampling a full *hāngi* feast, in which selected foods are cooked on hot rocks in an authentic earth oven, is part of the cultural experience. This delicious meal is served daily between 6:30pm and 10pm. Educational workshops are also held regularly on traditional Māori carving and weaving, performing arts, weaponry and warfare, and Māori food and health.

⑬

Blue Lake and Green Lake

🏠 Tarawera Rd

Eleven km (7 miles) southeast of Rotorua are the stunning Blue and Green lakes (Tikitapu and Rotokakahi). The narrow isthmus that divides the lakes provides a good vantage point to compare their contrasting hues. Lake Rotokakahi is sacred to Māori and is not accessible, but Lake Tikitapu

is the scene of many summer activities such as kayaking and waterskiing.

The Buried Village

🏠 Tarawera Rd 🕐 9am–5pm daily 🕐 25 Dec 💻 buriedvillage.co.nz

Fifteen minutes' drive from Rotorua and 2.5 km (1.5 miles) from Lake Tarawera is what remains of the village of Te Wairoa, devastated by the eruption of Mount Tarawera in 1886. A walk through parkland takes in the excavations of several sites and an interactive museum explains the eruption. A bush walk leads to the Te Wairoa waterfalls, while a walkway offers clifftop views.

TARAWERA ERUPTION

Months of underground rumbling culminated on 10 June 1886 with the eruption of Mount Tarawera, which left a deep crater. Lasting about three hours, the blast spread along a 17 km (10 mile) rift and killed 153 people. The eruption hurled red-hot volcanic bombs and bits of solidified lava 14 km (8.5 miles). The Māori villages of Te Ariki, Te Wairoa and Moura were buried under 20 m (65 ft) of mud.

INSIDER TIP
💬 **Take an Eco-tour**

Learn how the Māori in Whakarewarewa live in harmony with nature by taking an eco-tour (www.rotoruanz.com/visit/see-and-do/eco-tours). There are many other guided tours to choose from, including kayaking by starlight and waterfall hikes.

⑮ 🎿 Ⓜ 🍴 🖥 🛍

WHAKAREWAREWA

🅰 F3 🚌 No 2 CityRide from Rotorua 🏠 Te Puia: Hemo Rd; Te Whakarewarewa: Tryon St 🕐 Te Puia: 8am–5pm daily (to 6pm Sep–Apr); Te Whakarewarewa: 8:30am–5pm daily 🌐 tepuia.com; whakarewarewa.com

At Rotorua's southern edge, Whakarewarewa is a volcanic wonderland with geysers, boiling mudpots and steaming waters. It also offers rich experiences of Māori culture, society and tradition.

Within Geyser Flat, a 1 sq km (0.4 sq mile) silica terrace, there are more than 500 thermal features, including seven geysers; the largest is Pohutu ("Big Splash"), which erupts 10–25 times a day up to 30 m (100 ft) high. Don't miss the Leaping Frog mud pool and the Brainpot, a symmetrical basin said to have been used to boil the heads of enemies. Immerse yourself further in the mysteries and practicalities of Māori life at the Te Puia arts and crafts centre and Te Whakarewarewa Living Māori Village. Te Puia's attractions include carving, weaving and cultural performances; at Te Whakarewarewa, visitors can see a meeting house, cooking pools and a cemetery where the dead are interred in vaults above ground to keep them from the steaming earth.

↑ Ancient skills are passed to younger generations at Te Puia's carving school

←
Rushing geothermal
waters at awe-inspiring
Whakarewarewa

↑ The Meeting House at
Te Whakarewarewa,
the starting point for
excellent guided tours

←
Hypnotic swirling patterns
created in the simmering
mud pools, reminiscent of
linear Māori carvings

VOLCANIC FEATURES AT WHAKAREWAREWA

The volcanic activity
at Whakarewarewa
is a reminder of the
powerful tectonic
forces at work beneath
the earth's surface.
Here, volcanic gases
and heat break through
in spectacular and
sometimes dangerous
ways; superheated
steam emerges from a
vast chamber of boiling
water in roaring towers
of spray. Mud pools boil
and churn as gas and
hot water seek to
escape through the
surface, and steam
cascades over the
thermal pools and
brightly coloured
mineral-rich silica flats.

Three volcanoes forming
an interlocking landscape
of calderas and peaks ↑

❸

TONGARIRO NATIONAL PARK

▲E3 **🏠Ohakune** **🛈 National Park Visitor Centre, State Highway 48, Whakapapa Village; open 9am–5pm daily** **📮National Park Store, Carroll St** **🌐doc.govt.nz; Whakapapa and Turoa ski areas: www.mtruapehu.com**

South of Lake Taupo lies the magnificent 7,600 sq km (2,930 sq m) Tongariro, New Zealand's first national park and a dual UNESCO World Heritage Site, for both its natural and Māori spiritual and cultural value. It is a magnificent area for winter sports and summer trekking, but is also a volatile natural environment where caution is key.

The peaks of three active volcanic mountains – Ruapehu, Ngauruhoe and Tongariro – form the nucleus of the park, a winter playground for skiers and snowboarders, and a year-round wilderness walking, hiking and mountain-climbing area. The Tongariro Alpine Crossing, from Mangatepopo to Ketetahi, covers 18.5 km (11.5 miles) of varied and spectacular volcanic terrain and is often described as the best one-day trek in New Zealand. Round the Mountain is a four- to five-day hike around Ruapehu for those seeking solitude, magnificent views and a back-country experience. Park-and-ride shuttle services operate from the main visitor centre to the park.

VOLCANIC HAZARDS

Volcanic activity can occur in the park at any time and with little or no warning. Anyone intending to hike or climb on the upper slopes needs to first check the current alert status, exclusion zones and safety information with the nearest visitor centre. Be prepared for unpredictable weather, too; even in summer, storms are sudden and mists at dawn and dusk can obscure the path. Proper footwear and wind- and rain-proof clothing are essential.

① Hiking the Tongariro Alpine Track, with spectacular views of Lake Taupo.

② Snowboarding down steep, powdery slopes of Tongariro's Mount Ruapehu.

③ The scrubby Rangipo Desert on the eastern side is used for army training.

④

NAPIER

F4 🗺100 Marina Pde; www.hawkesbay.com
🚄5km (3 miles) NW of city 🚌Munto St

Perched on the edge of the Pacific Ocean, this elegant city is a memorial to a 1931 earthquake and fire that caused colossal damage and devastation. During rebuilding, architects adopted the fashionable Art Deco style, creating an endlessly stylish streetscape.

①

The National Aquarium of New Zealand

🏛Marine Parade 🕐9am-5pm daily 🌐national aquarium.co.nz

In a stingray-shaped building on Napier's foreshore, the aquarium's proximity to the ocean means that fresh sea-water can be pumped directly to its tanks. The ground floor has native marine life and other species such as the tuatara (a unique native reptile), while the upper floor is dedicated to creatures from different parts of the world. The Oceanarium is viewed from an underwater tunnel, and is home to sharks, stingrays, seahorses and east coast native fish. Visitors can watch divers feed the fish at 10am and 2pm every day, and there are opportunities to take part in a supervised swim with the sharks. There is also a nocturnal Kiwi House, for viewing the national bird.

②

MTG Hawke's Bay

🏛1 Tennyson St 🕐9:30am-5pm Mon-Sat 🌐mtg hawkesbay.com

MTG Hawke's Bay occupies three buildings that are home to a museum, a theatre and an art gallery. The museum has collections of Māori treasures, fine art, applied and decorative arts, and textiles, as well as artifacts relating to the lives of Hawke's Bay's early settlers. Visitors can also experience the devastation of the 1931 earthquake through audiovisual displays and ephemera.

③

Ocean Spa

🏛42 Marine Parade 🕐6am-10pm Mon-Sat 🔒25 Dec
🌐oceanspanapier.co.nz

This landscaped open-air spa complex has vast ocean views. Visitors can enjoy heated salt-water pools, a lap pool, two leisure pools and private spas, as well as a sauna, steam room and massage facility.

④

Bluff Hill Domain

🏛Lighthouse Rd

Prior to the 1931 earthquake, Napier comprised an oblong mass of hills (Scinde Island)

 PICTURE PERFECT
Pose at the Pier

Napier's striking Marine Parade makes a popular selfie-spot. The best background is beneath the viewing platform's graphic white canopy, which frames the ocean horizon behind you.

Aerial view of Napier town centre spreading out in front of the ocean

and Cape Kidnappers to the southeast, as well as the commercial port below.

---

 ⑤

Port Ahuriri

At Port Ahuriri visitors can watch fishing fleets being unloaded or enjoy the port's many bars and restaurants. A beach boardwalk meanders to the harbour at Perfume Point. Don't miss the Art Deco National Tobacco Building on nearby Ossian Street.

---

⑥

Botanical Gardens

🏠 Spencer Rd

On a hill in the middle of the city, these gardens form a charming oasis. As well as a

surrounded almost entirely by water. The lookout within Bluff Hill Domain will recreate this feeling if visitors imagine much of the low-lying area covered in water. Vantage points offer views of the Mahia Peninsula to the northeast, Kaweka and Ruahine ranges to the west

spacious aviary, there are long lawns bordered by flower beds, groves of stately trees and a stream with bridges.

Must See

EAT

Bistronomy
Sample seasonal produce infused with international flavours in cosy, modern surrounds.

🅰F4 🏠40 Hastings St, 🅦bistronomy.co.nz

$$⑤

Emporium Eatery & Bar
This elegant eatery in Napier's Art Deco Masonic Hotel offers up tasty sharing dishes and killer cocktails.

🅰F4 🏠2 Tennyson St 🅦emporiumbar.co.nz

$$⑤

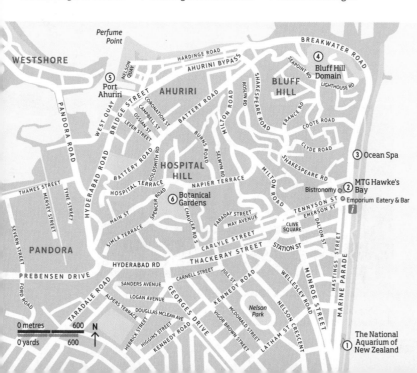

A SHORT WALK
NAPIER

Distance 1.5 km (0.8 mile) **Nearest bus stop** Napier, Carlyle St **Time** 25 minutes

Although they emerged from catastrophe, today, Napier's Art Deco buildings, with their pastel colours, bold lines and elaborate motifs, are internationally renowned for their aesthetic value. Take a stroll along the palm-fringed streets, admiring the striking façades as you go. Pay particular attention to the dates on each of the buildings to see how the city's style developed over time. The Art Deco Trust is responsible for protecting Napier's Art Deco buildings, and organizes walks and publishes information on tours, but you can easily navigate this pretty city on your own.

Purpose-built in 1922, the **Old Firehouse** was refurbished in Art Deco style after the earthquake; it now houses fashionable flats.

START

FINISH

TENNYSON

DALTON STREET

EMERSON STREET

The **Municipal Theatre**, built in 1938, is noted for its leaping nude wall panels flanking the stage.

Built in 1932, the **Countrywide Bank** has charming balcony windows framed by angular arches decorated with sunbursts and zigzags.

The **Public Trust Building**'s massive columns and internal oak fittings escaped earthquake damage.

Traffic bollards and seats topped with Art Deco motifs enhance pedestrian-friendly **Emerson Street**, the main shopping strip.

↑ Shops along pedestrianized, palm-tree-lined Emerson Street, Napier's central shopping district

↑ The neon-lit Art Deco façade of the Daily Telegraph building on Tennyson Street

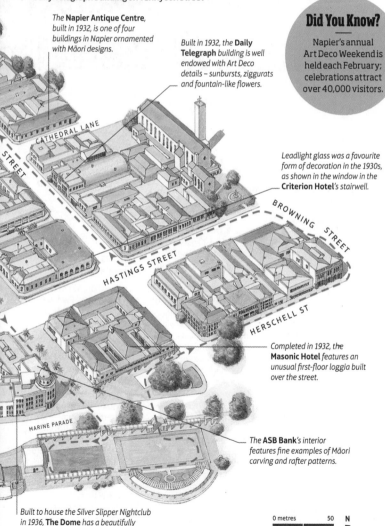

The **Napier Antique Centre**, built in 1932, is one of four buildings in Napier ornamented with Māori designs.

Built in 1932, the **Daily Telegraph** building is well endowed with Art Deco details – sunbursts, ziggurats and fountain-like flowers.

Leadlight glass was a favourite form of decoration in the 1930s, as shown in the window in the **Criterion Hotel**'s stairwell.

CATHEDRAL LANE

STREET

BROWNING STREET

HASTINGS STREET

HERSCHELL ST

Completed in 1932, the **Masonic Hotel** features an unusual first-floor loggia built over the street.

MARINE PARADE

The **ASB Bank**'s interior features fine examples of Māori carving and rafter patterns.

Built to house the Silver Slipper Nightclub in 1936, **The Dome** has a beautifully restored elevator.

| 0 metres | 50 |
| 0 yards | 50 |

N ↗

EXPERIENCE MORE

Raglan

 E3 ⬛ *i* 13 Wainui Rd;
www.raglan.org.nz

A laid-back coastal town with friendly locals and a thriving arts scene, Raglan fills with visitors during summer who are drawn to the watersports available in its harbour, its good swimming beaches and its excellent surfing. Te Kopua Beach and Te Aro Aro Bay, close to Raglan, are popular for swimming, while Manu and Whale Bays, a ten-minute drive south, are famous world-wide among surfers for their left-hand break, purportedly the longest in the world.

About 21 km (13 miles) southeast of Raglan, an easy ten-minute walk through bush leads to the Bridal Veil Falls. The 55-m (180-ft) waterfall plunges in a plume from a rock cleft to a deep pool below. A stepped track continues to the base of the falls, providing an even more dramatic vantage point with views across the pool and up at the falls.

Pirongia Forest Park

⬛ E3 *i* 798 Franklin St, Pirongia; www. hamiltonwaikato.com

This park, comprising four separate forest areas south and southeast of Raglan, offers a network of trails, from easy walks on the lower peaks to more strenuous hikes higher up. At 959 m (3,146 ft), Mount Pirongia, an ancient volcano, is the most obvious landmark in the park; its dramatic skyline and dark green forest contrast strongly with the surrounding farmland. Closer to Raglan, 756 m (2,480 ft) Mount Karioi rises sharply from the coastline. The park is home to native birds, and its streams host fish and a huge variety of aquatic invertebrates.

A hut on Mount Pirongia – Pahautea – holds 20 bunk beds. Hut tickets are available from the **Department of Conservation** in Hamilton. There is also a camping area alongside trout-filled Kaniwhaniwha Stream.

Department of Conservation
⬛ Level 4, 73 Rostrevor St, Hamilton ⬛ doc.govt.nz

Kawhia

⬛ E3 *i* Kaora St; www. kawhiaharbour.co.nz

On the coast 55 km (34 miles) to the south of Raglan, along winding but scenic back roads,

> 💬 INSIDER TIP
> ### Waingaro Hot Springs
> Waingaro Hot Springs are a short drive from Ngaruawahia. Sulphur-free thermal mineral water flows into four pools, reaching 41° C (106° F) in temperature. There is also a huge hydroslide that snakes down the contours of the Waingaro hills *(www.waingarohot springs.co.nz)*.

the small settlement of Kawhia comprises a jumble of cottages on the north side of Kawhia Harbour. The small but interesting **Kawhia Museum** here exhibits canoes and indigenous artifacts.

In former times, Māori prized the harbour and the fertile valleys running down to it and fought over rights to the area. The Māori migration canoe Tainui, which plied the coastline eight centuries ago, is buried on the slopes behind the Makatu meeting house. Stones placed 23 m (75 ft) apart above the bow and stern mark its position. The canoe was once moored to a pohutukawa tree, Tangi te Korowhiti, on the shore at the

end of Karewa Street. Now a large clump of pohutukawas, the tree is still revered by the Tainui people as signifying the beginning of their association with Aotearoa.

Kawhia Museum
📍 Ommitti St 📞 (07) 871 0161 🕐 11am–4pm Wed–Sun

---

⑧
Ngaruawahia

🅰 E3 🚌 ℹ 156 Great South Rd, Huntly; www. waikatodistrict.govt.nz

Situated where the Waikato and Waipa rivers meet at the edge of the central Waikato Basin, Ngaruawahia is one of the oldest and most historic settlements in Waikato and an important centre of Māori culture. On the northeastern bank of the river, off River Road, is Turangawaewae Marae, "the footstool" or home of the Waikato Tainui tribe – a significant location for Māori people. Turongo House, located within the *marae*, is the official residence of the reigning Māori monarch, Tuheitia Paki. *Marae* are sacred meeting places in Māori culture, and Turangawaewae Marae is not generally open to visits. The site, however,

allows public visits during the annual and well-known Turangawaewae Regatta on the river. The event has been running since 1896, and features *waka* (canoe) racing, *iwi* dance competitions and other activities.

The 1863–64 Waikato War was a pivotal moment in New Zealand's history. Māori united to protect their land and formed a resistance movement known as Te Kingitanga. The **Waikato War Driving Tour** is a useful app that guides visitors to the sites of signfinance.

In the Hakarimata Scenic Reserve, on the slopes of the Hakarimata Range to the north of Ngaruawahia, native rimu and kauri trees grow beside three well-marked tracks, which offer excellent hiking and stunning views of the Waikato Basin.

Waikato War Driving Tour
🌐 thewaikatowar.co.nz

> ### Did You Know?
> Turangawaewae Marae has hosted world leaders like Nelson Mandela.

↑ Fantastic surfing *(inset)* at Whale Beach in Raglan

↑ Māori canoes racing on the river during the Ngaruawahia Regatta at Turangawaewae Marae

Visitors exploring the themed collection in pleasant Hamilton Gardens

explore the Coromandel Forest Park wilderness area *(p132)*. Many buildings in the town owe their grandeur to wealth created during the gold-mining era.

The **Thames Historical Museum** features relics from the town's past, including the pioneering foundries that sprang up to support the mining industry, while the **Thames School of Mines and Mineralogical Museum** features 5,000 mineral samples and equipment used to process quartz ore and extract gold. Mine managers were taught in the school's classroom from 1885 to 1954.

A large World War I memorial stands on a hill above the town, off Waiotahi Creek Road, and affords panoramic views. At the

9 Hamilton

🅐 E3 ✈ 10 km (6 miles) S of city 🚌 ℹ Cnr Alexandra & Aro sts, Garden Place; www.visithamilton.co.nz

New Zealand's fourth largest metropolitan area and largest inland city, Hamilton straddles a meandering section of the Waikato River, at 425 km (264 miles) the longest in the country. The city has grown from a 19th-century military settlement into a bustling centre servicing the Waikato region, a huge undulating plain. Attractive parks and gardens, dissected by footpaths, border the river, and bridges connect the east and west banks. The Waikato River Explorer cruises the river daily from its landing at Hamilton Gardens Jetty, offering the best views of the area.

Perched on five levels above the river, the **Waikato Museum** features a large collection of New Zealand art, Waikato history and history of the local Tainui people. On permanent display is an impressive war canoe, Te Winika.

The **Hamilton Gardens**, located at the southern end of the city, are Hamilton's most popular visitor attraction with over a million visitors a year. Set along a scenic stretch of the Waikato River, they have pavilions showcasing the history of gardens through

time, including the Italian Renaissance, Indian Char Bagh, Modernist and New Zealand's only traditional Māori garden, Te Parapara.

Waikato Museum

🔄 🏛 🅐 1 Grantham St
🕐 10am–5pm daily
🌐 waikatomuseum.co.nz

Hamilton Gardens

🔄 🅐 Hungerford Crescent, SH1 off Cobham Drive
🕐 7:30am–dusk daily
🌐 hamiltongardens.co.nz

10 Thames

🅐 F2 🚗 2 km (1.2 miles) S of town 🚌 ℹ 200 Mary St; www.thecoromandel. com

At the southeastern corner of the Firth of Thames, against hills that 100 years ago rang to the sound of battery stamps pounding quartz ore to extract gold, Thames is the principal town of the Coromandel region. It services surrounding farmland and a swelling coastal population.

It is the gateway to the Coromandel Peninsula and an ideal base from which to

→

Hobbit Holes™ set in the bank and *(inset)* the Green Dragon Inn™, Hobbiton™

EAT

Palate Restaurant
Expect exquisite contemporary cuisine in sleek, pared-down surrounds at this renowned Hamilton restaurant.

🅐E3 🏠20 Alma St, Hamilton 🚫Sun & Mon 🌐palaterestaurant.co.nz

💲💲💲

small Karaka Bird Hide, built among mangroves off Brown Street on the edge of town, you can spot migratory wading birds, especially between high and low tides.

Thames Historical Museum
Ⓐ🕐🏠 🏠Cnr Pollen & Cochrane sts 📞(07) 868 8509 🕐10am–4pm daily

Thames School of Mines and Mineralogical Museum
Ⓐ🕐🏠 🏠101 Cochrane St 📞(07) 868 6227 🕐11am–3pm Wed–Sun (daily Jan–Feb) 🚫Good Fri, 25 Dec

---

⓫ 🖐🎬🍴🖥🛍

Hobbiton™ Movie Set

🅐F3 🏠501 Buckland Road, Hinuera, Matamata 🕐8:30am–3:30pm daily 🌐hobbitontours.com

One of New Zealand's most popular tourist attractions, the Hobbiton™ Movie Set recreates Middle-earth in convincing detail. Highlights include 44 Hobbit Holes™ set amid the verdant pastures of the Shire™, the iconic oak tree and the Green Dragon Inn, from Peter Jackson's epic *The Lord of the Rings* and *The Hobbit* trilogies.

Access to the site is limited to two-hour guided tours, which run daily, but should be booked well in advance. There is an evening banquet tour, including a feast of Middle-earth fare and a night-time visit to the Hobbit Holes™.

Tour buses transport visitors to the site from the Matamata tourist office and from the Hobbiton™ Movie Set Store in downtown Rotorua. Before starting the tour, make sure to head to the Shire's Rest™ Café in Hobbiton, which serves both second breakfast and elevenses, two of the six daily meals of a hobbit.

↑ Oyster catchers in the large aviary at Otorohanga Kiwi House

⓬

Otorohanga

🅐E3 🚉 ℹ️27 Turonga St; www.otorohanga.co.nz

About 50 km (31 miles) south of Hamilton lies Otorohanga, a small town whose main attraction is the **Otorohanga Kiwi House**. Three kiwi species are bred at the zoological park and 300 birds, representing 29 species, many of which can be viewed in the massive walk-through aviary.

Otorohanga Kiwi House
Ⓐ🕐🏠 🏠20 Alex Telfer Drive 🕐9am–5pm daily 🌐kiwihouse.org.nz

13

Port Jackson

F2 📍 85 Kapanga Rd, Coromandel Town; (07) 866 8598

At the tip of the peninsula, 56 km (35 miles) north of Coromandel Town, Port Jackson's long, lupin-backed beach comes as a surprise. The road, which is unsealed from the small settlement of Colville, the last supply point, ends at Fletcher's Bay, 6-km (4-miles) further on, a pretty pohutukawa-shaded cove with good fishing.

The Coastal Walkway, a 7 km (4.5 mile) track, leads from Fletcher's Bay to Stony Bay and takes about three hours to complete. Port Jackson, Fletcher Bay and Stony Bay all have camping grounds with toilets, cold showers and barbecue pits.

14

Coromandel Forest Park

F2 📍 Kauaeranga Valley, Thames; www.doc.govt.nz

This park stretches for 100 km (62 miles) along the peninsula's interior, but the most accessible part is the forested Kauaeranga Valley, with its well-developed network of scenic short walks, longer hikes, mountain bike trails and picnic areas.

The valley was a major source of kauri timber from the 1870s to the 1920s. The remains of dams, trestle bridges and river booms, used to flush kauri logs into the Kauaeranga River, are evident.

Anglers can fish for trout in the valley's streams. A rocky ridge known as the Pinnacles offers fine views of both coastlines. The Kauaeranga Kauri Trail features hikes along a pack track made by kauri bushmen. These were the men who felled the kauri forests of the North, working long hours for low wages with basic tools: the axe, the cross-cut saw, the maul and the wedge.

15

Hahei

F2 🏪 General Store, Hahei Beach Rd 🌐 hahei.co.nz

Hahei is the start of a two-hour return walk to the dramatic Cathedral Cove, Te Whanganui-A-Hei, Marine Reserve, where a cathedral-shaped cavern, accessible at low tide, cuts through a white headland. Reasonable fitness is required to reach the cove but panoramic clifftop views make the effort worthwhile. Hahei's beach is sheltered by offshore islands and tinged pink with broken shells. The area is popular with divers.

Just 6 kilometers (4 miles) south of Hahei, is the unique and astonishing Hot Water Beach, a stretch of shore along the Mercury Bay coastline where thermal waters bubble just beneath the golden sands. Head to the beach between low and mid-tides to dig your own personal spa pool and relax in the warm waters. Hote Water Beach is a site of particular cultural significance to the local Ngāti Hei Māori tribe, and so it is important that visitors behave respectfully when enjoying the waters –

> **Head to the beach between low and mid-tides to dig your own personal spa pool and relax in the warm waters.**

↑ Glorious views looking out across Coromandel Forest Park towards the sea

↑ Passengers travelling on the Driving Creek Railway, crossing a high bridge near Coromandel Town

do not to eat or drink in the pools, and make sure to take any litter away with you.

Coromandel Town

🅰F2 🚗3 km (2 miles) S of town 🚌 ℹ85 Kapanga Rd; www.coromandel town.co.nz

Coromandel Town, as it is called in order to distinguish it from the peninsula (referred to as The Coromandel), is a quiet fishing and crafts town about an hour's drive north of Thames (p130). It owes its name to the 1820 visit of HMS Coromandel, which called to load kauri spars for the British Royal Navy. Mining featured prominently in the town's formative years, and fine examples of Victorian and colonial architecture are a legacy of that era. The laid-back atmosphere and beauty of the area make it a haven for artists, and an ideal place in which to walk, fish or sail.

One of Coromandel Town's most popular attractions is the **Driving Creek Railway**

and Potteries, built by New Zealand potter Barry Brickell to convey clay and wood to his kiln, and to service a kauri forest replanting project. The mountain railway takes visitors on a one-hour round trip through native forest and tunnels and across bridges to a viewpoint high above Coromandel.

The **Coromandel Gold Stamper Battery** and a 100-year-old gold-processing museum, featuring a working water wheel, lie at the end of Buffalo Road to the north. The **Coromandel School of Mines and Historical Museum** has displays of early gold-mining and kauri logging, and an old jailhouse.

One of Coromandel's most innovative attractions, **the Waterworks**, located 9 km (6 miles) from Coromandel Town, showcase artist Chris Ogilvie's genius for inventing entertaining water-powered art forms and gadgets.

Just east of the Waterworks is a turn-off to Castle Rock. At 525 m (1,722 ft), it is the core of an old volcano on the "backbone" of the peninsula. Further along the road is the

Waiau Kauri Grove where magnificent kauri trees, protected for more than 100 years, can be seen a ten minutes' walk along a track on the left side of the road.

Driving Creek Railway and Potteries
⊘ⓘ 🅰380 Driving Creek Rd 🕙10am–4pm daily 🕔25 Apr, 25 Dec 🌐drivingcreek railway.co.nz

Coromandel Gold Stamper Battery
⊘🕙 🅰410 Buffalo Rd 🕙10am–3pm daily; tours on the hour 🌐coromandel stamperbattery.weebly.com

Coromandel School of Mines and Historical Museum
⊘ 🅰841 Rings Rd 📞(07) 866 8039 🕙Feb–Mar: 1–4pm daily; Apr–Jun & Oct–Jan: Sat & Sun only 🕔Jun–Oct

The Waterworks
⊘ⓘ 🅰471 The 309 Rd 🕙10am–4pm daily (to 6pm Nov–Apr) 🌐thewater works.co.nz

---

> ### GOLD FEVER IN THE COROMANDEL
>
> The first significant gold find on the Coromandel Peninsula occurred in October 1852 near Coromandel Town. Further discoveries near Thames in 1867 attracted 5,000 men into the surrounding hills. Soon Thames became a boom town and its population mushroomed to 18,000. Miners thronged the town on Saturdays, the three town theatres were hardly ever closed, and over 100 hotels sold liquor. However, by the 1870s it was all over, and interest shifted south-east to Karangahake Mountain and to Waihi.

Looking out over the Martha Mine, one of Waihi's most important gold mines

Stewart, but the district has since proved itself ideal for horticulture and dairy farming. Today, Katikati is thought of as an open-air "art gallery". More than 35 murals and other artworks decorate the town, all produced by local artists.

Sapphire Springs, set in a bush reserve 6 km (4 miles) from the town, has warm freshwater thermal springs for swimming or soaking.

Sapphire Springs
 274 Hot Springs Rd ☑ 8am–8pm daily ⒲ sapphiresprings.nz

---

⑲

Whitianga

🅐 F2 🚗 3 km (2 miles) SW 📧 ℹ 66 Albert St; www. whitianga.co.nz

Whitianga sits on the inner-most recess of Mercury Bay,

→

The beautiful Cathedral Cove at Whitianga, accessible only on foot or by boat

---

⑰

Waihi

🅐 F2 📧 ℹ Seddon St; www. waihi.org.nz

The history of Waihi has been linked with gold since Robert Lee and John McCrombie discovered a gold-bearing quartz reef in 1878. The Martha Mine, established on the site in 1882 was the most successful of many in the district. From 1988 onwards, substantial amounts of gold were extracted from the mine, but in 2015 and 2016, huge landslides within the pit caused activities to cease. In 2018, "Project Martha" was declared and mining restarted.

Learn about the rise of gold mining in Waihi at the nearby **Gold Discovery**

 INSIDER TIP
Whitianga Scallop Festival

The last weekend of September sees the opening of the scallop season in New Zealand at the annual Whitianga Scallop Festival. Music, parades and costumes enliven the serious business of tasting scallops and other fresh seafood *(www. scallopfestival.nz)*.

Centre. Visitors can operate mining equipment and watch pioneer miners come alive in the Ghost Theatre.

The **Goldfields Railway** operates vintage trains on 7 km (4 miles) of track between Waihi and Waikino, gateway to the Karangahake gold fields. The Karangahake Gorge Historic Walkway, a 5-km (3-mile) loop along the gorge, is signposted from the road. Waihi Beach, 11 km (7 miles) east of the town, is one of the most popular along the coast.

Gold Discovery Centre
126 Seddon St, Waihi ☑ 9am–5pm daily ⒲ golddiscoverycentre.co.nz

Goldfields Railway
30 Wrigley St ☑ 10am–3pm daily ⒲ waihirail.co.nz

---

⑱

Katikati

🅐 F3 ℹ 36 Main Rd; www. katikati.co.nz

Enthusiastic Irish colonizer George Vesey Stewart bought Katikati and its surrounding land in the 1870s and sold it to 406 Ulster families. Unfamiliar with the hard work needed to break in their land, these settlers initially resented

> **Sitting on the innermost recess of Mercury Bay, Whitianga was named by Captain Cook when he observed a transit of the planet Mercury on his 1769 visit to the area.**

named by Captain Cook when he observed a transit of the planet Mercury on his 1769 visit to the area. Whitianga provides safe boat launching, ideal during the big-game fishing season which occurs November to April. Major fishing contests occur in February and March. The Mercury Bay Boating Club, at the west end of Buffalo Beach, earned world fame when it spearheaded Auckland financier Michael Fay's unsuccessful 1988 challenge to the San Diego Yacht Club for the America's Cup.

The **Mercury Bay Museum** occupies a disused dairy factory on the Esplanade opposite the wharf. It documents the Polynesian chief Kupe, whose descendants are said to have occupied the town for more than 1,000 years. A short ferry ride across the narrow harbour entrance takes visitors to Ferry Landing, the original site of Whitianga, where there are walks and craft outlets. Whitianga Rock, upstream of Ferry Landing, was formerly a *pa* site of the Ngati

Hei tribe. Whitianga's Buffalo Beach is named after an 1840 shipwreck. The British ship *Buffalo*, which had delivered convicts to Australia and was to return to Britain with kauri spars, was blown by a storm onto the beach and destroyed. A cannon from the ship is mounted at the RSA Memorial Park in Albert Street.

At the northeast tip of the headland, 1.5 km (1 mile) from Ferry Landing, is Shakespeare Lookout, named after the bard. Here also, a memorial to Cook stands above Lonely Bay and Cooks Beach. Wave action at Flaxmill Bay, at the southwest end of Front Bay, has undercut the rock to form a natural soundshell.

The Te Whanganui-A-Hei Marine Reserve at Cathedral Cove extends from Cooks Bluff to Hahei Beach. It was established in 1992 to restore the area's marine environment to its former rich and varied condition. No fishing or gathering of shellfish is allowed, although visitors may swim, dive and sail in the reserve.

EAT

Harbour House Café
This vibrant, waterside café offers an inventive, quirky menu and delicious coffees. It's vegan-friendly too.

 F2 **11 The Esplanade, Whitianga** **(07) 866 4441**

$ $ $

Mercury Bay Museum
11A The Esplanade
Jul–Sep: 10am–3pm Tue–Sun; Oct–Jun: 10am–4pm daily 25 Dec mercurybaymuseum.co.nz

Verdant hills meet the coastline on The Coromandel

Fishing boats and other craft moored at Tauranga harbour ↑

 20

Mount Maunganui

🄰 F3 ⊞ 3 km (2 miles) S of town 🚌 𝕚 95 Willow St; (07) 578 8103

The town of Mount Maunganui sits on a narrow peninsula at the mouth of Tauranga Harbour, and is the main port for the central North Island timber industry. Overlooking the town is the 232-m (761-ft) cone-shaped Mount Maunganui, or Mauao, a sacred Māori site once home to historic *pa*. At the foot of Mauao, the **Mount Hot Pools**, saltwater pools heated by natural thermal water, make a great way to relax after a walk. The real highlight here is Mount Maunganui Beach, rated among New Zealand's best, which extends along the coastline towards Papamoa. Its waters are ideal for surfers and swimmers.

Mount Hot Pools

⊛ ⊕ 🄰 9 Adams Ave
🕒 6am–10pm Mon–Sat; 8am–10pm Sun
🅦 mounthotpools.co.nz

 GREAT VIEW
The Mount

The summit of Mauao affords breathtaking 360-degree vistas of the Bay of Plenty coastline and beyond. Climb the 3.4 km (2 mile) track which winds up the mountain to reach the peak.

 21

Tauranga

🄰 F3 ⊞ 3 km (2 miles) E of town 🚌 𝕚 95 Willow St; www.bayofplentynz.com

An important commercial centre and port, Tauranga lies along a section of Tauranga Harbour. On its seaward side, the city is sheltered by Matakana Island and to the west by the Kaimai Ranges.

Tauranga is a popular city, its benign climate and coastal location attracting retired New Zealanders and all those who enjoy year-round outdoor activities. Boating, surfing, parasailing, water-skiing, diving and deep-sea fishing are among its attractions. The Strand, in the centre of town, is the main shopping and restaurant area.

Originally a flax-trading and missionary town, Tauranga was the scene of fierce fighting during the New Zealand land wars in the 1860s. Many of the troops involved in a significant battle at Gate Pa, 5 km (3 miles) south of the city, were stationed at Monmouth Redoubt, a military camp built by British troops in 1864 to stop supplies reaching the Waikato Māori King Movement. Preserved earthworks and heavy artillery, are still in place.

McLaren Falls Park, off State Highway 29 on the road to Hamilton (*p130*), has walks through picturesque native bush interspersed with thousands of introduced trees. A river and Lake McLaren offer swimming. On scheduled days throughout the year, top white-water action takes place downstream on the Wairoa River when floodgates on the hydro-controlled waterway are opened. The park offers three backpacker hostels.

McLaren Falls Park

 McLaren Falls Rd
🕑 7:30am–dusk daily
🌐 tauranga.govt.nz

㉒

Whangamata

🅰 F2 🚌 ℹ️ 616 Port Rd;
www.whangamata
info.co.nz

The town of Whangamata, meaning "obsidian harbour", was named after the dark, glass-like volcanic rock washed ashore from Mayor Island, 30 km (19 miles) from the mainland. Whangamata is often referred to as "the surfing capital of New Zealand" because of the size of the waves in the area, particularly its sandbank surf break known as "the bar".

The hills and valleys behind Whangamata, a short drive from the town, offer many outdoor activities. Within the Tairua Forest lie the Wentworth Valley, Taungatara Recreation Reserve and Parakiwai Valley. These are crisscrossed with walking tracks that make the most of stony streams and pockets of native bush. A popular walk takes in the "Luck at Last" gold mine and the remains of ore processors, water races, and even a baker's oven. Details are available from the Whangamata information centre and forestry company Matariki Forests, which may close access when it is conducting forestry operations.

㉓

Mayor Island

🅰 F2 🚗 35 km (22 miles) from Tauranga Harbour
🚢 From Tauranga or Whangamata ℹ️ 95 Willow St, Tauranga; www.waihi
beachinfo.co.nz

Located off the coast of the Bay of Plenty, Mayor Island (Tuhua) is hilly and bush-clad, with few landing places around its steep cliffs. Its highest peak, Opauhau, reaches 354 m (1,161 ft) above the circular island 4 km (3 miles) across. At its heart, a dormant volcano rises from beneath the sea floor, crowned with two crater lakes.

The island's most striking feature is its black obsidian, a natural glass formed by rapid cooling of silica-rich lava. In pre-European times, Māori prized obsidian and fought battles over the island.

An 18-km (11-mile) walking track circles the island, and there are a camping ground and cabins. Visitors must take food and water as supplies on the island are limited. All sea life is protected within a marine reserve on the island's northern coastline.

㉔

Te Puke

🅰 F3 🚌 ℹ️ 130 Jellicoe St; www.tepuke.co.nz

Like Katikati (p134), Te Puke was originally settled with Irish folk by Ulsterman George Vesey Stewart in the 1880s. Early farming of sheep and cattle in the area was hampered by "bush sickness," a cobalt deficiency that dogged farming in central North Island regions. Sheep and dairy farming predominated until interest in horticulture strengthened in the 1960s.

Pioneering horticulturists experimented with what was then known as the Chinese gooseberry, and developed an international market for it under a new name – kiwifruit. Since then Te Puke has been hailed as the "kiwifruit capital of the world". The export kiwifruit orchard and horticultural park **Kiwifruit Country** showcases the fruit with creative exhibits. There is an orchard of kiwifruit vines on site.

Tours that run from the area explore the extraordinary productivity and abundance of the Bay of Plenty region, taking in spectacular horticultural estates that most visitors don't get to see. Longer trips include the coastlines of the Bay of Plenty and highlights of Tauranga.

Kiwifruit Country

♿ 🅿 🍽 📷 🛍 🅰 State Hwy 33, Paengaroa 🕒 9am–5pm daily 🌐 kiwifruit
countrytours.co.nz

↑ A giant kiwifruit sign representing the Bay of Plenty near Te Puke

---

Whangamata is often referred to as "the surfing capital of New Zealand" because of the size of the waves in the area, particularly its sandbank surf break known as "the bar".

Whakatane

F3 🚌 ℹ Cnr Quay St & Kakahoroa Drive; www.whakatane.com

Resting in the coastal heart of the eastern Bay of Plenty, Whakatane is one of New Zealand's sunniest locations, enjoying more than 2,500 hours of sunshine a year. With its coastside location within easy reach of nearby islands, the town makes an ideal base from which to enjoy a range of marine activities, such as diving, or watching marine wildlife like the dolphins that frequent the Bay's waters.

The **Whakatane Museum and Art** gives an insight into the lifestyles of early Māori and European settlers. It contains a pictorial history of the district as well as displays of Māori artifacts.

There are several excellent local walkways. One, the Nga Tapuwae O Toi Walkway, provides beautiful views of the sea and coastal pohutukawa trees. Access to the route, which takes seven hours to complete, is from Seaview Road above the town. The first landmark is Kapu te Rangi ("ridge of heaven"), which features some of the country's oldest earthworks.

Whale Island, set 10 km (6 miles) north of the harbour entrance, is a wildlife refuge. Island excursions are organized by the volunteer-run Whakatane Coastguard over the Christmas–New Year period; trips can be booked at the Whakatane Visitor Centre.

East of Whakatane, idyllic Ohope Beach stretches 12 km (7.5 miles) from Otarawairere, its western extremity, to the mouth of tidal Ohiwa Harbour.

MAORI MIGRATION AND SETTLEMENT

According to legend, three migration canoes travelling from Hawaiki landed in the eastern Bay of Plenty in the 14th century. Mild weather and abundant seafood encouraged Māori to settle along the coastal margins. Today, Māori continue to form a high proportion of the population in the Bay of Plenty area, and red-framed Māori meeting houses, important spiritually and as decision-making centres, are scattered around the countryside.

Whakatane Museum and Art

⊗ 🏛 51–55 Boon St 🕙 10am–4pm daily 🚫 1 Jan, Good Fri, 25 & 26 Dec 🅦 whakatanemuseum.org.nz

---

White Island

F2 🏔 50 km (31 miles) N of Whakatane 🅦 whiteisland.co.nz

New Zealand's most active volcano, White Island lies at the northern end of the Taupo–Rotorua volcanic fault line. It can be reached by boat or helicopter or simply viewed from the air.

The island's terrain is likened to that of the moon or Mars. Visitors can get up close to roaring steam vents, bubbling pits of mud and an amazing lake of steaming acid – the yellow and orange resulting from the abundant sulphur on the island. The island was mined for sulphur until 1914, when a night-time eruption killed all the miners. Remains of mining can still be seen.

There is a large gannet colony on the island and it suffers no ill-effects from the ash fall-out. The island also offers excellent diving.

↑ The moon-like active volcano White Island, giving off white sulphur

↑ Hiker gazing up at the trees in dense rainforest, Te Urewera Park

㉗
Te Urewera Park

🅰F3 🚌 ℹ6249 Lake Rd, SH 38, Te Urewera; www. doc.govt.nz

A national park until 2014, this protected area remains the biggest tract of untouched native forest remaining on the North Island. For centuries its dense rainforest sheltered the industrious and resilient Tuhoe people. At the centre of Te Urewera is the deep Lake Waikaremoana ("the lake of rippling waters"), formed 2,200 years ago by a landslide. A 46-km (28-mile) track around the lake takes three to four days to complete (booking through the

> **INSIDER TIP**
> **Kayak up Waioeka River**
>
> From the river wharf in the town of Opotiki, there's easy kayaking southwards along the Waioeka River. The harbour and estuary offer tranquil, sheltered waters, perfect for beginners, though further south there are rapids and wild scenery (www.wharfhub.com).

Aniwaniwa Visitor Centre is mandatory). There are also beautiful short walks into the park from the main road.

㉘
Opotiki

🅰F3 🚌 ℹ70 Bridge St; www.opotikinz.com

Situated at the confluence of the Waioeka and Otara rivers, Opotiki is the gateway to the East Cape and the last major town before Gisborne. In 1865, at Opotiki, the Reverend Carl Sylvius Völkner was hanged and then decapitated by Māori who were convinced he had passed information about their movements and fortifications to Governor George Grey. Hiona St Stephen's Anglican Church, where the incident took place, lies at the northern end of the Church Street business area.

→ Statue of Captain James Cook located in Gisborne

A key is held at the **Opotiki Museum**, which is full of early settlers' items and has a separate grocery and hardware store museum nearby.

The warm, temperate rainforest of the Hukutaia Domain, home to over 2,000 native tree species, can be reached from the western end of Waioeka Bridge along Woodlands Road.

Opotiki Museum
♦♦ 🅰123 Church St
🕙10am-4pm Mon-Sat
🆆opotikimusesum.org.nz

㉙
Gisborne

🅰G3 ✈4 km (2.5 miles) NW of town 🚌 ℹ209 Grey St; www.tairawhiti gisborne.co.nz

Gisborne is renowned for its warm summers, its farming, viticulture and horticulture, its surf beaches at Midway, Wainui and Makorori, and its history. A monument and reserve on Kaiti Hill are named in honour of Captain James Cook who made his first New Zealand landfall at Gisborne's Kaiti Beach on 9 October 1769.

The **Tairawhiti Museum** houses fine European and Māori artifacts. On the bank of the Taruheru River, but part of the museum complex, rests the salvaged wheelhouse from the *Star of Canada*, which sank off Kaiti Beach in 1912. Statues of Captain Cook and Young Nick, at the mouth of the Turanganui River, commemorate Nicholas Young, the first crewman on board Cook's ship, the *Endeavour*, to sight New Zealand.

Tairawhiti Museum
♦♦♦♦ 🅰10 Stout St 🕙10am-4pm daily (from 1:30pm Sun)
🆆tairawhiti museum. org.nz

Wai-O-Tapu Thermal Wonderland

F3 **201 Waiotqapu Loop Rd** **8:30am-5pm daily** **waiotapu.co.nz**

This is the country's most diverse geothermal area and is home to the reliable Lady Knox Geyser, named in 1904 after Governor-General Lord Ranfurly's daughter. The geyser shoots water and steam up to 21 m (69 ft) into the air at 10:15am daily. A good place to start the self-guided tour is at the visitor centre, which provides background information about the 1886 blast of Tarawera volcano.

Other main attractions include the Artist's Palette, a panorama of hot and cold pools, boiling mud pools and hissing fumaroles in a variety of changing colours, and the Champagne Pool, with its ochre-coloured petrified edge. The Primrose Terraces are also naturally tinted and have delicately formed lacework patterns. Walks through the geothermal area, over board-walks and along signposted paths, take 30 to 75 minutes.

↑ Jet-boating on the swirling rapids of Huka Falls in Wairakei Park

Wairakei Park

F3 **10 km (6 miles) N of Taupo** **wairakeitourist park.co.nz**

Just north of Taupo (p145) is the area loosely referred to as Wairakei Park. The biggest attraction is the Huka ("foam") Falls, where the Waikato River is channelled through a narrow rock chute before hurtling over an 11-m (36-ft) bluff to a foaming cauldron below. Access down the Waikato River from Taupo to the Huka Falls is possible by jet-boat, or by the more sedate paddlewheeler, built in 1908. A 7-km (4-mile) path leads from the falls down the right-hand side of the river to the Aratiatia Rapids, also accessible by road. Floodgates to the dam above the rapids are opened several times a day.

At Craters of the Moon, at the end of Karapiti Road, 2 km (1.2 miles) south of Wairakei, steaming craters and boiling mud pits can be viewed for a charge ($8 for adults) amid a bush-covered landscape.

The country's only prawn farm, off Huka Falls Road, uses geothermally heated river

↑ The Champagne Pool at Wai-o-Tapu Thermal Wonderland

water to raise giant prawns for its restaurant, Huka Prawn Park Restaurant. Tours of the farm are conducted hourly.

Waimangu Volcanic Valley

A F3 **@** 587 Waimangu Rd
© 8:30am–5pm daily
w waimangu.co.nz

Created on 10 June 1886 as a result of the Tarawera Eruption (p119), Waimangu is the only hydrothermal system in the world wholly formed within historic times. An easy, mostly downhill, walk passes geothermal features at the southern end of the 17-km (10-mile) rift created by the eruption.

Frying Pan Lake, a large hot water spring, emits steam over its entire area and is

> **Access down the Waikato River from Taupo to the Huka Falls is possible by jet-boat, or by the more sedate paddle-wheeler, built in 1908.**

dominated by the red-streaked Cathedral Rocks. The lake was formed by a 1917 eruption that buried a nearby tourist hotel.

The steaming water and delicate silica clay terracing of the Inferno Crater should not be missed, even though it requires a short detour from the main path. The water reaches 80° C (176° F) in the lake and rises and falls 8 m (26 ft) over a 38-day cycle.

At the end of the walk lies Lake Rotomahana, submerging what remains of the Pink and White Terraces (p119), presided over by Mount Tarawera. The lake shoreline can be explored by a boat excursion, taking in fumaroles and geysers, and the unusual thermal plants that fringe the water's edge. Allow two to three hours for the volcanic valley walk and the boat cruise.

Orakei Korako Geyserland

A F3 **@** 28 km (17 miles) N of Wairakei **©** 8am–4:40pm daily **w** orakeikorako.co.nz

Orakei Korako, or "The Hidden Valley", as it is known, lies at

the southern end of Lake Ohakuri, fed by the Waikato River as it flows northward from Lake Taupo. Reaching the valley's geothermal attractions requires a boat trip (included in admission price) across the lake to the imposing Emerald Terrace, the largest silica feature of its kind in the country. Beyond is a 60-minute walk taking in a geyser, more silica terraces, hot springs, a cave and mud pools. A café with a large deck overlooking the lake serves snacks and drinks.

STAY

Huka Lodge

Luxury without opulence, understated elegance in harmony with nature and exceptional service make this one of the most highly regarded riverside retreats in the country.

🅐F3 🅐271 Huka Falls Rd, Taupo
🅦hukalodge.co.nz

$$$

Grand Mercure Puka Park Resort

Romantic private chalets are set along the native forest slopes of Mount Pauanui at this elegant luxury retreat. Outdoor dining is available.

🅐F2 🅐Pauanui Beach
🅦pukapark.co.nz

$$$

Turangi

🅐F3 🚍 🅲Ngwaka Place;
www.turangi.co.nz

At the southeastern end of Lake Taupo, Turangi was a small fishing retreat until it was developed in 1964 to accommodate workers for the Tongariro Hydro-Electricity Scheme. It remains a great resort area for anglers, kayakers and skiers.

South of Turangi is the **Tongariro National Trout Centre**, a hatchery and research facility. A 15-minute walk takes you through the hatchery to an underwater viewing chamber to see trout.

Tongariro National Trout Centre

🅐257 State Hwy 1 🅲10am-3pm daily 🅲1 Jan, 25 Dec
🅦troutcentre.com

Cape Kidnappers

🅐F4 🅐30 km (19 miles) S of Napier

The Māori believe that the crescent-shaped bay and

jagged promontory of Cape Kidnappers represent the magical jawbone hook used by Maui to pull the North Island from the sea like a fish. In October 1769, Captain Cook anchored off the headland naming it Cape Kidnappers after Māori attempted to carry off his Tahitian translator.

At the cape, yellow-headed Australasian gannets surf wind currents metres from onlookers. The best time to see them is from November to February. Access is closed during the early nesting phase from July to October. At low tide, visitors can walk 8 km (5 miles) along the beach to the colony – check times with the local visitor centre. Guided tours by coach and tractor-trailer are also available.

← Quadbikers enjoying the sands at crescent-shaped Cape Kidnappers

← Dawn mists rising over Hastings' ridgeline, seen from majestic Te Mata Peak

36 Hastings

F4 ✈ 25 km (15 miles) N of town *i* Cnr Russel St North & Heretaunga St; (06) 873 5526

Set on the Heretaunga Plains, 20 km (12 miles) south of Napier, Hastings is the centre of a large fruit growing and processing industry, including wine making – established in 1998, the **Craggy Range Winery** offers tastings.

Rebuilt after the 1931 earthquake, it is the only city in New Zealand with streets laid out on the American block system. It has some fine Spanish Mission buildings, the most notable being the Hawke's Bay Opera House.

Between Hastings and the eastern coastline, Te Mata Peak rises 399 m (1,309 ft). Māori legend describes the Te Mata ridgeline as the body of chief Te Mata O Rongokako, who choked and died eating his way through the hill, a task set him by the beautiful daughter of another chief. From Hastings the "bite" that killed him can be clearly seen, as can the chief's body, which forms the skyline.

Craggy Range Winery

⌂ 253 Waimarama Rd, Havelock North 4294
🕐 11am–5pm daily
🌐 craggyrange.com

Did You Know?

"Trolling" is a method of fishing from a slow-moving boat. You can spot anglers trolling trout on Lake Taupo.

37 Taupo

F3 ✈ 8 km (5 miles) S of town 🚌 Gascoigne St Travel Centre; (07) 378 9005 *i* 30 Tongariro St; www.lovetaupo.com

The town of Taupo is located at the northeastern end of Lake Taupo, New Zealand's largest lake, which was formed by a volcanic explosion in AD 186. Sheltered rocky coves and white pumice beaches surround the lake, which covers 619 sq km (239 sq miles). On a clear day, the distant volcanic peaks of Mounts Tongariro and Ngauruhoe and the snow-capped Ruapehu provide a spectacular backdrop to the lake. Taupo services surrounding farms and forests and an important tourist industry. All year round the town attracts large numbers of holiday-makers who come for its excellent lake and river fishing, sailing and water-sports, and local geothermal attractions. There is a wealth of accommodation in the town, much of it with lakeside views, and good dining and shopping. Many hotels have their own hot pools.

The wide selection of outdoor activities includes bungy jumping, boating and rafting, horse riding, mountain biking, tandem skydiving, flightseeing and golf. The bungy, set in majestic surroundings above the Waikato River off Spa Road, is a big draw. Details of the operators offering outdoor recreation may be obtained from the information centre in Taupo.

→ Bungee jumping from a gantry overhanging Waikato River

A DRIVING TOUR
EAST CAPE

Length 334 km (207 miles) **Stopping-off points** Opotiki, Te Araroa, Tolaga Bay **Terrain** Windy coastal highway

Skirting the rugged hills of the East Cape peninsula, this section of the Pacific Coast Highway offers exceptional scenery. From Opotiki northeast to East Cape, the road clings to rocky coastline cloaked with pohutukawa trees. The second part of the route heads south to Gisborne along an inland farming route with secondary roads providing access to the coast. Most beaches and bays are suitable for swimming, fishing and diving. There are also opportunities for jet-boating, horse trekking and hiking. Māori marae and churches dot the route.

Built in 1894, the Anglican **Raukokore Church**, with its distinctive roofline, stands between road and sea.

The **Motu River**, banked by steep hills and forest, is a magnificent setting for jet-boating, rafting and fishing.

Raukokere

Te Kaha

Motu River

35

BAY OF PLENTY

START

Opotiki

*Begin this drive in the small town of **Opotiki**, the gateway to the East Cape.*

Waioweka

Motu River

2

Motu

Matawai

Whatatutu

2

Te Karaka

| 0 kilometres | 10 |
| 0 miles | 10 |

N ↑

←

Set beside the sea, the picturesque Raukokore Church

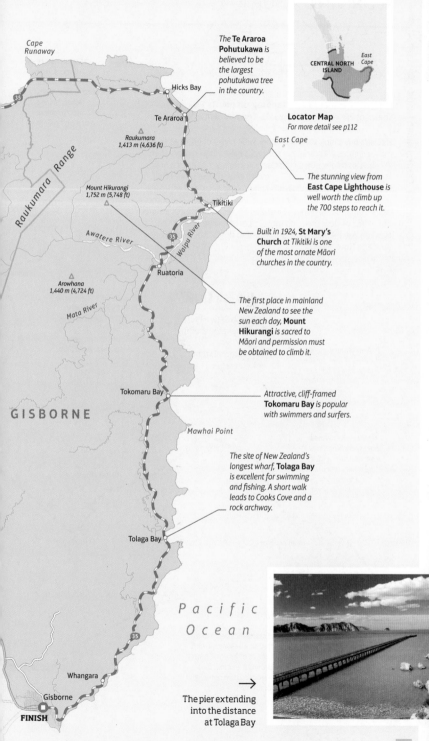

The **Te Araroa Pohutukawa** is believed to be the largest pohutukawa tree in the country.

Locator Map
For more detail see p112

The stunning view from **East Cape Lighthouse** is well worth the climb up the 700 steps to reach it.

Built in 1924, **St Mary's Church** at Tikitiki is one of the most ornate Māori churches in the country.

The first place in mainland New Zealand to see the sun each day, **Mount Hikurangi** is sacred to Māori and permission must be obtained to climb it.

Attractive, cliff-framed **Tokomaru Bay** is popular with swimmers and surfers.

The site of New Zealand's longest wharf, **Tolaga Bay** is excellent for swimming and fishing. A short walk leads to Cooks Cove and a rock archway.

CENTRAL NORTH ISLAND

East Cape

Cape Runaway

Hicks Bay

Te Araroa

Raukumara 1,413 m (4,636 ft)

East Cape

Mount Hikurangi 1,752 m (5,748 ft)

Tikitiki

Awatere River

Waipu River

Ruatoria

Arowhana 1,440 m (4,724 ft)

Mata River

Raukumara Range

Tokomaru Bay

GISBORNE

Mawhai Point

Tolaga Bay

Pacific Ocean

Whangara

Gisborne

FINISH

→ The pier extending into the distance at Tolaga Bay

A DRIVING TOUR
HAWKE'S BAY VINEYARD

Length 70 km (44 miles) **Stopping-off points** Pick from the many Hawke's Bay Vineyards **Terrain** Gentle hills

Hawke's Bay's long sunshine hours, wide range of growing microclimates and variety of soil types have allowed more than 70 wineries to develop all the classical grape varieties to a high standard. Traditionally a fruit-growing area, Hawke's Bay's fruit is sourced from varied vineyard and orchard sites, and wines are made using both modern and traditional techniques. The success of the region's wine is not only evident in its international awards, but in one of New Zealand's most important wine events, the Hawke's Bay F.A.W.C! Food and Wine Classic festival, held every June and November.

Mission Estate Winery, New Zealand's oldest winery, offers sales, winery tours, a gourmet restaurant and a craft gallery.

START Mission Estate Winery

Taradale

Mediterranean-style **C J Pask Winery** produces grapes with very ripe fruit flavours across a range of premium varieties.

Te Awa Winery, named "River of God" for the large aquifer beneath the plains, makes fine Bordeaux-blend red wines.

Ngatarawa's Wines makes excellent wines in an attractive setting – the winery is housed in stable buildings near a lily pond.

Did You Know?
Mission Estate Winery was established in 1851 by a group of French Catholic missionaries.

Ngaruroro River

OMAHU ROAD
PAKOWHAI ROAD
Te Awa Winery
C J Pask Winery
HASTINGS
50A
Ngatarawa Wines
MARAEKAKAHO ROAD
Sileni Estates

Sileni Estates has benefitted from massive investment which has produced a showcase winery incorporating a gourmet food store, wine education centre and restaurant/café.

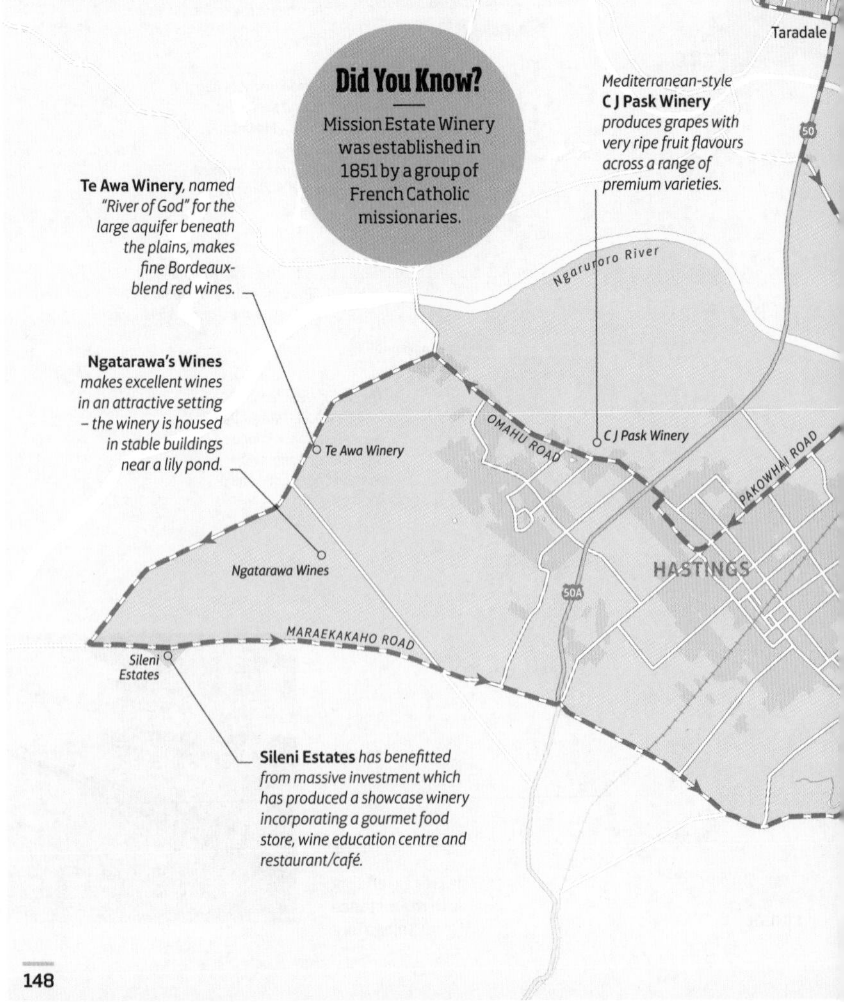

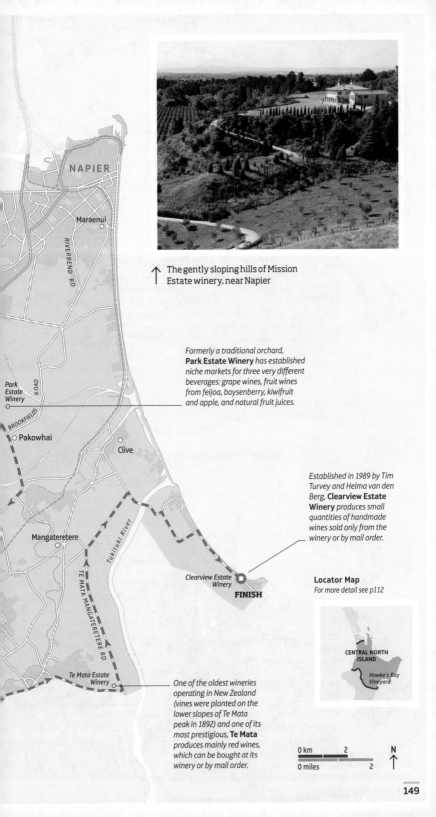

↑ The gently sloping hills of Mission Estate winery, near Napier

Formerly a traditional orchard, **Park Estate Winery** has established niche markets for three very different beverages: grape wines, fruit wines from feijoa, boysenberry, kiwifruit and apple, and natural fruit juices.

Established in 1989 by Tim Turvey and Helma van den Berg, **Clearview Estate Winery** produces small quantities of handmade wines sold only from the winery or by mail order.

Locator Map
For more detail see p112

One of the oldest wineries operating in New Zealand (vines were planted on the lower slopes of Te Mata peak in 1892) and one of its most prestigious, **Te Mata** produces mainly red wines, which can be bought at its winery or by mail order.

CENTRAL NORTH ISLAND

Hawke's Bay Vineyard

| 0 km | | 2 |
| 0 miles | | 2 |

N

NAPIER

Maraenui

RIVERBEND RD

Park Estate Winery

BROOKFIELDS ROAD

○ Pakowhai

Clive

Tukituki River

Mangateretere

TE MATA MANGATERETERE RD

Clearview Estate Winery

FINISH

Te Mata Estate Winery

WELLINGTON AND THE SOUTH

Wellington is New Zealand's capital, a compact city that hugs Lambton Harbour. The settlement was founded in 1840 by the New Zealand Company, which employed less-than-truthful advertising to lure pioneers to southern towns. In the late 19th century, a financial and mercantile district grew on land reclaimed from Wellington's harbour, and in 1865, New Zealand's capital was moved here from Auckland, bringing parliament closer to the economically powerful South Island goldfields. Between the 1870s and 1910s, the country's biggest forest clearance programme turned thousands of hectares of forest north of Wellington into raw farmland to await the toils of European settlers. Small towns along the railway enjoyed periods of importance before the sawmillers moved on. By 1907, milling output had passed its peak, leaving a landscape of rich, rolling farmland pocked by areas of industry.

Today, harbour-fringed Wellington is still this region's main city, the centre of government, business and performing arts, with a cosmopolitan atmosphere and thriving café and bar scene. Numerous surrounding small farming towns make for charming, friendly stopover points.

SUGAR LOAF ISLANDS
MARINE PARK

17 **4** NEW PLYMOUTH

Oakura

Egmont   Inglewood

*Cape
Egmont*

EGMONT
NATIONAL PARK

3

15

*Mount Taranaki
2,518 m (8,261 ft)*

STRATFORD

Oaonui   **65**

Eltham

18

OPUNAKE   T A R A N A K I

Manaia

19

HAWERA

Kakaramea

Patea

WELLINGTON
AND THE SOUTH

Must Sees

1 Wellington
2 Palmerston North
3 Egmont National Park
4 New Plymouth
5 Whanganui

Experience More

6 Whanganui National Park
7 Kapiti Island Nature Reserve
8 Paekakariki
9 Paraparaumu
10 Waikanae
11 Martinborough
12 Masterton
13 Pukaha Mount Bruce
National Wildlife Centre
14 Featherston
15 Stratford
16 Levin
17 Sugar Loaf Islands Marine Park
18 Opunake
19 Hawera

*Stephens
Island*

*Cape
Stephens*

*D'Urville
Island*

*Marlborough
Sounds*

French Pass

*Motuara
Island*

*Arapawa
Island*

Canvastown

Picton

MARLBOROUGH
AND NELSON
p178

Tuamarina

Renwick

Wellington's lights twinkling at twilight, from Mount Victoria ↑

WELLINGTON

🅰 E5 ✈ 8km (5 miles) S of city 🚻 Cnr of Wakefield and Victoria sts; www.wellingtonnz.com

Known as "Windy Welly", New Zealand's cool capital remains unruffled by the frequent gales that plague the city. Wellington's compact centre, lying between the hills and mountain-encircled harbour, magnifies its attractive buzz. It's packed with stylish shops, trendy restaurants and hipster galleries, but the city is perhaps best known for its café culture.

Civic Square

🏛 Wakefield St 🌐 welling tonnz.com

The heart of the city's cultural scene, this extensive paved, plaza-style courtyard was opened in the early 1990s, making use of an area that was previously a busy street. The pink and beige square is an open space that features various sculptures and provides a link to a number of institutions bordering it. These include the City Gallery Wellington, Visitor Information Centre, City Council Buildings, City Gallery Wellington and the capital's main concert venues, the Town Hall and Michael Fowler Centre.

The square harkens back to its previous role as a thoroughfare. It brings together Wellington's central business district with the city's cultural and social side: the Museum of New Zealand Te Papa Tongarewa, the Opera House, theatres, cinemas and shops, as well as the bars and restaurants of the city's night-time entertainment area, Courtenay Place (p156). The square has become a central meeting place for Wellingtonians. Visitors to the square will often find themselves among street theatre performers and at outdoor concerts, exhibitions and rallies of all kinds.

EAT

Nikau Café
Set beside Wellington's City Gallery, this stylish café serves breakfast and lunch with wholesome, seasonal ingredients.

🅰 E5 🏠 101 Wakefield St 🌐 nikaucafe.co.nz

Logan Brown
Bright red doors open into an old bank building. Upscale and ambitious, the menu here invites indulgence.

🅰 E5 🏠 192 Cuba St 🌐 loganbrown.co.nz

The Larder
Irresistible brunch dishes and a friendly atmosphere draws a loyal crowd at this local favourite.

🅰 E5 🏠 133 Darlington Rd 🌐 thelarder.co.nz

②

City Gallery Wellington

☐ Te Ngākau Civic Square
☐ 10am–5pm daily ☐ city gallery.org.nz

Housed in a striking Art Deco building fitted with original kauri doors, marble finishes, handrails and steel windows, the building that for decades served as the city's Public Library is now home to the country's leading art gallery.

The gallery has a distinctive character, specializing in bringing to Wellington the best contemporary art and design shows from around the world. Exhibitions here have covered a diverse range of media and subjects, including painting, sculpture, film and video, industrial and graphic design, and architecture.

The building has been extended to include an auditorium, a gallery of Māori and Pacific art, and the enlarged Michael Hirschfield Gallery, which is dedicated to exhibiting works by Wellington artists.

---

③

Michael Fowler Centre

☐ 111 Wakefield St ☐ (04) 801 4231 ☐ For concerts

Designed by Christchurch's Sir Miles Warren and named after a former mayor and prominent architect, this semicircular complex is internationally renowned for its ability to distribute sound throughout its 2,550-plus seat concert chamber. Rock concerts, conventions and even political rallies are staged in what has become the city's premier concert hall and home of the New Zealand Symphony Orchestra. Many events associated with the increasingly popular New Zealand Festival (*p55*), which attracts thousands of visitors to Wellington, are held here.

---

④

Town Hall

☐ Wakefield St

Ongoing restoration of this sedate 1904 Edwardian brick building has returned the hall to much of its former glory. Works have included seismic strengthening of the building, uncovering wrought-iron balustrades, manufacturing lights and fittings from original samples, and repairing the auditorium's pressed zinc ceiling. The hall's "shoe box" auditorium is regarded as one of the world's leading venues for the performance of classical music.

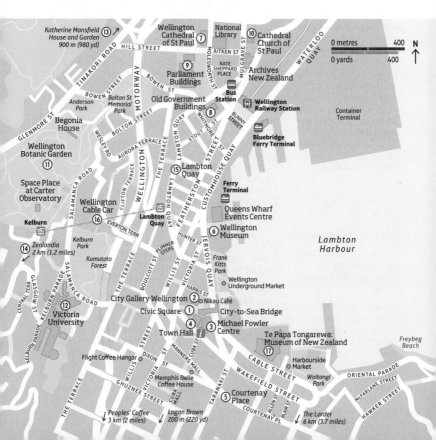

⑤

Courtenay Place

Lined with a concentrated strip of sophisticated night-clubs, trendy cafés and restaurants, and professional theatres, Courtenay Place and the streets leading from it form the night-time entertainment heart of the city.

You'll find eateries serving nearly every cuisine style here, and there's something to suit every budget, from cheap-and-cheerful outlets to award-winning restaurants. But the fun doesn't stop with the end of dinner. Live music inside packed cafés and bars is matched by a lively street scene, where crowds thread their way through the buskers and performers that add to the area's relaxed and endlessly cool atmosphere.

⑥

Wellington Museum

🏛 3 Jervois Quay ⏰ 10am-5pm daily ⛔ 25 Dec 🌐 museumswellington. org.nz

Housed in the former customs house, which was constructed in 1892, the fascinating Wellington Museum gives an insight into the capital's rich maritime, cultural and social history. The museum uses model ships, ships'

instruments, relics from wrecks, maritime paintings, old maps and sea journals, as well as holographic re-creations and videos to tell the story of Wellington in the context of its harbour and surrounding coast. One of the most interesting exhibits in the museum's collection of ship models is the inter-island ferry, the *Wahine*. This vessal sank off the Wellington suburb of Seatoun in April 1968 during a storm. A photo-graph exhibit documents the tragedy. The Plimmer's Ark Gallery displays part of the excavated remains of the ship *Inconstant*, built in 1848.

The museum also features a 12-minute show on Māori creation legends and looks at early Māori and European settlement. A 20th century gallery explores how the city has changed. There is also an education room for children.

⑦

Wellington Cathedral of St Paul

🏛 Cnr Molesworth and Hill sts ⏰ 8am-5pm Mon-Fri, 10am-4pm Sat, Sun 8am-6:15pm 🌐 wellington cathedral.org.nz

After a building programme spread over several decades, including a number of exterior and interior design changes

↑ Catching up with friends at a café on vibrant Courtenay Place

and reversals, the Wellington Cathedral of St Paul was finally completed in 1998. Standing in the parliamentary precinct opposite the Law Courts and the National Library, the Romanesque-style cathedral houses various unique etched and stained-glass windows, memorials to historic events, and a 4,000-pipe organ. The Lady Chapel, which was formerly a parish church on the Kapiti coast north of Wellington, was relocated to the site in 1998 to complete the cathedral complex. There is a pleasant café behind the church.

⑧

Old Government Buildings

🏛 15 Lambton Quay 📞 (04) 472 7356 ⏰ 9am-5pm Mon-Fri ⛔ 1 & 2 Jan, Easter Sun, 25 Apr, 25 & 26 Dec

The largest wooden building in the southern hemisphere, and one of the largest such buildings in the world, the Old Government Buildings was built in the 1870s in a style imitating stone.

Originally used in the early 20th century by New Zealand's

parliamentary cabinet and then by government departments until 1990, the restored buildings are now filled with law school students. The original cabinet room on the first floor and historic displays on the ground floor are open to the public.

↑ Wooden roof trusses adorn the Cathedral Church of St Paul

⑨

Parliament Buildings

🏛 Molesworth St 🕐 9:30-4:30pm daily 🚫 1 & 2 Jan, 6 Feb, Good Fri, 25 & 26 Dec 🌐 parliament.nz

New Zealand's Parliament is made up of four main buildings: the Edwardian Neo-Classical style Parliament Building (1922); the Parliamentary Library (1899); the Beehive occupied since 1979 and so-called for its shape; and the modern Bowen House. Free guided tours take in all three buildings (photo ID is required). They stand next to each other on the site that has housed the country's parliament since 1865, 400 m (1,300 ft) away from the earthquake fault line that runs through Wellington. Historic trees have been retained in the grounds, which also feature a rose garden.

⑩

Cathedral Church of St Paul

🏛 34 Mulgrave St 🕐 Daily 🚫 To tourists Good Fri, 25 Dec 🌐 oldsaintpauls.co.nz

Known as Old St Paul's, the Cathedral Church of St Paul is a fine example of an early English Gothic-style cathedral. Built on the site of Pipitea Pā, a Māori settlement on the waterfront, the church was consecrated in 1866, and is made of native timber, including its nails.

SHOP

Wellington Underground Market
This vibrant market beside Wellington's waterfront attracts over 100 stalls and street food vendors. Spot young fashion designers hawking their latest creations, alongside local artists and craftspeople selling their wares.

🅰 E5 🏛 Jervois Quay 🕐 10am-4pm Sat 🌐 underground market.co.nz

Harbourside Market
For over a century, Wellington's busiest outdoor market has thronged with some 25,000 fruit and veg seekers each Sunday. Entertainers add to the bustling atmosphere. There is also a kindergarten on site.

🅰 E5 🏛 Cnr Cable and Barnett sts 🕐 7:30am-2pm Sun 🌐 harbourside market.co.nz

The grand Beehive, one of Wellington's Parliament Buildings ↓

11

Wellington Botanic Garden

Tinakori Rd Sunrise to sunset daily wellington.govt.nz

Established in 1868, this garden has protected native forest, conifer plantings and plant collections. A seasonal bedding programme includes a massed display of 30,000 tulips in spring and early summer. The Lady Norwood Rose Garden has 106 formal beds, including recent introductions and old favourites. The Begonia House features tropical and temperate plants, a lily pond, seasonal displays of orchids, and a collection of epiphytic and carnivorous plants. The Treehouse Visitor Centre can be accessed via a tower lift or a steep path.

The **Space Place** is housed in Carter Observatory, New Zealand's national observatory. It stands in the Botanic Garden complex near the terminus of the cable car. Astronomical displays, audiovisual shows and a planetarium are special features of the attraction.

Space Place
40 Salamanca Rd, Kelburn 4-11pm Tue & Fri, from 10am Sat, 10am-5:30pm Sun museumswellington.org.nz

12

Victoria University

Kelburn Parade victoria.ac.nz

Opened in 1897, Victoria University's main campus has occupied its Kelburn site overlooking downtown Wellington since 1904. The Faculties of Law and Commerce, as well as the School of Architecture and Design, are among the campuses located in the city.

13

Katherine Mansfield House and Garden

25 Tinakori Rd 10am-4pm Tue-Sun Good Fri, 25 Dec katherinemansfield.com

This 1888 villa is the birthplace and childhood home of the famous author Katherine Mansfield. It contains period photographs, excerpts from Mansfield's writing and antique furniture.

14

Zealandia

53 Waiapu Rd 9am-5pm daily visitzealandia.com

The world's first, and biggest, wildlife sanctuary located in a densely urban area, Zealandia is named after the "missing" eighth continent hidden beneath New Zealand. Set around a picturesque reservoir, some 50 threatened species are protected within the park. Zealandia's mission is to restore its sanctuary grounds to a state similar to that of 700 years ago, before mammalian predators were introduced to New Zealand's shores.

One of the park's most notable residents is the nocturnal kiwi bird. Your best chance of spotting this notoriously shy creature is by joining a night tour of the grounds, led by experienced

→ Wellington cable car climbing the hillside to the Botanic Garden

Must See

guides who know every hiding spot. There are also special tours for kids aged five plus.

⑮
Lambton Quay

Wellington's premier shopping street runs through the heart of New Zealand's political and commercial life. Its 1,100 m (3,600 ft) route is lined with arcades, plazas and elevated walkways. Most of Lambton Quay and its seaward parts are sited on reclaimed land. While steep steps lead up to the slopes on the west, the side streets on the east offer flat access to the harbourfront.

↑ Relaxing in the sun beside Wellington's sparkling harbourfront

⑯
Wellington Cable Car

🚗 Car Cable Car Lane , 280 Lambton Quay ⏰ Museum: 7am-10pm Mon-Fri, from 8:30am Sat-Sun 🚫 25 Dec 🌐 wellingtoncablecar.co.nz

The very first Wellington cable cars were put into service in 1902, and electricity replaced steam power in 1933. The current system dates from 1979 and still links the hillside suburbs with the city centre.

Stops along the route include Victoria University, with access to the Botanic Garden and Space Place at the top. The Kelburn terminus, perched high above the city has glorious views over the city and harbour.

DRINK

Peoples' Coffee
Sip organic fairtrade brews at this trendy suburban spot, which has links to coffee coops around the world.

 E5 🏠 12 Constable St 🌐 peoplescoffee.co.nz

$ $ $

Flight Coffee Hangar
So serious about coffee the owner here bought their own farm in Columbia. Huge breakfast menu.

 E5 🏠 119 Dixon St 📧 flightcoffee.co.nz

$ $ $

Memphis Belle Coffee House
At this quirky haunt, it's all about the coffee, be it cold pressed, a silky flat white or a classic, smooth espresso.

 E5 🏠 38 Dixon St 📧 flightcoffee.co.nz

$ $ $

⑰ Ⓜ ⓨ ⬚ 🛍

TE PAPA TONGAREWA: MUSEUM OF NEW ZEALAND

🅐 E5 **🅐 55 Cable St** **🕐 10am–6pm daily** **🚍 Courtney Place** **🅦 tepapa.govt.nz**

With exhibition space equivalent to three football pitches, Te Papa Tongarewa ("Container of Treasures") is one of the largest museums in the world. Committed to telling the stories of all cultures in New Zealand, Te Papa, as it is referred to locally, houses New Zealand's National Art Collection, including significant Māori works of art, as well as a unique 21st-century carved meeting house.

The diversity of exhibits here is astonishing, ranging from ancient Māori treasures to immersive contemporary installations. The museum's extensive natural history collections even include a rare colossal squid specimen. At the Te Taiao | Nature exhibition, visitors can encounter interactive displays that delve into New Zealand's unique natural history, and examine the environmental challenges faced by the islands today. In the History Collections, inspect dinosaur fossils and Polynesian artifacts; and admire a superb dress and textiles collection. See how New Zealanders experienced World War I's Gallipoli campaign; compare the stories of early migrants and present-day refugees, and experience an earthquake simulator. Te Papa is set amid attractive grounds known as Bush City, with lush native ferns and a glowworm cave. The museum's top level outdoor terrace affords sweeping views of the city and harbour.

Did You Know?

Te Papa's *marae*, Te Hono ki Hawaiki ("the link back to Hawaiki"), recalls the ancestral land of Māori.

↑ Portraits of Māori leaders and Europeans, National Art Collection

GALLERY GUIDE

The excellent high-tech interactive exhibitions begin with Te Taiao | Nature on level 2, where there is also access to Bush City. On level 3 is the exhibition Blood, Earth, Fire: Whangai, Whenua, Ahi Ka, telling the story of human impact on New Zealand's unique flora and fauna. Exhibitions reflecting the country's multicultural heritage, including the Māori, Pacific and European influences on modern-day life, are found on level 4. Art from the National Collection is mainly on display over levels 4 and 5. The roof terrace is on level 6.

← All aspects of the nation's history are exhibited at Te Papa

→ The capacious museum buildings, which opened in 1998, on their waterfront site

↑ The spectacular interpretation of a traditional Māori meeting house

A DRIVING TOUR
MARINE DRIVE

Length 28 km (17 miles) **Stopping-off points** Scorching Bay, Worser Bay, Lyall Bay **Terrain** Flat coastal roads

Hugging the coastline from Oriental Bay, southeast of the city centre on the inner harbour, to Owhiro Bay on the outer shoreline facing Cook Strait, this route is one of New Zealand's great coastal drives. It is both picturesque on cloudless days and awe-inspiring when Wellington's famous southerly gales whip up pounding waves. The route takes visitors past numerous small bays and beaches. It also passes through several suburbs where wooden villas perch on what seem precarious sites high above the road, and around steep, uninhabited hillsides covered with trees that come down to the water's edge.

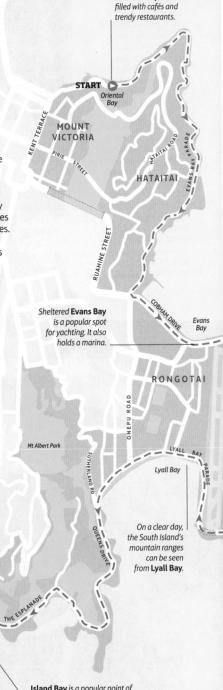

Begin this drive at **Oriental Bay**, an area filled with cafés and trendy restaurants.

START — Oriental Bay

MOUNT VICTORIA

KENT TERRACE

PIRIE STREET

HATAITAI

HATAITAI ROAD

EVANS BAY PARADE

RUAHINE STREET

COBHAM DRIVE

Evans Bay

Sheltered **Evans Bay** is a popular spot for yachting. It also holds a marina.

RONGOTAI

ONEPU ROAD

LYALL BAY PARADE

Lyall Bay

Mt Albert Park

SUTHERLAND RD

QUEENS DRIVE

On a clear day, the South Island's mountain ranges can be seen from **Lyall Bay**.

↑ Relaxing on the soft sand beach of fashionable Oriental Bay

Owhiro Bay

FINISH

THE ESPLANADE

THE ESPLANADE

Island Bay

Taputeranga Island

End this drive at **Owhiro Bay**, the gateway to the south coast.

Island Bay is a popular point of departure for fishing trips to the Cook Strait and beyond.

One of the smallest and most sheltered bays along the route, **Mahanga Bay** is fringed with pine trees.

WELLINGTON AND THE SOUTH

Marine Drive

Locator Map
For more detail see p152

Mahanga Bay

MASSEY ROAD

MASSEY RD

Mount Crawford
163 m (534 ft)

Scorching Bay

Popular with swimmers, **Scorching Bay** allows good views towards Somes and Ward islands and the Cook Strait.

MAUPUIA

KARAKA BAY ROAD

SHELLY BAY ROAD

DARLINGTON RD

PARK ROAD

PARA ST

Karaka Bay is named after the native orange-berried karaka trees found along its edge. It has a pier and a number of elegant wooden summer houses.

Karaka Bay

MIRAMAR AVENUE

Worser Bay

The eastern suburbs of Seatoun are home to **Worser Bay** the city's thriving film industry, including Peter Jackson's Weta Workshop (see p44).

MIRAMAR

HOBART STREET

IRA STREET

MARINE PARADE

SEATOUN

BREAKER BAY RD

BROADWAY

STRATHMORE PARK

Wellington International Airport

MOA POINT

MOA POINT ROAD

Breaker Bay

Little blue penguins can sometimes be seen crossing the road at **Breaker Bay** to nest noisily under nearby houses.

Moa Point

Palmer Head

↑ Quiet Breaker Bay, a scenic place to sun-bathe on pristine sand

0 metres	1000
0 yards	1000

N ↑

↑ Red skies at night over the Manawatu River, Te Apiti - Manawatu Gorge

②

PALMERSTON NORTH

F4 ℹ (06) 350 1922; www.manawatunz.co.nz

Manawatu's largest city, Palmerston North lies in the centre of a broad, fertile coastal plain that encompasses a varied landscape of valleys, plateaus and rivers. The city is a growing hub for the lower North Island. New Zealand's largest university, Massey University, and several colleges and research institutes are based here, giving Palmerston North a pleasant and diverse student atmosphere.

①

The Square

Laid out in 1866, this tranquil, garden zone at the heart of the city provides welcome relief to the busy commercial centre. Originally bisected by New Zealand's main trunk railway, the Square has clipped lawns, flower beds, trees and shrubs, ornamental ponds and fountains. These features, as well as its war memorial and chiming clock tower, attract plenty of visitors all year round. The surrounding shops and buildings reflect the diversity of styles in New Zealand's architectural history.

②

New Zealand Rugby Museum

🏠 326 Main St ⏰ 10am-5pm daily 🚫 1 Jan, Good Fri, 25 & 26 Dec 🌐 rugbymuseum.co.nz

Founded in 1968, this was the first museum in the world devoted to New Zealand's national sport – rugby. It contains exhibits and memorabilia relating to the game's legends and explores the history of rugby in New Zealand from the first game played in the country, at Nelson in 1870, to the present.

There are also exhibits from other rugby-playing countries.

The paraphernalia on display includes caps, jerseys, trophies, badges, autographed balls, ties, posters and photographs. Interactive exhibits allow visitors to explore the aspects of rugby that interest them most and test their rugby skill, plus famous international games can be watched on screen. Also on display is a broken protestor's shield, a legacy of the bitter 1981 tour to New Zealand by the South African Springbok rugby team. The tour divided the country and caused bloody protests.

↑ Displays in the New Zealand Rugby Museum

Te Apiti – Manawatu Gorge

📍1631 Napier Rd, Ashhurst 🌐teapiti.com

East of the city, the Manawatu River runs through the imposing Te Apiti – Manawatu Gorge. Offering one of North Island's most well-known day walks, Te Apiti is a stunning, culturally rich, structure formed over time. The river seems to defy geographical logic by rising on the eastern slopes of the Tararua Range, then turning back on itself to reach the Tasman Sea to the west. The gorge is popular with jet-boaters, kayakers, walkers and campers. A sculpture of ancient warrior Whatonga stands 6-m- (20-ft-) tall along one of the walking tracks.

Cross Hill Gardens

There are a number of beautiful gardens around the city and region. One of these is the Cross Hill Gardens, a 45-minute drive north, which has one of New Zealand's largest and most varied collections of rhododendrons.

Te Manawa Art Gallery

📍326 Main St ⏰10am–5pm daily 🚫1 Jan, Good Fri, 25 & 26 Dec 🌐temanawa.co.nz

First opened in 1959 as the Palmerston North Art Gallery, this gallery was renamed and rehoused in a modern building near the Square in 1977. The entrance displays local artist Paul Dibble's striking sculpture, Pacific Monarch, reputedly the largest bronze work cast in New Zealand.

The gallery's strength lies in its contemporary art, but it also houses a permanent collection of paintings, sculpture, prints, drawings, photographs and ceramics by prominent New Zealand artists. The gallery is part of the Te Manawa complex, which includes a museum and science centre.

EAT

Moxies
Popular for breakfast and desserts. Order at the counter.
🅰F4 📍67 George St 📞06 355 4238

💲💲💲

The Bean Cafe
Japanese, Korean, Chinese and Malaysian dishes, plus bubble tea.
🅰F4 📍92 Broadway Ave 🌐thebeancafe. business.site 🚫Sun & Mon

💲💲💲

Cafe Jacko
Breakfast and lunch spot highly praised for its brunches.
🅰F4 📍8 George St 📞06 359 3303

💲💲💲

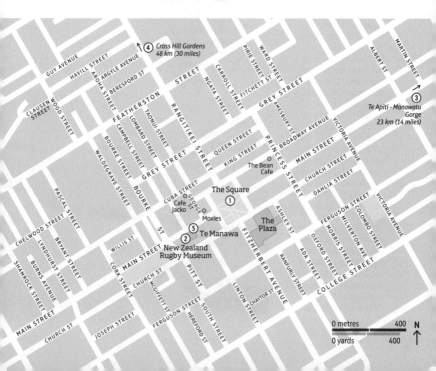

EGMONT NATIONAL PARK

⚠ E3 🛈 North Egmont Visitor Centre, (06) 756 0990; Dawson Falls
Visitor Centre, (027) 443 0248 🚉 Stratford Depot 🖥 doc.govt.nz

With 13 entrances, the national park surrounding Mount Taranaki/Egmont
is one of the most easily accessed in New Zealand. Its 193 km (119 mile)
network of tracks offers ample recreation for the average walker, plus
excellent climbing, hiking and some skiing for the fit and well prepared.

The centrepiece of the park is the solitary 2,518 m (8,261 ft) Mount Taranaki/Egmont, a dormant volcano. Almost year-round, snow and ice cover its peak and upper slope. Sacred to local Māori, it is believed to have formed after a volcanic eruption more than 70,000 years ago; the last eruption was in 1775. Ice and snow routes lead to the summit from the northern slopes, where visitors will find a useful resource at the North Egmont Visitor Centre, a short drive from Egmont Village. The centre has interesting displays on the park and mountain, an audiovisual show and café. For less strenuous walking on the lower slopes, a good starting point is the Dawson Falls/Te Rere O Noke Visitor Centre, which has a model of the park's volcanic features and exhibits on the park's flora and fauna; the plant life here is diverse, from tall rimu and kamahi trees at lower altitudes, to dense subalpine shrubs and an alpine herbfield with plants unique to the park. The falls are a 20-minute walk from the centre.

WALKS IN EGMONT NATIONAL PARK

The park has an extensive network of walking tracks leading to the summit or around the mountain. Shorter tracks start off from the three roads heading up the mountain. These range from easy to difficult and take from 30 minutes to several hours. The popular two-day Pouaki circuit offers walkers a taste of everything Egmont has to offer: rainforest, tussock land, an alpine swamp and volcanic features. This track can be accessed from the North Egmont visitor centre. Simple refuge huts are situated along the tracks; hut passes can be bought from information centres and Department of Conservation offices.

Did You Know?

The near-symmetrical Mount Egmont stood in for Mount Fuji during filming of the movie *The Last Samurai*.

1 Te Rere O Noke, the Dawson Falls, drop 18 m (60 ft) down an ancient lava flow.

2 Hiking towards Fathams Peak; weather conditions can change quickly on the mountain, so it is vital to be well equipped.

3 Gnarled, mossy native trees, abundant on the lower slopes, where the wet mountain climate promotes luxurious vegetation.

↑ Mount Taranaki/ Egmont shrouded in a pink veil of morning cloud

4

NEW PLYMOUTH

⊞E3 ✈12 km (7.5 miles) NE of city ⊞Queen St ℹ65
Aubyn St (Puke Ariki foyer); www.visitnewplymouth.nz

The principal centre of the Taranaki region, New
Plymouth is set around a deep-water port, surrounded
by surfing beaches along the North Taranaki Bight. The
massive cone of Mount Taranaki/Egmont towers behind
the city, which is recognized for its many beautiful
parks, gardens and reserves. The area is the base for the
country's major oil, gas and petrochemical industries.

① Taranaki Cathedral Church of St Mary

🏛37 Vivian St 📞(06) 758
3111 🕐9am-5pm daily

Consecrated in 1848, this
Anglican church is the oldest
stone church in New Zealand.
It is a fine example of 19th-
century architecture, and has
some outstanding stained-
glass windows, an impressive
vaulted timber ceiling and
historic artifacts.

② Len Lye Art Centre

🏛40 Queen St 🕐10am-
5pm daily 🌐lenlyefoun
dation.com

Opened in 1970 as a contemporary art museum, the
Govett-Brewster Art Gallery
was the gift of local
benefactor

Monica Brewster. Its main
strengths lie in its collection
of abstract art from the 1970s
and 1980s and in its contemporary sculpture. It became
the site of the Len Lye Archive
containing the kinetic sculptures, paintings and films of
this New Zealand multimedia
artist, painter and film-maker
(1901–80), and was renamed
in his honour in 2015.

③ Puke Ariki

🏛1 Ariki St 🕐9am-6pm
daily 🌐pukeariki.com

Built on what was the most
notable Māori site in Taranaki,
Puke Ariki comprises a library,
museum and information
centre. The centre provides a
venue for the display of the
museum's heritage collection,
including 6,000 nationally
important Māori *taonga*
(treasures), such as

💬 INSIDER TIP
Go WOMAD

Every March, the New
Zealand chapter of the
World of Music, Arts and
Dance festival (WOMAD)
comes to Brooklands
Park, New Plymouth.
Book tickets in advance
to enjoy the festivities
(*www.womad.co.nz*).

paintings, photographs,
cartoons, maps and coins.
Puke Ariki overlooks a 12-km
(7-miles) New Plymouth
coastal walkway.

④ Richmond Cottage

🏛2-6 Ariki St 📞(06) 759
6060 🕐11am-3:30pm
weekends and public hols

Richmond Cottage, built in
1853 of stone instead of the
customary timber, was the
residence of the Richmond
family. Many of the furnishings
on display in the beautifully

←

Striking façade of the Len Lye
Art Centre, setting the scene
for the contemporary art inside

↑ New Plymouth suburb with Mount Taranaki/Egmont in the distance

restored cottage belonged to these former owners. During the 1880s, the cottage offered accommodation to seaside holiday-makers.

---

 ⑤

Puke Ariki Landing

🏠 **Ariki St** 📞 **(06) 759 6060**

An oasis of green oasis in the central city, Puke Ariki Landing opened in 1990 when train tracks previously fronting the coastline were removed. This attractive park stands where surfboats, which carried people and supplies from ships, used to come ashore.

 ⑥

Pukekura Park

🏠 **Liardet St** 🕐 **7:30am–dusk daily** 🌐 **pukekura.org.nz**

Dense native bushland, native and exotic trees, and fern gullies beside freshwater lakes and streams define Pukekura Park. A fernery, fountain, waterfall, playground and boats for hire are other attractions. From the Tea House there is a dramatic view of Mount Taranaki/Egmont. During the Festival of Lights (mid-December to late January), the park is transformed at night into a fairyland by thousands of coloured lights.

 ⑦

Brooklands Park

🏠 **Brooklands Park Drive** 🕐 **7:30am–dusk daily**

Brooklands is an English-style park with sweeping lawns and formal gardens. Highlights include a huge 2,000-year-old puriri tree, 300 varieties of rhododendron and a children's zoo. The Bowl of Brooklands plays host to concerts.

EAT

Social Kitchen
A trendy bistro serving small plates and sizzling charcoal-cooked dishes.

🗺️ **E3** 🏠 **40 Powderham St** 🌐 **social-kitchen.co.nz**

💲💲💲

Monica's Eatery
This light bright modern café offers fresh Italian-inspired cuisine.

🗺️ **E3** 🏠 **42 Queen St** 🌐 **monicaseatery.co.nz**

💲💲💲

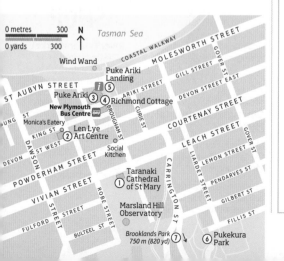

The cityscape and the
Whanganui River at dusk,
seen from Durie Hill ↑

5

WHANGANUI

⚑ E4 ✈ 8 km (5 miles) SE of city 🚉 165 Ridgway St
ℹ 31 Taupo Quay; www.visitwhanganui.com

**First settled by Māori in about AD 1100, Whanganui
was colonized in the mid-19th century when land
around Wellington became scarce. Today it enjoys a
healthy business economy and a lively arts scene.**

Cooks Gardens

⚑ Maria Place

This popular outdoor venue
has a wooden velodrome and
an attractive old bell tower. It
was here, in 1962, that New
Zealander Peter Snell ran the
mile in under four minutes,
breaking the record held by
Britain's Roger Bannister.

Victoria Avenue

The preserved buildings,
cinema, gaslights, wrought-
iron street furniture and palm
trees make Victoria Avenue,
Whanganui's central city
shopping area, a charming
spot for visitors. In summer,
around 1,000 floral baskets
are hung on streetlights and
verandahs to celebrate the
Whanganui in Bloom festival.

Whanganui Regional Museum

⚑ 62 Ridgway St
🕐 10am–4:30pm Mon–Sat
🌐 wrm.org.nz

Established by local naturalist
and jeweller Samuel Drew, the
Whanganui Regional Museum
opened in 1895. Its collection
is focused on the geology
and natural and social history
of the city and surrounding
region. Among the treasures
on display are paintings of the
Māori by Gottfried Lindauer
(1839–1926), who managed to
avoid service in the Austro-
Hungarian army by settling
in New Zealand; Te Mata-o-
Hoturoa, a Māori war canoe
carved from a single totara

SHOP

River Traders Market
The tradition of "river
traders" dates back to
pre-European times. On
Saturday mornings you
will find over 100 stalls
selling everything you
can eat, wear or collect
at Moutoa Quay in the
heritage precinct.

⚑ 7 Taupo Quay
🌐 therivertraders.co.nz

19th and 20th centuries. It houses the Denton photography collection and World War I posters and cartoons.

⑤ Moutoa Gardens

🅰 Market Place

Located at the site of the settling of Whanganui as a town, the beautiful Moutoa Gardens feature monuments set within mature specimen trees and flower beds. They're perfect for a rest stop on Saturday mornings, after a stroll through the lively River Traders Market on the quay. Since the early 1990s, the gardens have been a political rallying point. In 1995, Māori tribes protesting about land and river rights occupied the gardens for 79 days.

⑥ Waimarie Centre

🅰 1A Taupo Quay 🕙 10am–3pm daily 🌐 waimarie.co.nz

This centre houses the salvaged and restored Victorian paddle steamer *Waimarie*. Built in London in 1899, it plied the Whanganui River, carrying goods and passengers, for 50 years. Cruises on the restored steamer leave from here.

⑦ Durie Hill

🅰 42 Anzac Parade 📞 (06) 345 8525 🕙 8am–6pm daily

Located opposite the city bridge at the end of Victoria Avenue, Durie Hill is known for its historic elevator, which rises 66 m (216 ft) inside the hill to the summit. Opened in 1919, it is the only such elevator in New Zealand. A pedestrian tunnel leads to the elevator. It takes about a minute to rise to the top, where you'll find the 34 m (110 ft) Durie Hill Memorial Tower, a memorial to World War I. A climb up the 176 steps of the spiral staircase inside affords even finer panoramic views of Whanganui, Mount Taranaki/Egmont to the northwest *(p166)*, Mount Ruapehu to the east *(p122)* and the Tasman Sea.

tree; and an intact egg, one of very few in the world, from the extinct New Zealand moa.

④ Sarjeant Gallery

🅰 38 Taupo Quay 🕙 10am–4:30pm Mon–Sat 🌐 sarjeant.org.nz

This gallery features a highly regarded collection of New Zealand oil paintings, watercolours and prints from the

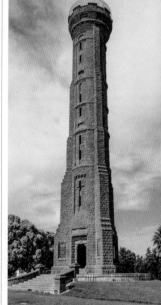

↑ The Durie Hill tower, built from blocks of fossilized seashell rock

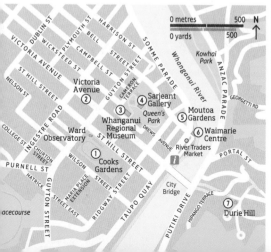

 Majestic Whanganui river meandering through the national park

EXPERIENCE MORE

❻

Whanganui National Park

🄰 E4 🆆 doc.govt.nz

Established in 1987, the three main sections of this park lie within the catchment of the mystical Whanganui river, the longest navigable river in New Zealand. The 290-km (180-mile) river begins its journey high up on Mount Tongariro and meanders through Whanganui National Park all the way to the Tasman Sea. The great waterway has eroded through mudstone to form the park's striking gorges, bluffs, razor-sharp ridges and valleys. Broadleaf podocarp forest surrounding the river forms the heart of the park.

The park is lush with tree ferns and riverside plants, and there is abundant birdlife here, including the beautiful whio (blue duck). The river is rich in fish, with 18 native species frequenting its waters.

Visitors can choose from a variety of activities including canoeing, kayaking, mountain biking and hiking. For a more leisurely trip, take a cruise on the 19th-century paddle steamer *Waimarie*.

❼

Kapiti Island Nature Reserve

🄰 E4 🚆 Paraparaumu
🛈 Department of Conservation, Waikanae Field Centre, 10 Parata St, Waikanae; www.doc.govt.nz

Kapiti Island lies about 6 km (4 miles) from the mainland, dominating the Kapiti Coast. The 10-km- (6-mile-) long island has been a protected wildlife reserve since 1897, and is home to birds like saddlebacks and takahe which are rare or absent from the mainland. Less rare are the cheeky kakas that will steal anything left unattended.

 A whio and duckling, a species native to Whanganui

Access to the island itself is limited, and special tours can be booked through the Department of Conservation's visitor centre in Wellington. But the waters surrounding the island can be enjoyed on diving and swimming trips at any time without the need to arrange a tour in advance.

❽

Paekakariki

🄰 E4 🚉🚌 🛈 i-SITE, Rimu Rd, Paraparaumu; (04) 298 8195; www.naturecoast.co.nz

Situated on the Kapiti Coast, 40 minutes' drive north of Wellington, Paekakariki is

> **The main centre on the Kapiti Coast, Paraparaumu has shorefront shops, cafés and restaurants. It also has a developed beach, with a park and playgrounds.**

the first township on 40 km (25 miles) of sandy coastline known as the "nature coast".

A main attraction here is Queen Elizabeth Park, which encompasses a stunning coastline, sand dunes, peat swamps and bush walks. From MacKays Crossing north of Paekakariki, a tram ride takes in the park. At the **Wellington Tramway Museum**, visitors can view some of the forerunners of the trolley buses that still run on Wellington's streets.

Wellington Tramway Museum
 ☐ Queen Elizabeth Park
🕙 11am–4:30pm Sat & Sun
ⓦ wellingtontrams.org.nz

---

❾ Paraparaumu

Ⓐ E4 🏠🚃🚌 ℹ️ Coastlands; (04) 298 8195

The main centre on the Kapiti Coast, Paraparaumu has shorefront shops, cafés and restaurants. It also has a developed beach, with a park and playgrounds. The town is the departure point for boat trips to Kapiti Island.

The area's major attraction is the **Southward Car Museum**, which holds the southern hemisphere's largest collection of vintage and veteran vehicles. The collection of bicycles includes an 1863 boneshaker. Marlene Dietrich's limousine is one of more than 250 classic and quirky vehicles dating from 1895. Racing boats, homemade vehicles, motorcycles, early motoring curios and traction engines are also housed on the site. A highlight is a 1950 Cadillac Gangster Special, once owned by an employee of Al Capone and Lucky Luciano. It boasts a bomb-proof floor, armour-plated doors, and bullet-proof windows.

The **Lindale Village**, set around a New Zealand farm, is ideal for families. The centre offers sheep shearing demonstrations as well as other events, and a night market with food stalls, and music. A shop showcasing gourmet Kapiti Cheese and Kapiti Ice Cream is located on the site, along with galleries and cafés. There is also space for allocated for picnics and barbecues.

Southward Car Museum
🚗🕙🏠🚻🍴 ☐ Otaihanga Rd, Paraparaumu 🕙 9am–4:30pm daily ⓦ southward carmuseum.co.nz

Lindale Village
🚗🕙🏠🍴🚻 ☐ State Hwy 1, Paraparaumu 🕙 9am–9pm daily 🚫 Good Fri, 25 Dec
ⓦ lindale.co.nz

---

❿ Waikanae

Ⓐ E4 🏠🚌 ℹ️ Rimu Rd, Paraparaumu; (04) 298 8195

Nestled between the foothills of the Tararua Range and the Kapiti Coast, Waikanae is primarily a retirement centre, known for its craft shops and magnificent gardens. The formally designed English-style Burnard Gardens is located here.

The town's highlight is the **Waikanae Estuary Scientific Reserve**, home to over 63 species of birds, such as shags, dabchicks, Caspian terns, royal spoonbills and pukeko. Fires, hunting and mountain and trail biking are forbidden.

Waikanae Estuary Scientific Reserve
☐ Paraparaumu Beach, Waikanae ⓦ doc.govt.nz

TE RAUPARAHA

Kapiti Island was once the base of Te Rauparaha (1768–1849), chief of the Ngati Toa tribe and one of the greatest Māori generals of his era. After years of warfare in the Waikato and Taranaki areas, he moved to Kapiti Island in the 1820s, dominating the southwestern part of the North Island and the north of the South Island until the 1840s. He is credited with composing the well-known haka (war chant) that is often performed by the All Blacks before international rugby matches.

↑ Veteran car on display at the Southward Car Museum

Grapevines growing
in the countryside
around Martinborough

sheep-shearing displays for groups of ten or more. The town also has a recreation centre with swimming pools, and the region's art and history musem, Aratoi. Queen Elizabeth Park has a children's playground, a miniature train, mini-golf and a skatepark.

Masterton is close to the beach resorts of Castlepoint and Riversdale, popular for surfing, fishing and walking.

The Tararua Forest Park, located within the rugged Tararua Range, can be accessed at Holdsworth, 15 km (9 miles) from State Highway 2, via Norfolk Road just south of Masterton. The park has bush walks ranging from easy to difficult, while Grassy Flats beside the Atiwhakatu Stream are ideal for picnics and barbecues.

The Wool Shed

 12 Dixon St
10am–4pm daily
Anzac Day, Good Fri, 25 Dec
thewoolshednz.com

13

Pukaha Mount Bruce National Wildlife Centre

E4 30 km (19 miles) N of Masterton 9am–6pm daily 25 Dec pukaha. org.nz

This centre conserves some of New Zealand's rarest and most endangered wildlife. Most famously, it is home to three white kiwi and features a Kiwi House where the birds are hatched, hand-raised and fed from October to April. Other bird species include the stitchbird, kokako and takahe. Visitors can take a walking tour through native bush, including a last remnant of forest once known as "Forty

11

Martinborough

E5 18 Kitchener St; www.wairarapanz.com

Established in 1881 by Irish immigrant John Martin, Martinborough was once reliant on the surrounding farming community for its prosperity. Since the late 1970s, the town has become internationally known for its grape growing and wine making. It is now a fashionable weekend destination for those attracted by its premium wines, vineyard cafés, boutique stores, quality accommodation and award-winning restaurants. Most of the town's boutique wineries are within walking or cycling distance of its picturesque town square. New Zealand's first commercial wind farm, Hau Hei Wind Farm is 21 km (13 miles) southeast of Martinborough. Although the farm is on private land, the sails can be seen from a public viewing area.

12

Masterton

E4 10 Dixon St; www.wairarapanz.com

Ninety minutes' drive from both Wellington and Palmerston North, Masterton is Wairarapa's largest town. It hosts a number of events during the summer, including a biennial air show and an annual sheep-shearing competition known as the Golden Shears.

Masterton is home to **The Wool Shed**, a national museum dedicated to New Zealand's shearing heritage, with live

---

DRINK

Tirohana Estate

One of Martinborough's oldest vineyards, Tirohana is open daily for tastings, and is popular for lunch and dinner – it's best to book in advance.

E5 42 Puruatanga Rd tirohana estate.com

Palliser Estate

One of the country's largest wine producers, Palliser hosts exceptional dinners at its on-site cooking school. Sample the signature Great Riddler Chardonnay.

E5 96 Kitchener St, Martinborough palliser.co.nz

Mile Bush", containing native rimu, rata and kamahi trees, nocturnal kiwi and tuatara. It is also possible to watch eels being fed near the centre's river bridge and kaka being fed each afternoon.

 14

Featherston

🅐 E4 🚌 🛈 Old Courthouse, Main St; www.wairarapanz.com

Situated at the foot of the Rimutaka Range, Featherston is the southern gateway to the Wairarapa area for those arriving from the Wellington side of the divide. Known for its antique shops and colonial buildings, the town also houses the **Fell Locomotive Museum**, home to the world's only surviving steam-powered Fell locomotive. Running on three rails, these ingenious engines used to climb up and over the Rimutaka Range.

On the right side of the road from Wellington, before reaching Featherston, a signpost points the way to a lookout. There are also terrific walks that provide splendid views across Lake Wairarapa to the ranges of Haurangi (Aorangi) Forest Park and Palliser Bay. The lake is home to internationally recognized wetlands, which are the third largest in New Zealand. Both native and migratory breeds of bird gather at the lake.

Southeast of the lake is Cape Palliser where, next to a public road, visitors can find one of the country's largest breeding colonies for the New Zealand fur seal, one of nine fur seal species found worldwide. Seals can be seen throughout the year, with breeding from November to January.

Another spectacular sight in the area is the Putangirua Pinnacles, which were formed in the past 120,000 years by heavy rain eroding an ancient gravel deposit. Some of the pinnacles could be over a 1,000 years old.

Wairarapa has a mulitude of cycle routes running along the region's expansive rural landscape and rugged coastlines. The 115-km (71-mile) south coast Rimutaka Cycle Trail begins in Wellington and takes riders through the Rimutaka Ranges to Wairarapa Valley before coming to an end at Orongorongo.

Cyclists travelling Wairarapa's rugged Rimutaka Cycle Trail ↓

GOLDEN SHEARS COMPETITION

The Golden Shears International Shearing and Woolhandling Championships are held for four days in Masterton in early March each year. Initiated by the Wairarapa District Young Farmers' Club, the competition was originally envisaged to form part of the local Agricultural and Pastoral Show. Since the inaugural competition in 1961, the Golden Shears has become a national institution, attracting hundreds of competitors from around the world and thousands of observers. Although several smaller shearing competitions now take place around the country, this remains the pre-eminent show in New Zealand.

Fell Locomotive Museum
♿ Ⓜ 🅐 Cnr SH2 & Lyon sts ⏰ 10am–2:30pm Tue–Fri, 10am–4pm Sat–Sun 🆑 Anzac Day (am only), 25 Dec 🆆 fellmuseum.org.nz

⑮
Stratford

Ⓐ E3 🚌 ℹ 61-63 Miranda St; www.stratford.govt.nz

Lying to the east of Mount Taranaki/Egmont (p166), Stratford is named after Shakespeare's birthplace, Stratford-upon-Avon, and many streets are named after Shakespearean characters. The **Taranaki Pioneer Village** in the town comprises restored or recreated buildings, including a school house, old-fashioned jail, railway station and about 50 other buildings that relate to the area's local and provincial history.

Perhaps one of the best ways to appreciate this region is to drive the 150-km-(93-mile-) long Forgotten World Highway, which connects Stratford to the small town of Taumarinuione. Following colonial bridle tracks, the route travels through a truly memorable landscape and includes an eerie one-lane tunnel and a sinuous journey through a river gorge. Part of this road is unsealed gravel, and the only significant settlement here is Whangamomona.

Taranaki Pioneer Village
Ⓐⓒⓕ 🚗 State Hwy 3, Stratford South 🕐 10am–4pm daily 🌐 pioneer village.co.nz

⑯
Levin

Ⓐ E4 🚌 🚐

Levin sits on a fertile plain that is one of the largest vegetable-producing areas in the country. Its main street, lined with shops that service its farming hinterland, epitomizes much of traditional small-town New Zealand. Owner-operated outlets on the outskirts of the town offer "pick-your-own" freshly grown produce direct from the fields and orchards.

⑰
Sugar Loaf Islands Marine Park

Ⓐ E3 🚢 From Lee Break-water, New Plymouth 🌐 doc.govt.nz

Established as a protected area in 1991, the Sugar Loaf Islands, or Ngā Motu, lie between 700 m (2,300 ft) and 1.5 km (1 mile) off New Plymouth's Port Taranaki breakwater. The spectacular reefs that make up the islands are the oldest volcanic features in Taranaki. Of the eleven island groupings, the two largest are Motumahanga and Moturoa, often referred to as the "outer islands". Four rocky islets close to the mainland at Paritutu are known as the "inner islands".

The islands support a wealth of wildlife and plants. Fur seals are present all year round, with common and Maui's dolphins and killer, pilot and humpback whales also seen at times.

Although the best way to explore the islands is by charter boat, Round Rock, one of the "inner islands", can be accessed on foot from the beach during mid- to low tide. Snapper Rock, another "inner island", is accessible from the shore only when the spring tides are very low.

The deep water, wide variety of marine life and underwater scenery make the park a good spot for diving. Recreational fishing is also popular, but restricted to defined areas. Game fishing further offshore for tuna and marlin takes place in summer and early autumn.

⑱
Opunake

Ⓐ E3 🚌 ℹ 55 High St; www.opunake.co.nz

The thriving centre of a rich dairy-farming district, Opunake is the largest town on the west side of Mount

← With rolling hills rising behind, the sleepy town centre of Stratford

> The Opunake Walkway takes visitors around the beautiful coastline and beach front, as well as around the nearby Opunake Lake.

↑ The Taranaki coast's Back Beach, overlooking the Sugar Loaf Islands

Taranaki/Egmont. The beach at Opunake, situated along from small Middleton Bay, is regarded as one of Taranaki's best. It teems with tourists attracted to its safe swimming and surfing during summer. The Opunake Walkway takes visitors around the beautiful coastline and beach front, as well as around the nearby Opunake Lake, an excellent spot for watersports. The 7-km (4-mile) route can be accessed from a number of points along the way.

19
Hawera

🄰E4 🚌 🛈55 High St; (06) 278 8599

Part of Taranaki's rural heartland, Hawera boasts many interesting places. The 38,000-sq-m (409,000-sq-ft) **Hollard Gardens** were laid out in the late 1920s by farmer Bernard Hollard and presented to the Queen Elizabeth II National Trust in 1982.

Hawera and its surroundings can be viewed from the top of the town's water tower, built after a series of fires in the 1880s, one of which razed most of the main street. In 1914, a month after the tower was erected, an earthquake caused it to list 75 cm (30 inches) to the south. The fault has been reduced to 8 cm (3 inches).

The **Tawhiti Museum** recreates many aspects of early life in south Taranaki. Exhibits range from the early land wars to the development of the dairy industry, and there is a traders and whalers experience, where visitors may take an underground canal boat to explore the region's history. The life-like figures in the exhibits, modelled on the faces of local volunteers, were cast at the museum's on-site workshops. A bush railway takes passengers on a reconstruction of the logging railways that used to operate in Taranaki.

Hollard Gardens

⊛ 🄰1686 Upper Manaia Rd 🕐7am-dusk daily 🔳trc. govt.nz/gardens

Tawhiti Museum

⊛⊛⊜🄰 🄰401 Ohangai Rd 🕐10am-4pm Fri-Mon 🔳tawhitimuseum.co.nz

STAY

Whangamomona Hotel
Famous for its classic car rallies and vintage decor, this hotel has charm in spades, and makes for a good stop along the Forgotten World Highway.

🄰E3 🄰6018 Ohura Rd, Whangamomona 🔳whanagamomona hotel.co.nz

$$$

Wharekauhau Country Estate
A two-hour drive from Wellington, you'll find unrivalled luxury on a working farm, with a spa and gourmet dining.

🄰E5 🄰4132 Wharekauhau Rd, Palliser Bay 🔳wharekauhau.co.nz

$$$

MARLBOROUGH AND NELSON

Archaeological evidence dates Māori occupation of Marlborough to at least AD 1280, with the early Polynesian navigators Kupe and Rakaihautu also known to have spent time here. In 1642, Dutch explorer Abel Tasman and his crew sailed into Golden Bay, becoming the first Europeans to sight New Zealand. A confused and ultimately fatal confrontation with Māori left four of the crew dead, and the Dutch sailed off without ever making landfall in the country. No European visited New Zealand until 1770, when James Cook sailed to Ship Cove in the Marlborough Sounds.

Following the signing of the Treaty of Waitangi in 1840, the New Zealand Company established its Nelson settlement. In 1858, Nelson was declared New Zealand's second city, a year before Marlborough gained identity as a separate province. Marlborough's warm climate and low rainfall would later provide the perfect climate for viticulture, and in the 1970s, the Wairau Valley flourished as the country's largest wine growing region.

Today, northern Nelson makes the perfect base for exploring the spectacular nearby Abel Tasman, Kahurangi and Nelson Lakes national parks. This rich hinterland, peopled by artists, vitners and horticulturalists, extends south through lush Marlborough vineyards to the great Southern Alps.

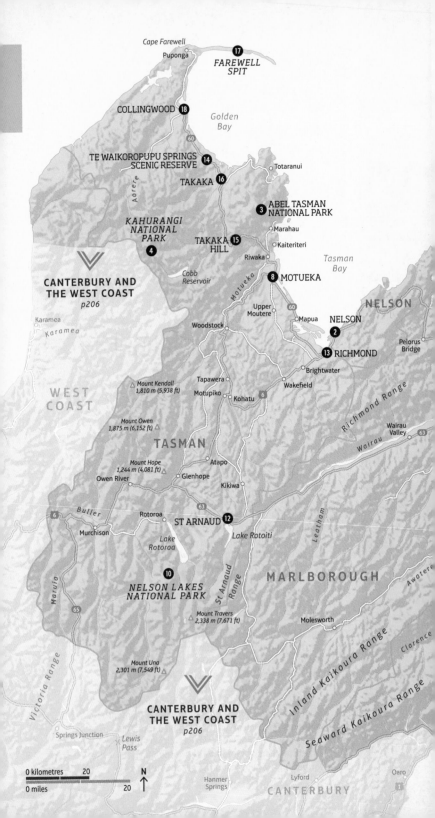

MARLBOROUGH AND NELSON

Must Sees

① Marlborough Sounds
② Nelson
③ Abel Tasman National Park
④ Kahurangi National Park

Experience More

⑤ Queen Charlotte Drive
⑥ Havelock
⑦ Picton
⑧ Motueka
⑨ Kaikoura
⑩ Nelson Lakes National Park
⑪ Blenheim
⑫ St Arnaud
⑬ Richmond
⑭ Te Waikoropupu Springs Scenic Reserve
⑮ Takaka Hill
⑯ Takaka
⑰ Farewell Spit
⑱ Collingwood

WELLINGTON
AND THE
SOUTH
p150

Did You Know?

The Sounds are home to the entire breeding population of the king shag, New Zealand's rare cormorant.

The forested ridges and drowned valleys of the outer Sounds ↑

①

MARLBOROUGH SOUNDS

△E4 ❑ Picton: The Foreshore, (03) 520 3113; Havelock: Cnr Te Aute and Middle rds, (03) 574 2161 ⛴ From Picton and Havelock ⓦ marlboroughnz.com

The Marlborough Sounds region is an intricate tracery of pretty bays, sheltered inlets and hidden coves rich in walking tracks, wildlife, historic whaling sites and unsurpassed views. Campsites, waterside lodges and B&Bs abound in this peaceful holiday area, where water transport rules.

Picton *(p195)* and Havelock *(p194)* are the Sounds' two main towns. Launch services from both provide the best access to the secluded bays and accommodation by the sea. Picton gives access to the easterly Queen Charlotte Sound, the most popular for kayaking and sailing, as well as marine life; boat tours also depart from Picton to see orcas, humpback whales and five species of dolphin that cruise the waters here. The scenic Queen Charlotte walking and cycling track, 71 km (44 miles)

long, runs along the sound's westerly side all the way out to Ship Cove, where a short trip across the water gives access to Motuara Island wildlife reserve, where a myriad birds can be seen from the walkways.

Havelock is the gateway to quieter Kenepuru Sound, a popular spot for walking, fishing and camping, and to the more remote area beyond Pelorus Sound, including forested Tennyson Inlet and, beyond the treacherous French Pass strait, unspoiled d'Urville Island.

HOW THE SOUNDS WERE FORMED

The Sounds region appears as a series of ridges rising above the water but is, in fact, a series of valleys drowned by the ocean. A combination of changing sea levels (due to world climate changes), movement along faultlines and tilting of the landmass has caused inundation by the sea. The last significant surge in sea level was at the end of an Ice Age about 12,000 years ago. The Sounds were the site of New Zealand's first whaling stations, and today are used by North-South Island crossing ferries from Wellington, which cruise up the channels to dock at Picton.

① A walker pauses to take in the view from the Queen Charlotte Track.

② Cormorants are among the many bird species that feed from these rich waters.

③ Kayaking in the sheltered waters, where each headland rounded reveals another attractive cove or bay.

②

NELSON

🅰 D4 ✈ 15 km (9 miles) SW of city 🚌 27 Bridge St
ℹ 77 Trafalgar St; www.nelsonnz.com

The second settlement developed by the New Zealand Company, Nelson was granted city status in 1858 by royal decree, and today is a vibrant art, crafts and festival centre with a superb climate, fine beaches and boutique hotels. The compact city centre teems with galleries, craft shops and heritage attractions.

↑ Spring flowers and palm trees in Anzac Park, perfect for a stroll

① Centre of New Zealand

🏛 Cnr Milton & Hardy sts

An easy walk beginning at the Botanical Reserve leads up Botanical Hill to a lookout and monument known locally as "the centre of New Zealand" – the "zero-zero" point from which topographers first began to survey the country. The hill provides good views of the city, harbour, Maitai Valley and the Maitai River. A path follows the river downstream through a pleasant park and past Riverside Pool, a modern heated pool with a historic façade.

② Suter Art Gallery

🏛 A208 Bridge St
🕘 9:30am–4:30pm daily
🚫 1 Jan, Good Fri, 25 Dec
🌐 thesuter.org.nz

One of New Zealand's oldest galleries (1899), the Suter Art Gallery holds a nationally important permanent collection, including paintings by Sir Tosswill Woollaston (one of the founders of New Zealand modern art), Frances Hodgkins, Colin McCahon and Jane Evans. It also houses the collection of Andrew Suter, the city's bishop from 1866 to 1891. He donated early colonial paintings, including

many by the colonial watercolourist John Gully, to the people of Nelson.

③ Anzac Park

🏛 Cnr Rutherford and Halifax sts

The beautifully landscaped Anzac Park, with its pretty flowerbeds, tall palms and cenotaph, is Nelson's main war memorial. A horse-drawn passenger carriage ran alongside the park until 1901, using a section of New Zealand's first railway line. Auckland

The Matai river, which flows through Nelson to the harbour

were formally established in 1887. Albion Square borders the gardens and was once the political centre of Nelson when provincial government buildings dominated the square. Some historic buildings remain, such as a powder magazine, trout hatchery and fire station. A still-in-service 1864 postbox and surveyors' test chain complete the picture.

⑤

The Nelson Provincial Museum

🏠 Cnr Trafalgar & Hardy sts
🕐 Daily 🗓 Good Fri, 25 Dec
🌐 nelsonmuseum.co.nz

Nelson's first European settlers set up this museum in 1842, and today's modern building occupies the same city block. The lower gallery focuses on the natural and social history of the Nelson and Tasman region. Here, you'll find a huge range of geological and fossil specimens and displays. Māori artifacts and *taonga* (treasures such as weapons and ornaments) also form a large part of the collection, along with ceramics, glass and silverware, and textiles from colonial times to the present. On top of this, there's a fascinating collection of early photographs chronicling Nelson and New Zealand's early colonial history. The upper gallery hosts special exhibitions on a wide range of subjects, for which there is often an entry charge. Entry to the main museum is free for locals, but there is a small fee for visitors.

Point nearby was once the site of a Māori fortification. A winding track to the summit provides excellent city views.

④

Queens Gardens and Albion Square

The main focus of the city's heritage precincts remains the Queens Gardens. Some of the trees date back to the 1850s although the gardens

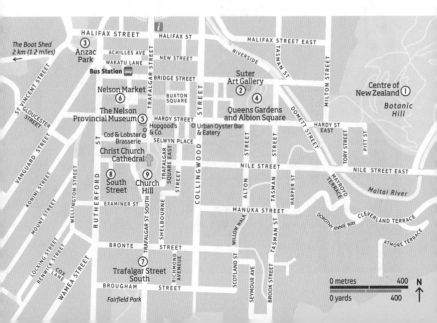

HALIFAX STREET
HALIFAX ST
HALIFAX STREET EAST

The Boat Shed 2 km (1.2 miles)

③ Anzac Park
ACHILLES AVE
WAKATU LANE
🚌 Bus Station
NEW STREET
RIVERSIDE

Nelson Market ⑥
BRIDGE STREET
BUXTON SQUARE

Suter Art Gallery ②

Centre of New Zealand ①
Botanic Hill

The Nelson Provincial Museum ⑤
HARDY STREET
Hopgood's & Co.
Urban Oyster Bar & Eatery

Queens Gardens and Albion Square ④

Cod & Lobster Brasserie
SELWYN PLACE
HARDY STREET EAST

Christ Church Cathedral

⑧ South Street
⑨ Church Hill
EXAMINER ST
NILE STREET
NILE STREET EAST

Maitai River

MANUKA STREET

BRONTE
STREET

⑦ Trafalgar Street South
BROUGHAM STREET
RICHMOND AVENUE

Fairfield Park

ATMORE TERRACE
CLEVELAND TERRACE

0 metres 400
0 yards 400
N

⑥
Nelson Market

🏠 Montgomery Square
📞 (03) 546 6454 🕐 8am–
1pm Sat, 9am–1pm Sun
🗓 1 Jan, 25 Dec

On weekends the car park at
Montgomery Square is
transformed into a colourful
marketplace. Shoppers and
buskers bring the market to
life, creating a busy spectacle
that has become a key part of
life in Nelson, for locals and
visitors alike. On Saturdays,
there are also offerings from
local artisans selling everthing
from handmade soaps, hats
and toys to ceramics and
jewellery, while the Sunday
market brings second-hand
clothes, books, and home-
wares as well as antiques and
collectables. On both days,
street food stalls and carts
provide a delicious range of
snacking opportunities, and
the typical produce and plant
stalls sell their wares.

NELSON'S THRIVING ARTS SCENE

A warm climate and a
relaxed environment has
attracted many artists to
Nelson. The city abounds
with opportunities to
explore their work in
the many galleries and
studios of glass-blowers,
painters, jewellers, textile
artists, woodworkers and
ceramic artists. It is also
becoming known for
music and performance
events, such as the Nelson
Jazz Festival and the
Nelson School of Music
Winter Festival.

⑦
Trafalgar Street South

Nelson's main street, Trafalgar,
extends south of the cathedral. Trafalgar Street South
leads to Fairfield Park and a
small cemetery with the
graves of some early settlers.

Close by are two colonial era
houses, Melrose and Fairfield.
Melrose House, which was built
around 1878, is a grand home,
constructed in the Italianate
style. Equally imposing,
Fairfield House (1873) is
crowned by its viewing tower,
a replica of one used by its

original owner, Arthur Atkinson, to house his telescope. A prominent lawyer, he was also a keen amateur astronomer, while his wife was active in the suffragette movement. This connection is interesting as New Zealand was the first country in the world to give women the vote. Outside the house, the gardens are beautiful, with many exotic trees and some plantings made by the Dalai Lama during his 1996 visit to New Zealand.

South Street

To the west of Church Hill is the historic precinct of South Street, comprising a collection of workers' cottages built between 1863 and about 1867. Sixteen of the charming little wooden buildings remain intact and have been carefully restored, making this New Zealand's oldest fully preserved street.

Church Hill

Church Hill is dominated by the Anglican Christ Church Cathedral, the third church built on a site which has also been a survey base, pa, fort and immigration barracks. The present building is noted for its belltower, added in 1957. Its openwork design and modern construction material – its made out of reinforced concrete – at first provoked outrage among many, but with time it has become a distinctive city landmark. Church Hill is linked to Trafalgar Street by the impressive granite Cathedral Steps, one of many gifts to the city by Thomas Cawthron, a philanthropist. Panels explain the history of Church Hill and some notable trees still shade those who climb the stairs, while the remains of the old fort are visible near the cathedral entrance.

Did You Know?

The first rugby union match ever played in New Zealand took place in Nelson, on 14 May 1870.

EAT

Hopgood's & Co

A charming Victorian building with a cosy inside and an outdoor patio. Sophisticated food is on the menu here, including good vegetarian and vegan options.

284 Trafalgar St

$$$

The Boat Shed

This Nelson institution perched on the water's edge offers sumptuous fresh fish and seafood.

D4 350 Wakefield Quay boatshed cafe.co.nz

$$$

Cod & Lobster Brasserie

Seafood is the speciality here, as the name implies, and gin is the tipple of choice. Inside, expect white tablecloths; outside is a more casual brick patio.

300 Trafalgar St codandlobster.com

$$$

← The belltower of Christ Church Cathedral seen from Trafalgar Street

ABEL TASMAN NATIONAL PARK

🅰 D4 🏠 79 Trafalgar St, Nelson 🚌 To Marahau and Totaranui from Nelson and Motueka 🚢 From Kaiteriteri and Marahau 🌐 doc.govt.nz

Nestled at the far north of the South Island, Abel Tasman is the country's smallest national park. Its pristine golden beaches, sandy estuaries and crystal-clear waters backed by forest are a true wilderness reserve, and a sanctuary for a diversity of animal, bird and marine life.

Named for the Dutch navigator who was the first European to reach New Zealand (*p56*), Abel Tasman National Park is best known for the winding 60 km (37 mile) Coast Track. The track is accessible from Marahau, Totaranui and Wainui and can be walked in either direction between Marahau and Wainui Bay – the waters of Tonga Island Marine Reserve are roughly halfway. Huts and campsites dot the route (advance booking is necessary – check website), although water taxis and sea shuttle services make a day trip possible, too. The more rugged 41 km (25 mile) Inland Track treks through native forest, and has an optional side-trip to the vertical shaft of Harwoods Hole and can be combined with the Coast Track to create an epic week-long tramp. Abel Tasman is also one of New Zealand's best sea kayaking destinations and a day or two on the water is well spent exploring rocky granite outposts and spotting seals, penguins, dolphins and birds.

→ Pristine coastline of Abel Tasman National Park, where fur seals (*inset*) are often found basking in the sun

TOP 5 WILDLIFE AT ABEL TASMAN

Little Blue Penguin
At 25–30 cm (10–12 in), these are the smallest of all penguins.

Bottlenose and Dusky Dolphins
Playful dolphins often cruise in the wake of boats, especially early in the morning.

Orca Whale
Rarely spotted here, but identified by their tall, dominant dorsal fin.

Bellbird
Captain Cook described their song as "small bells exquisitely tuned".

Fur Seals
A common sight on the park's shorelines.

↑ The arresting Split Apple Rock (Tokangawhā), fractured by two gods in Māori legend

→ Walking the 60 km (37 mile) Coast Track

Did You Know?

Tides on the Abel Tasman coast can rise and fall up to 5.2 m (15 ft) between high and low tide.

STAY

Camping and hut stays are an essential part of the national park experience.

The Barn Backpackers and Campground

A year-round shady campsite plus 4- and 6-bed dorms and purpose-built private cabins can be found here, with all the facilities a weary traveller might need.

🗺D4 🏠14 Harvey Road, Marahau, Rd 2 Motueka 🌐barn.co.nz

Totaranui Campground

A huge DOC campground next to gorgeous Totaranui beach and the estuary, with 269 unpowered and vehicle accessible sites. Campers are responsible for their own rubbish. Reservations required.

🗺D4 🏠Totaranui 🌐doc.govt.nz

Awaroa Lodge

The most stylish accommodation in the park has no road access; arrival is by water taxi, light plane or helicopter. While surrounded by native bush, this upscale option has all the comforts of home.

🗺D4 🏠11 Awaroa Bay 🌐awaroalodge.co.nz

Never too young for adventure: ↑ on the trails through lush forest at Abel Tasman National Park

Exploring on Foot

Tramping in Abel Tasman is incredibly varied. As well as the world-famous 3–5 day Coast Track and strenuous 3-day Inland Track, Abel Tasman has several shorter trails, such as Wainui Falls (1 hour 20 minutes), Harwoods Hole (1 hour 30 minutes) – which leads to the deepest shaft in the country – and tramps of varying lengths and difficulties around Totaranui, one of the main access points for the park. The DOC (Department of Conservation, responsible for national parks) has huts and campsites along the Coast Track that need to be booked in advance. Operators such as Wilsons offer combined water taxi, kayak and walking tours from half a day to multi-day trips – and

↑ Kayakers enjoying an organized group trip paddling the calm waters of the coastline

Did You Know?

Much of the lower shrubby layer of Abel Tasman's vegetation is manuka, source of the healthful honey.

→
Wainui Falls, reached by a short detour from the Coast Track

have their own beachfront lodges in the park. A couple of sections of the Coast Track can only be tackled at low tide so independent trekkers must consult tide timetables.

Kayaking Expeditions

Guided trips typically include exploring coves and lagoons, wildlife watching, and a visit to a beach and short hike; on multi-day tours food and accommodation are included. Specialists Abel Tasman Kayaks offer guided tours from their base facilities at Marahau, as well as kayak hire. For something a little different, Māori-owned Waka Tours, operating from Kaiteriteri, use single- or double-hulled outrigger canoes paddled by a crew, who teach a formidable waka salute and a little about Māori culture *(wakaabeltasman.nz)*. You can also explore the coastline on your own; but read the warnings first.

Water Taxi Services

Water taxis operate on fixed timetables and by private charter to points along the Coast Track from Mārahau and Kaiteriteri. Marahau Water Taxis drop off at all the main beaches and will organize pickup further along the coast. Abel Tasman Sea Shuttle offers a raft of cruises and a flexible 3-day pass; its sister company is Kaiteriteri Kayak, so consider combining tours.

 INSIDER TIP
Adventure Arrangers

Intrepid explorers should join an Abel Tasman Canyons tour: groups are led to remote bush locations where adventurers can abseil, slide and swim through pristine rivers, waterfalls and explore narrow canyons. Free pickups are from Motueka, Riwaka, Kaiteriteri and Marahau *(www.abel tasmancanyons.co.nz)*.

KAHURANGI NATIONAL PARK

🅐D4 📍20 Wallace St, Motueka; www.doc.govt.nz

Covering more than 4,500 sq km (1,740 sq miles) on the region's west coast, Kahurangi, New Zealand's second largest national park, has a wealth of magnificent natural habitats just waiting to be explored.

Kahurangi can be translated as "treasured possession", and it's not hard to see why this pristine landscape is so highly prized. Three peaks – Mount Arthur, Mount Peel and Mount Lodestone – surround a plateau of high, rocky moor called the Tableland. In the 19th century, gold-prospectors set up camps here, but today the treasures hidden amid the tussocky grasses are a rich array of native flora – 80 per cent of New Zealand's alpine species can be found in the park's alpine herbfields. Rushing river valleys cut down from glacial lakes in the high ground into ancient beech forests, lush

with mosses and ferns and rich in birdlife: fantails, bellbirds and fearless South Island robins flourish. On the coast, groves of nikau palms give the forest a semi-tropical look.

The stunning wilderness can be traversed along an extensive network of tracks studded with refuge huts, making it prime trekking and mountain-biking territory; there are plenty of gentler walking routes too. Kayaking, caving, rafting and fishing are also popular activities along the Karamea River. The main gateway to the park is Motueka, but access is also possible from Karamea, Murchison and Golden Bay.

Rare alpine plants, many found only on Kahurangi, grow on the high ground →

1

2

1 A historic wooden refuge hut in Kahurangi's verdant Cobb valley.

2 The great-spotted kiwi (pictured) and tiny rock wren, both threatened species, thrive in the park's rich vegetation.

3 Cycling along the coastline on a lush stretch of the Heaphy Track.

3

Did You Know?

Kahurangi is home to the *powelliphanta*, a rare carnivorous snail that can grow up to 10 cm (4 in) long.

THE HEAPHY TRACK

This 82-km (50-mile) intermediate walking trail takes 4–5 days of tramping and is immensely popular. The route meanders through Kahurangi's lush tropical rainforest, over rocky alpine terrain and across sub-alpine scrubland to palm-fringed beaches. It requires no technical expertise, but a fair amount of effort.

EXPERIENCE MORE

⑤
Queen Charlotte Drive

E4

The best-known road in the Marlborough Sounds, Queen Charlotte Drive is a scenic route connecting Picton and Havelock. With stopovers, it can take up to half a day to complete the 35-km (21.5-mile) journey on the sealed but narrow and winding road. Leaving Picton, the Queen Charlotte Drive passes lookout points above the town and at Governors Bay, 8 km (5 miles) from Picton, with excellent views up and down Queen Charlotte Sound. Beaches and pleasant picnic and swimming areas can be found along the route that passes through the settlements of Ngakuta and Momorangi bays. At Ngakuta Bay, **Sirpa Alalääkkölä's Art Studio** showcases her large, bright paintings, many of them inspired by the Sounds.

Continuing west, a turn-off 12 km (8 miles) from Governors Bay leads to historic Anakiwa, where the Queen Charlotte Track begins. A shelter and picnic area are provided and an easy stroll along the track leads through beech forest to Davies Bay.

The drive continues through Linkwater with the road following the waters of the Mahakipawa Arm, the innermost reaches of Pelorus Sound. The walking tracks and viewpoint at Cullen Point provide another perspective on the waterways below, before the road's final descent into Havelock.

Sirpa Alalääkkölä's Art Studio

 Phillips Rd, Ngakuta Bay (03) 573 7775
By appointment

⑥
Havelock

D4 📧 📧 ℹ 46 Main Rd; www.havelocknz.com

The self-styled green lip mussel capital of the world, the village of Havelock receives a growing number of visitors attracted by its history and the success of its mussel-farming industry. Havelock was established in the 1850s on the Nelson–Blenheim track near the uppermost navigable reaches of Pelorus Sound. Timber milling

💬 INSIDER TIP
Pelorus Bridge

Stop off between Havelock and Nelson at Pelorus Bridge, once the site of fierce Māori tribal battles, and more recently where the dwarves floated down-river in Peter Jackson's *The Hobbit*. Today it is a stunning scenic reserve.

and gold mining were its first industries; now fishing and aquaculture (the cultivation of shellfish) dominate. The main street still retains something of its pioneer character. Highlights of a walk around the waterfront are the stately 1880s home of timber miller William Brownlee, the stone St Peter's Church, and the old primary school (now a hostel) attended by Lord Ernest Rutherford in the 1870s. A number of cafés can be found in the town along with many interesting shops selling antiques, jewellery, carvings, crafts and Māori art.

Tours and activities such as sea kayaking begin in Havelock,

with the scenic mail run (where mail is delivered by boat) being perhaps the easiest and most popular way to get to the outer sounds. The **Havelock Museum** preserves relics from the pioneer era and Rutherford's time.

Havelock Museum
 🏛 Main St ⏱ 10am–4pm daily 🌐 havelockmuseum.nz

---

⑦
Picton

🗺 D4 🚆 Koromiko, 9 km (6 miles) S of town 🚗 🚌 🚢 ℹ The Foreshore; www.picton.nz.com

Set in the upper reaches of Queen Charlotte Sound, Picton is the South Island terminus for ferries that cross Cook Strait. The buzz of port and railway activity dominates this town nestled between the sea and the hills. The port is popular for its safe anchorages.

Picton's wide streets and historic buildings along the waterfront reflect its European beginnings. Formerly known as Waitohi, Picton was chosen to become the port for the Wairau district, and in 1859 became the capital of the newly formed province of Marlborough. That status shifted to Blenheim in 1866. An inter island ferry service was first mooted in 1899 and the first rail and car ferry began operating in 1962.

The **Picton Museum** focuses on the whaling era, beginning in the 1820s, and on the 1770s visit of Captain James Cook to Queen Charlotte Sound. At one end of the foreshore, stands the sailing ship **Edwin Fox**, built in 1853 and now preserved in a dry dock beside a museum. The last Australian convict ship and the last East Indiaman clipper in existence,

↑ The remains of the hulking *Edwin Fox*, preserved in dry dock at Picton

it provides a fascinating look at New Zealand's extensive shipping history.

Along the Picton waterfront is **EcoWorld Aquarium and Wildlife Rehabilitation Centre**, home to native local species to be seen throughout Marlborough Sounds such as rescued Little Blue Penguins, turtles and seahorses.

A number of walks and cycling tracks in Picton begin near Shelly Beach on Picton Harbour where a lookout affords excellent views of the town. A short uphill walk from here leads to Victoria Domain, a bushy reserve. A longer walk past Bob's Bay passes a panoramic view of Queen Charlotte Sound. The Tirohanga and Essons Valley tracks allow exploration of the forest behind the town.

Just a short boat ride from Picton Harbour is the **Kaipipu Wildlife Sanctuary**, set on an island just off shore. The sanctuary is home to a variety of birdlife, including Little Blue Penguins. A 3-km (2-mile) walking track circles the island, with great views and bird watching opportunities.

← Queen Charlotte Drive, overlooking the lush green Malborough Sounds

Did You Know?

Jutting out from Picton is the Snout, a cape known in Māori as "Te Ihumoeoneihu" (nose of the sand worm).

Picton Museum
 🏛 9 London Quay ⏱ 10am–4pm daily 🌐 pictonmuseum-newzealand.com

Edwin Fox
🏛 Dunbar Wharf ⏱ 9am–5pm daily 🌐 edwinfoxsociety.com

EcoWorld Aquarium and Widlife Rehabilitation Centre
🏛 Picton Waterfront ⏱ 9:30am–5pm daily 🌐 ecoworldnz.co.nz

Kaipupu Wildlife Sanctuary
🏛 Kaipupu Point ⏱ 7am–6pm daily; boats run daily 9am–5pm 🌐 kaipupupoint.co.nz

EAT

Kaikoura Seafood BBQ

A caravan shell dispensing the freshest mouthwatering crayfish, scallops, mussels and prawns in Kaikoura.

D5 Fyffe Quay, Kaikoura
027 376 3619

$$$ $$$ $$$

Brancott Estate Cellar Door

Dine on seasonal produce, followed by a tour, wine tasting or even a helicopter flight over this Marlborough estate.

D5 180 Brancott Rd, Marlborough
brancottestate.com

$$$ $$$ $$$

8

Motueka

D4 20 Wallace St;
(03) 528 6543

Motueka has a diverse horticultural industry and is the country's most prolific orcharding area. Kiwifruit, apples, berries, hops, pears and grapes are just some of the produce grown here. The town is also a base for trips to the Abel Tasman and Kahurangi national parks.

Kaiteriteri, 14 km (9 miles) north of Motueka, is known for its stunning golden beaches. South of Motueka are the coastal villages of Tasman and Mapua. Inland is Upper Moutere village, established in the 1840s by German settlers. Each village has its own artists, shops, wineries, cafés and boutique accommodation.

9

Kaikoura

D5 Westend; www.kaikoura.co.nz

The name Kaikoura means "meal of crayfish" and reflects the importance of the sea throughout the area. Captain Cook sailed past the Kaikoura Peninsula in 1770, naming the place "Lookers On" because of the reticence of local Māori.

While Kaikoura's plentiful marine life once attracted whalers to the town's shores, today these gentle creatures draw wildlife enthusiasts. The town has seen a considerable rise in tourism and now hosts a plethora of whale watching trips. The visitor centre has extensive displays and an audiovisual show. About 6 km (4 miles) south of town is historic **Fyffe House**, Kaikoura's oldest building and last remnant of the town's colonial-era whaling station – whale bones were used as part of the house's foundations. It also has pleasant gardens. At the beachfront, is the Garden of Memories with a walkway encased with pairs of whale ribs.

Above town, Scarborough Street has a lookout point, a remnant *pa* and the Gold Gallery with wall sculptures gilded with gold leaf. On the southern edge of Kaikoura is **Māori Leap Cave**, a limestone cave full of stalagmites and stalactites. Inland roads lead to Mount Fyffe, where walking tracks through the forest and mountains afford great views.

In 2016, Kaikoura was struck by a 7.8 magnitude earthquake, which severely impacted local communities, and left the coastline uplifted by 5 m (16 ft) in places. The town has since rebounded, with roads and transport links rapidly repaired.

Fyffe House

62 Avoca St (03) 319 5835 Oct-Apr: 10am-5pm daily; May-Sep: 10am-4pm Thu-Mon Good Fri, 25 Dec

Māori Leap Cave

State Hwy 1 (03) 319 5023 10:30am-3:30pm daily

←

Built in colonial style and painted pink, the charming Fyffe House in Kaikoura

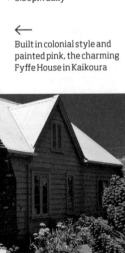

↑ Playful dusky dolphins leap through the waters off the coast of Kaikoura

KAIKOURA'S MARINE LIFE

The deep, nutrient-rich waters off the coastline of Kaikoura have created an ideal feeding ground for an incredible diversity of marine life. The main attraction here is sperm whales, seen as they rest at the surface between dives, as well as orca and dolphins. Visitors can witness the habits of animals like whales, seals and dusky dolphins for themselves from the shore, the air and on the water on a variety of eco-tours.

Whales

Most whales seen at Kaikoura are toothed whales, humpback whales and sperm whales. Unlike baleen whales, which feed by filtering plankton, toothed whales hunt for their prey, including fish, krill and giant squid. Sperm whales hunt the deep seas, diving down to depths of 1,000 m (3,280 ft), and can hold their breath for over an hour.

↑ A young humpback whale breaches into the ocean

Seals

New Zealand fur seals can be observed at a colony at Ohau Point, 23 km (14 miles) north of Kaikoura. The Department of Conservation recommends maintaining a distance of at least 20 m (65 ft) from seals at all times.

Dolphins

Hector's dolphin, a small species found exclusively in New Zealand, spends most of its time close to the shore, in pairs or small groups. The inquisitive and playful dusky dolphin can be spotted around the shorelines of Kaikoura, where large groups are present year-round.

Birdlife

Species of seabirds found in Kaikoura include the royal albatross, wandering albatross, grey petrel and the Antarctic fulmar. The black-browed mollymawk is one of the most common marine bird species to be seen within easy reach of the shores of Kaikoura.

WILDLIFE WATCHING

It's important to be mindful of the unpredictable nature of wild animals: seals for example can attack if people get between them and the sea. Try to minimise disturbance when possible, especially during breeding season. It's best to view wildlife with an experienced guide: the DOC offers advice for walking routes and tours (doc.govt.nz).

A whale descends into the deep waters at Kaikoura

Nelson Lakes National Park

Ⓐ D5 🚌 **Ⓦ doc.govt.nz**

The twin, glacier-formed lakes Rotoiti and Rotoroa dominate the 1,017 sq km (393 sq miles) of this park at the northern tip of the Southern Alps. A water taxi is the easiest form of access to the high passes, forests, valleys and basins. The lakes and rivers are popular for kayaking, boating, swimming and trout fishing. Winter pastimes include ski touring. There are many trails including the 80-km (50-mile) Travers–Sabine Circuit, which includes two major valleys, an alpine pass, the wetland Speargrass area and both main lakes.

PICTURE PERFECT
Lake Rotoiti

For a perfect snap, make for alpine Lake Rotoiti in Nelson Lakes National Park. Not far from the visitors' centre, a wooden jetty juts out over the lake granting near-symmetrical shots of the glacial mountains and crystal blue waters.

Blenheim

Ⓐ D5 ✈ **6 km (4 miles) W of city** 🚌 **ⓘ Railway Station, Sinclair St; www.marlboroughnz.com**

The largest settlement in the Marlborough region, Blenheim is known as the gateway to the Wairau Valley, New Zealand's most celebrated wine-making region (p204). The annual Blenheim food and wine festival is a major draw.

The town centre makes for a pleasant place to stroll; Seymour Square has pretty gardens and the Clock Tower. Blenheim's only public art gallery, the **Millennium Art Gallery** houses works by local artists and sculptors, while the **Marlborough Museum** exhibits archaeological finds, textiles and photographs. On the southern edge of town, Brayshaw park has a miniature railway, and reconstructed colonial village. Nearby is **Wither Hills Farm Park** where a network of well-marked foot and cycling tracks criss-cross the working farm.

Five km (3 miles) outside of Blenheim, the **Omaka Aviation Heritage Museum** showcases a collection of WWI and WWII aircraft and rare artifacts with displays by film director Peter Jackson and Wingnut Films.

Millennium Art Gallery

🅿♿🅿 Ⓐ Cnr Seymour & Alfred sts ⏱ 10:30am-4:30pm Mon-Fri, 1-4pm Sat & Sun 🅀 Public hols Ⓦ marlboroughart.org.nz

Marlborough Museum

♿ Ⓐ 26 Arthur Baker Place 📞 (03) 578 1712 ⏱ 10am-4pm daily

Wither Hills Farm Park

Ⓐ Rifle Range Place, off Taylor Pass Rd 📞 (03) 577 8080

Omaka Aviation Heritage Museum

🅿♿🅿 Ⓐ 79 Aerodrome Rd, Omaka Ⓦ omaka.org.nz

→

Hiker following Paddy's Track on Mount Robert, near St Arnaud

←

Heading out on the water in Nelson Lakes National Park

 12

St Arnaud

⚑D5 🚌 *i* View Rd; (03) 521 1806

Approximately 90 minutes' drive from Blenheim or Nelson this small town, nestled on the shore of Lake Rotiti, is a service centre for the outdoor activities on offer in nearby Nelson Lakes National Park. Hikes include Paddy's Track, a walk for advanced trampers which begins in St Arnaud and offers views over the lake.

St Arnaud is the closest town to the **Rainbow Ski Area**, where the terrain is suitable for novice and intermediate snowboarders and skiers. In summer, the terrain offers great hiking trails, and the ski field access road continues to Hanmer Springs *(p228)*.

Rainbow Ski Area

🎿 😊 ⚑ Wairau Valley 🕑 Jun-Oct daily 🌐 skirainbow.co.nz

 13

Richmond

⚑D4 ✈ Nelson, 8 km (5 miles) W of town *i* 22 Gladstone Rd; (03) 543 9521

This busy town serves the productive horticultural lands to its south and west. Highlights are the Washbourne Gardens, complete with 1862 jailhouse, and the Redwood Stables restaurant, built using bricks from New Zealand's first racing stables. Visitors can observe the art of glass making at **Höglund Art Glass** where Ola and Marie Höglund create their renowned colourful glassware. Just south of Richmond, at Brightwater, is a memorial to New Zealand's best known scientist, atom-splitting Lord Ernest Rutherford, born here in 1871. Also at Brightwater is the **McGlashen Pottery**, a gallery and studio of the renowned Richmond-born master ceramicist, Royce McGlashen.

Höglund Art Glass

🎨 🏛 ⚑ 52 Lansdowne Rd 🕑 10am–5pm daily 🌐 hoglundartglass.com

McGlashen Pottery

🏛 ⚑ 128 Ellis St 🕑 10am–5pm daily 🌐 roycemcglashen.co.nz

STAY

Alpine Lodge
Ideal for families, with a spa and playground amid stupendous scenery and comfy rooms. A backpacker annex offers family and dormitory budget rooms.

⚑D5 ⚑ 79 Main Rd, St Arnaud 🌐 alpinelodge.co.nz

💲💲💲

14 Te Waikoropupu Springs Scenic Reserve

D4

About 7 km (4 miles) north of Takaka on State Highway 60, a turnoff leads to the Te Waikoropupu Springs Scenic Reserve. The splendid waters here at New Zealand's largest freshwater springs are exceptionally clear, coming from an underground cave system that is connected to the kaarst features on Takaka Hill and at Riwaka Resurgence. The springs are best viewed from the curved viewing platform, which is reached by an easy walk through beautiful forest. Swimming is prohibited as the water is considered *wahi tapu* (sacred).

Just beyond the springs (at the end of the road), the Pupu Hydro Walkway is a track that follows the line of a water race originally built to serve a gold-mining claim. An impressive piece of engineering, the water race was later used (and still is) to generate electric power. The loop walk is about 5 km (3 miles) long and is Golden Bay's most popular day walk. The climb to the water race is a little steep but the first section to the power station is easier.

15 Takaka Hill

D4

Takaka Hill is often referred to as "the marble mountain" because of its large marble deposits that contrast sharply with the granite hills and headlands of adjoining Abel Tasman National Park (p190). There are many caves and sinkholes to explore in the area, including **Ngarua Caves** (booking required Jun–Sep) near the summit of Takaka Hill, where a lookout offers views north to D'Urville Island and east towards Nelson city. Tours of the only cave open to visitors are available and bones of the flightless giant moa, a now-extinct prehistoric bird, can be seen. Visible below the caves is Marahau's golden beach located in Abel Tasman National Park.

To the west of Ngarua Caves, Canaan Road leads to Canaan car park, the starting point for walking tracks, including the Rameka Track, one of Nelson's better mountain-bike rides. An easy walk leads to the impressive Harwoods Hole, a 176-m (577-ft) vertical shaft. A short steep side track leads to the Harwood Lookout with a fine

↑ Steep cliffs dotted with caves and concealing a cove at Farewell Spit

viewpoint inland to the Tablelands in Kahurangi National Park (p192).

Ngarua Caves

⊕⊛🅿 🏔 Main Rd, Takaka Hill ⏰10am–4pm daily; tours only 🌐ngaruacaves.co.nz

16 Takaka

D4 🚌6 km (4 miles) N of town 🚌 🛈 Willow St; www.nelsonnz.com

Takaka is the main shopping and business area for the Golden Bay region and an access point to Abel Tasman National Park. The townspeople are a mix of "alternative life-stylers" and farming folk – dairy farming is one of the region's largest industries. The town's **Golden Bay Museum** is excellent, and best known for its displays on Abel Tasman and the story of Golden Bay's many extractive industries. Several galleries operate in the area and many artists near Takaka show their works.

At **Anatoki Salmon**, visitors can catch Chinook salmon and get it smoked to eat or take it away. It is also home to tame

↑ Admiring the beautiful clear waters at Te Waikoropupu Springs Scenic Reserve

> **Farewell Spit is a nature reserve with restricted access and has been designated a Wetland of International Importance.**

eels and farm animals. River walks and picnics in the park are other attractions.

Golden Bay Museum

◈ ⊛ 🏛 73 Commercial St ⏱ 10am-4pm daily 🚫 Sun Jun-Sep, public hols 🌐 golden baymuseum.org.nz

Anatoki Salmon

◈ ⊜ ⊚ 🏛 230 McCallum's Rd ⏱ 9am-4:40pm daily 🌐 anatokisalmon.co.nz

Farewell Spit

🅰 D4 ⏱ Daily 🌐 farewell spit.com

At the northern tip of the South Island, a 35-km (22-mile) sandspit sweeps east into the sea. Farewell Spit is a nature reserve with restricted access and has been designated a Wetland of International Importance. During late spring, tens of thousands of migratory waders arrive from the northern hemisphere, joining the year-round residents before returning home in autumn to breed. Black swans, Canada geese, Australasian gannets, Caspian terns, oystercatchers, black shags and eastern bartailed godwits are among the species to be seen in summer. As the region is a protected area, the only way to visit the spit is on a guided tour with the licensed tour operator based in Collingwood.

18 Collingwood

🅰 D4 🚌

A quiet village at the mouth of the Aorere River, Collingwood was designated a port of entry in the 1850s gold rush and was considered as the site for New Zealand's capital city. Despite several devastating fires, the courthouse, post office and the Anglican St Cuthbert's Church remain to remind visitors of the town's moment of glory. Collingwood is a base for tours to Farewell Spit and for buses serving the Heaphy Track in Kahurangi National Park (p192).

STAY

Westhaven Retreat

On a private peninsula, luxury awaits at this secluded lodge that overlooks pristine beaches and forests.

🅰 D4 🏠 336 Te Hapu Rd, Golden Bay 🌐 west havenretreat.com

$$$

Te Hapu Coastal Cottages

Three delightful self-catering cottages set amid splendid scenery.

🅰 D4 🏠 429 Te Hapu Rd, Collingwood 🌐 tehapu.co.nz

$$$

A DRIVING TOUR
WAIRAU VALLEY VINEYARD

Length 36 km (22 miles) **Stopping-off points** Blenheim Visitor Centre, Renwick **Terrain** Flat paved roads

Well known for its Sauvignon Blanc, the Wairau valley is New Zealand's largest and best-known wine region. In the early 1970s, grape planting was begun by Montana Wines. Now, 130 wineries operate in the area. The wines of the Wairau are celebrated with the annual Marlborough Wine and Food Festival each February. West of Blenheim is the Brancott Estate Cellar Door and Restaurant, a visitor's centre covering all aspects of the wine experience.

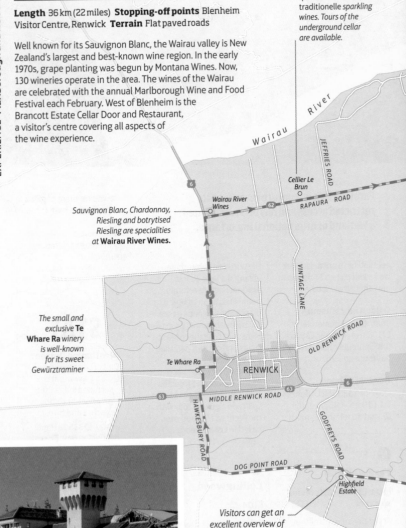

Cellier Le Brun specializes in méthode traditionelle *sparkling* wines. Tours of the underground cellar are available.

Sauvignon Blanc, Chardonnay, Riesling and botrytised Riesling are specialities at **Wairau River Wines.**

The small and exclusive **Te Whare Ra** *winery is well-known for its sweet Gewürztraminer*

Visitors can get an excellent overview of the vineyard district from the Tuscan-style tower of **Highfield Estate**.

← Highfield Estate's iconic pink Tuscan tower

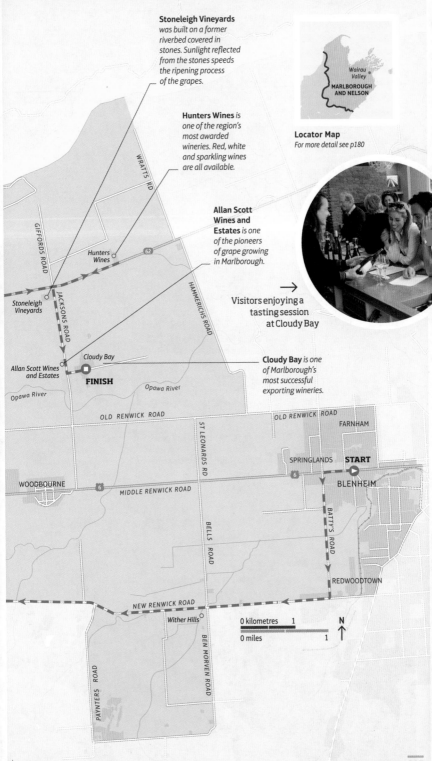

Stoneleigh Vineyards was built on a former riverbed covered in stones. Sunlight reflected from the stones speeds the ripening process of the grapes.

Hunters Wines is one of the region's most awarded wineries. Red, white and sparkling wines are all available.

Allan Scott Wines and Estates is one of the pioneers of grape growing in Marlborough.

Locator Map
For more detail see p180

Wairau Valley

MARLBOROUGH AND NELSON

→ Visitors enjoying a tasting session at Cloudy Bay

Cloudy Bay is one of Marlborough's most successful exporting wineries.

WRAITS RD

62

GIFFORDS ROAD

Hunters Wines

JACKSONS ROAD

Stoneleigh Vineyards

HAMMERICHS ROAD

Cloudy Bay

Allan Scott Wines and Estates

FINISH

Opawa River

Opawa River

OLD RENWICK ROAD

OLD RENWICK ROAD

FARNHAM

ST LEONARDS RD

SPRINGLANDS

START

WOODBOURNE

6

MIDDLE RENWICK ROAD

BLENHEIM

BATTY'S ROAD

BELLS ROAD

REDWOODTOWN

NEW RENWICK ROAD

Wither Hills

0 kilometres 1

0 miles 1

N ↑

PAYNTERS ROAD

BEN MORVEN ROAD

CANTERBURY AND THE WEST COAST

When European settlers began arrving in this region in 1850 – lured first by the promise of pastoral farmland and later by the discovery of gold and coal – both Canterbury and the West Coast were dominated by the Ngai Tahu tribe. By 1860, the bulk of the tribe's land had been acquired by the government in a series of dubious sales transactions, leaving the Ngai Tahu impoverished and unable to participate equally in the new settler economy – it wasn't until 1997 that the Ngai Tahu received compensation from the New Zealand government.

This vast and varied region's main settlement is Christchurch (Ōtautahi), first inhabited by Māori in the 13th century. In 1850, four European settler ships sailed into the whaling port of Lyttelton, carrying on board 800 settlers and the hopes of the Canterbury Association to found a middle-class Anglican community. The city grew and prospered, with agriculture in the surrounding plains its primary industry. Between 2010 and 2012, Christchurch suffered a series of devastating earthquakes, but in the years since, the city has undergone extensive renewal and has rebounded as a hub of activity and culture.

CANTERBURY AND
THE WEST COAST

Must Sees

1. Christchurch
2. Westland Tai Poutini National Park
3. Arthur's Pass National Park
4. Aoraki/Mount Cook National Park

Experience More

5. Port Hills
6. Lyttelton
7. Banks Peninsula
8. Timaru
9. Lewis Pass
10. Hanmer Springs
11. Reefton
12. Akaroa
13. Karamea
14. Westport
15. Paparoa National Park
16. Greymouth
17. Hokitika
18. Arthur's Pass
19. Mount Hutt
20. Ashburton
21. Geraldine
22. Lake Tekapo
23. Twizel
24. Lake Pukaki
25. Waipara Vineyards
26. Rakaia
27. Lake Ohau

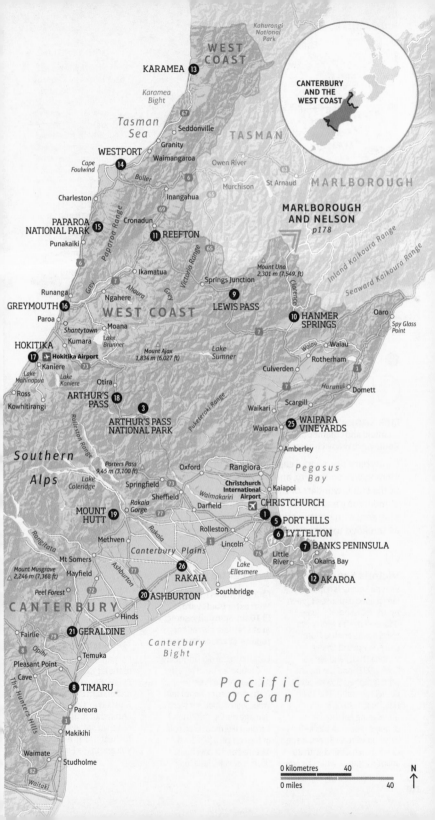

❶

CHRISTCHURCH

🅐 D6 ✈ 10 km (6 miles) NW of city 🚉 Troup Dr 🚌 Cnr of Lichfield and Colombo sts 🛈 Arts Centre, Worcester Boulevard; www.christchurchnz.com

Canterbury's provincial capital, Christchurch is a vibrant, welcoming city, and the principal gateway to the scenic wonders of the South Island. A mix of modernity and quaint, colonial style, the city is scattered with pretty parks and historic buildings, all threaded together by the winding Avon River.

① Victoria Square

Victoria Square is a beautifully landscaped expanse of green north of Cathedral Square, bounded by the Avon river. Focal points are the Floral Clock, statues of Queen Victoria (1901) and James Cook (1932), and the much-photographed Bowker and Ferrier fountains. The Town Hall, built in 1972, is still undergoing earthquake damage repairs. A block away, on Victoria Street, is the Christchurch Casino, with its stylized roulette wheel façade.

② Arts Centre

🅐 Cnr of Rolleston Ave & Worcester Boulevard
🕐 10am–5pm daily; some areas remain closed for repairs 🖥 artscentre.org.nz

Located in the old University of Canterbury buildings, the Arts Centre is a lively arts, crafts and performance hub. While it sustained substantial damage during the 2011 earthquake, more than half of the complex has been restored and it now houses dozens of galleries, studios and shops, performance spaces and an art cinema. There are some attractive eateries, and a popular market on Sundays.

Construction of the Gothic Revival-style buildings began in 1877. They were designed by a succession of architects, including Mountfort, who was responsible for the Clock Tower building, Great Hall and Classics block. It is on these heritage buildings that the next phase of restoration work will focus.

🏔 **GREAT VIEW**
Hitch a Lift

For panoramic views of the city, Canterbury Plains, Banks Peninsula and distant Southern Alps, take a ride on the Christchurch Gondola cable car (gondola.co.nz) to the top of an extinct volcano in the Port Hills.

←

The Chalice, an eye-catching sculpture, towers over Cathedral Square

③

Bridge of Remembrance

 Cnr of Cashel St & Oxford Terrace

A commemoration of New Zealand's soldiers, this bridge stands at the head of City Mall, the city's central shopping area. Damaged during the earthquakes, the Bridge underwent extensive repairs and is now restored to its former glory.

↑ The Bridge of Remembrance, a monument to Canterbury gunners who served in the two World Wars

④

Canterbury Museum

 Rolleston Ave ⏰9am–5pm daily (to 5:30pm Oct–Mar) 🚫25 Dec 🌐canterbury museum.com

Built between 1869 and 1876, Canterbury Museum is considered to be one of Mountfort's most successful adaptations of the Gothic style for secular purposes. It contains the world's most comprehensive collection of Antarctic items. Other halls feature oriental art, a reconstruction of a typical 19th-century Christchurch street and a Māori cultural section.

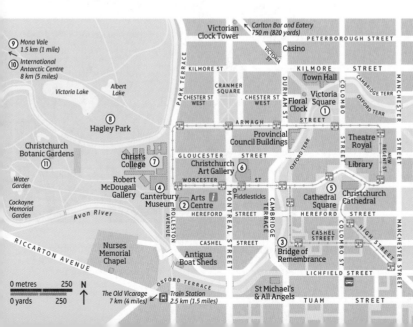

Must See

EAT

The Old Vicarage
Home-style cooking served in the timbered interior and pretty garden. Pork belly with crackling is a favourite.

📍335 Halswell Rd
🌐theoldvicarage.co.nz

$$$

Fiddlesticks
A contemporary bar and restaurant with an all-day "grazing menu" and good wines.

📍48 Worcester Blvd
🌐fiddlesticksbar.co.nz

$$$

Carlton Bar and Eatery
Butcher's block tables signal the focus on meat dishes. Friendly service.

📍1 Papanui Rd
🌐carltonbar.co.nz

$$$

9 Mona Vale
1.5 km (1 mile)

10 International Antarctic Centre
8 km (5 miles)

Victoria Lake

Albert Lake

Victoria Clock Tower

Carlton Bar and Eatery 750 m (820 yards)

PETERBOROUGH STREET

Casino

KILMORE ST

KILMORE STREET

Town Hall

CRANMER SQUARE

CHESTER ST WEST

CHESTER ST WEST

Floral Clock

Victoria Square ①

Hagley Park 8

ARMAGH STREET

Christchurch Botanic Gardens 11

Christ's College 7

GLOUCESTER STREET

Provincial Council Buildings

Theatre Royal

Library

Water Garden

Robert McDougall Gallery

Christchurch Art Gallery 6

WORCESTER ST

Christchurch Cathedral

Cockayne Memorial Garden

Canterbury Museum 4

Arts Centre 2

Fiddlesticks

Cathedral Square 5

HEREFORD STREET

HEREFORD STREET

Avon River

RICCARTON AVENUE

Nurses Memorial Chapel

Antigua Boat Sheds

CASHEL STREET

CASHEL STREET

Bridge of Remembrance 3

LICHFIELD STREET

0 metres 250
0 yards 250
N

The Old Vicarage
7 km (4 miles)

Train Station
2.5 km (1.5 miles)

St Michael's & All Angels

TUAM STREET

⑤
Cathedral Square

In the heart of the city, Cathedral Square is still dominated by the fenced-off ruins of Christ Church Cathedral. The cathedral survived the earthquake of September 2010 with only minor damage, but during 2011's quake the iconic spire toppled into Cathedral Square, leaving the main entrance surrounded by broken masonry.

Despite this, the square remains vibrant and filled with daily activity, the heart of a resilient city. Children play with a giant open-air chess set, and crowds gather for frequent festivals and concerts. There is also a popular Friday night food-truck market. The 1867 statue of Robert Godley, founder of the city, has been restored and returned to its plinth.

On the edge of Cathedral Square, Turanga, the central library, features the Discovery Wall. Here, a touch-sensitive digital wall lets you swipe through screens showing the city's unique history. A Lego playground for kids and an espresso bar make Turanga a lively meeting ground. Even newer in the square is Te Pae, an integrated convention and exhibitions facility including shops and art galleries.

Steps away on Latimer Square is Christchurch's "temporary" Cardboard Cathedral, itself an intriguing architectural structure. Designed by architect Shigeru Ban, it opened in 2013 and quickly became a symbol of hope and community for the city. A 700-seat steel-and-timber-clad A-frame structure supported by 90 cardboard tubes, it is expected to have a lifespan of about 50 years.

⑥

Christchurch Art Gallery (Te Puna o Waiwhetu)

📍 Cnr of Montreal St & Worcester Blvd ⏰ 10am–5pm daily 🌐 christchurchartgallery.org.nz

Situated close to Cathedral Square, this is the city's principal art gallery. It houses an impressive collection of 5,000 contemporary New Zealand and international works of art, which are complemented by touring exhibitions. The gallery's large, permanent display features historical European artworks, with an extensive collection of Dutch, French, Italian and British paintings, drawings, prints, sculpture and ceramics.

The New Zealand collection is one of the most comprehensive in the country, and brings Canterbury artists to the forefront. The collection encompasses works by noted Canterbury portrait and landscape artist William Sutton, as well as other prominent New Zealand painters, including Doris Lusk, Colin McCahon, Rita Angus, Charles Goldie, Frances Hodgkins, Dick Frizzell and Seraphine Pick.

 INSIDER TIP
Riverboating

The Antigua Boat Sheds (boatsheds.co.nz), on the banks of the Avon, have been providing river recreation since 1882. Canoes, paddle boats and punts can all be hired here for water-borne trips upstream.

← Christchurch's Transitional Cathedral with its brightly coloured stained glass

7

Christ's College

📍 Rolleston Ave 🕐 For guided tours only, Oct–Feb 🌐 christscollege.com

Amid serene old buildings, schoolboys in black-and-white-striped blazers trot between their lessons, but while this may resemble an English public school, Christ's College is both progressive and diverse, offering a thoroughly modern education. The school's Gothic Revival buildings, dating to 1863, can be toured on weekdays in summer (book ahead).

8

Hagley Park

📞 (03) 941 6840 🕐 7am–dusk daily

Hagley Park, a green expanse in the heart of Christchurch, serves as the city's lungs. Within its boundaries are a golf course, polo grounds, tree-lined walking and cycling tracks, artificial lakes and the city's Botanic Gardens (p214).

When the early colonists laid out the site for their new town, they set aside 2 sq km (0.80 sq mile) for a public park, and in 1856 an ordinance was passed declaring it "reserved forever" for public recreation and enjoyment. By the early 1870s, the settlers had replaced the park's native flora with European plants, grasses and trees.

9

Mona Vale

📍 63 Fendalton Rd 🕐 10am–late afternoon Wed–Sun 🌐 monavale.nz

The impressive homestead of Mona Vale was built between 1899 and 1900. The historic home is situated among sweeping lawns, mature trees and landscaped gardens to the northwest of Hagley Park, with the Avon River meandering through the property's garden. Visitors are invited to stroll through the gardens and feed the ducks.

10

International Antarctic Centre

📍 38 Orchard Rd 🕐 9am–5:30pm daily 🌐 iceberg.co.nz

About 20 minutes from the city centre by free, hourly Penguin Express shuttles from outside the Canterbury Museum, is the International Antarctic Centre, a fascinating and fun place to visit, especially for families. There are imaginative interactive exhibits, huskies to pet and cute blue penguins, and a 4D theatre which blows mist in your face. In the Storm Room you'll experience -18° C (0°F) windchills (protective clothing provided), and there's the opportunity to ride Antarctic vehicles.

 A summer punt trip on the Avon river through Hagley Park

ONGOING RESTORATION

In addition to the cathedral, historic sites still closed for repairs include the Provincial Council Buildings, Old Chief Post Office and the Town Hall. Those now rebuilt include the Edwardian Regent Theatre (now the Isaac Theatre Royal), the Gothic Press Building and Oxford Terrace (now The Terrace). The city's charming trams are back in service.

⑪ Ⓜ ▢ 🛍

BOTANIC GARDENS

🅰 D6 🏠 Rolleston Ave (main entrance) 🕐 Gardens: dawn to dusk daily; conservatories: 10am–4pm daily 🚫 25 Dec 🚌 Worcester Boulevard 🌐 wellington.govt.nz

The earthquake of 2011 damaged many of the trees and buildings in Christchurch's Botanic Gardens, but replanting and restoration have worked wonders to bring them back to their former, tranquil glory.

So many of the Botanic Gardens' features speak to Christchurch's sense of Victorian "Englishness": the lawns and rose gardens, the bandstand and the host of golden daffodils that surround it in spring, the fountains and ornamental lakes on which model boats are raced, and the wrought-iron tracery of the principal glasshouse. Yet there are also carefully curated displays and plantings of indigenous flora, including a conservatory dedicated to magnificent ferns. The visitor centre features interactive plant displays, and guided tours are offered in summer.

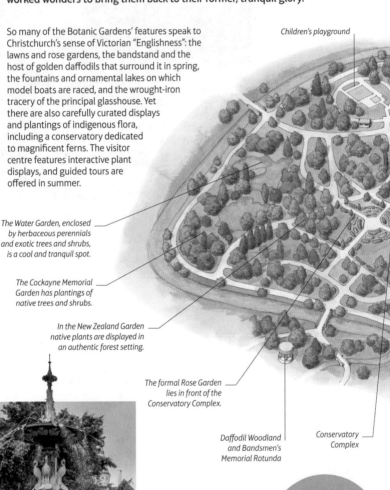

Children's playground

The Water Garden, enclosed by herbaceous perennials and exotic trees and shrubs, is a cool and tranquil spot.

The Cockayne Memorial Garden has plantings of native trees and shrubs.

In the New Zealand Garden native plants are displayed in an authentic forest setting.

The formal Rose Garden lies in front of the Conservatory Complex.

Daffodil Woodland and Bandsmen's Memorial Rotunda

Conservatory Complex

← The ornate cast-iron Peacock Fountain at the eastern entrance

Did You Know?

The blaze of yellow daffodils surrounding the rotunda dates back to 1933, when 16,000 bulbs were planted.

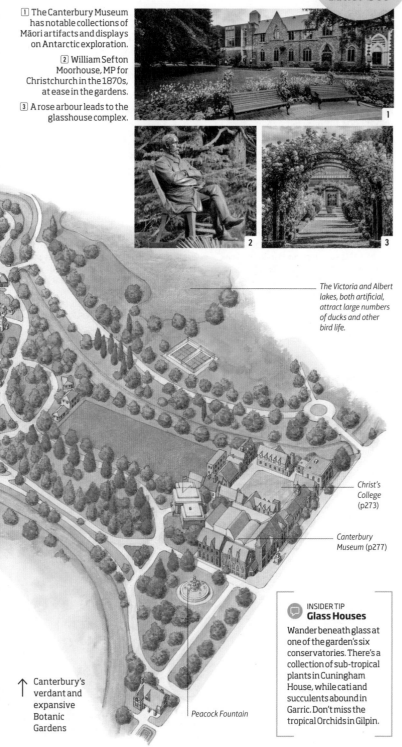

1 The Canterbury Museum has notable collections of Māori artifacts and displays on Antarctic exploration.

2 William Sefton Moorhouse, MP for Christchurch in the 1870s, at ease in the gardens.

3 A rose arbour leads to the glasshouse complex.

The Victoria and Albert lakes, both artificial, attract large numbers of ducks and other bird life.

Christ's College (p273)

Canterbury Museum (p277)

↑ Canterbury's verdant and expansive Botanic Gardens

Peacock Fountain

INSIDER TIP
Glass Houses

Wander beneath glass at one of the garden's six conservatories. There's a collection of sub-tropical plants in Cuningham House, while cati and succulents abound in Garric. Don't miss the tropical Orchids in Gilpin.

2 ⓂⒹ

WESTLAND TAI POUTINI NATIONAL PARK

🅐C5 🚌 𝒾 Franz Josef Glacier village (03) 752 0796; Fox Glacier village, (03) 751 0044 🅦 doc.govt.nz n

Stretching from the top of the Southern Alps in the east to the Tasman Sea in the west, this 1,270 sq km (490 sq mile) national park is renowned for its soaring mountain peaks, dramatic glaciers, dense green rainforest, coastal lagoons and beautiful lakes.

Despite the intrusions of the West Coast gold rush of the 1860s and pastoral farming on the river flats, this vast area has remained largely unspoiled. In the east stand New Zealand's two highest peaks, Mounts Tasmin and Cook, while rising in front are Franz Joseph Glacier and the impressive Fox Glacier, the largest glacier in the park. Walking tracks crisscross the area; one of the best winds up the Waiho River from Franz Josef Glacier village, leading to the terminal face. The Copland Valley Track, accessible from State Highway 6, is popular with hikers. For experienced climbers, the track continues over the challenging Copland Pass and ends at Mount Cook village. Gillespies Beach, once a historic gold-mining settlement 20 km (12 miles) from Fox Glacier, offers walks along an early miners' track and to a fur seal colony along the beach. The park's extremely high rainfall (5,000 mm or 200 inches a year at Franz Josef village) supports lush, ferned lowland podocarp forest, featuring local species. Lake Mapourika stands at the northern end of the park and nearby is Okarito Lagoon.

MOVEMENT OF A GLACIER

A glacier is a large body of ice that forms on land and moves slowly downhill at a rate of about 1.5 m (5 ft) a day. Glaciers are fed by snow accumulating in high-altitude basins (névés) where it condenses to form bluish ice. This ice field flows downhill under its own weight, cracking into deep crevasses and collecting moraine (debris), which scours the mountain sides to form U-shaped valleys. The glacier ends at a terminal where the ice melts. The Franz Josef Glacier, 11 km (7 miles) long, and Fox Glacier, 13 km (8 miles) long, are unique in that they descend from regions of perpetual snow to rainforest located close to the coast.

↑ Okarito Lagoon, home to abundant birdlife, including rare white herons

→ The peaceful waters of tranquil Lake Mapourika

💬 INSIDER TIP
Take a Heli Hike

Take to the skies on a once-in-a-lifetime helicopter ride, then descend to the mountains to hike through blue ice crevasses. Combined heli-hike trips can be enjoyed at both Fox *(www.foxguides.co.nz)* and Franz Josef glaciers *(www.franzjosefglacier. com).* At Franz Joseph, trips include a free soak in the thermal pools.

↑ Two hikers walking towards the towering icy mass of the Fox Glacier

Skiing down snowy slopes on Arthur's Pass

INSIDER TIP
Be Prepared

The valleys, alpine passes and mountainsides of the park offer a range of graded walks. The climate in the park is highly changeable and many routes rudimentary, so it is important for hikers and climbers to register their intentions with the visitor centre at Arthur's Pass village.

Fertile foothills and steep slopes of Arthur's Pass, the heart of the Southern Alps

3 🍴 🍵 🏛

ARTHUR'S PASS NATIONAL PARK

🔺C5 📍153 km (95 miles) from Christchurch 🚌 🚂 ℹ️ Arthur's Pass village; www.doc.govt.nz

Straddling the Southern Alps, the 1,147 sq km (443 sq mile) Arthur's Pass National Park is a place of huge geological and climatic contrasts, providing a rich and nurturing habitat for diverse flora and fauna.

Sixteen mountain peaks in Arthur's Pass National Park exceed 2,000 m (6,560 ft). On the western side of the alps, where the rainfall is high, the park is clad in dense and varied rainforest through which steep, boulder-strewn rivers rush. Seen from the main road, the 131-m (430-ft) Devil's Punchbowl Waterfall is a one-hour walk to the base from Arthur's Pass village (p232). On the drier eastern side, mountain beech forests and tussock-covered river flats predominate, with Temple Basin at the core.

Further south, the valleys give way to steep, craggy hills as the road approaches Bealey Spur village, on the fringes of the national park, marked by a cluster of rustic holiday homes.

The park offers the well-equipped outdoor enthusiast superb mountain climbing and hiking opportunities, as well as many shorter walks suitable for people of all ages and fitness levels. The Dobson Nature walk on the Arthur's Pass summit gives an excellent introduction to the area's alpine and subalpine plants.

1 Dramatic limestone rock formations at Castle Hill.

2 Spires of purple lupins that thrive in the west of the park.

3 Sinuous strands of the Waimakariri River transport rock and shingle from the Southern Alps.

FLORA AND FAUNA

As well as the notable mountain beech forests in the east and mixed rainforest in the west, the park contains a wide variety of alpine and subalpine plant species, including tussock, snow grass, alpine daisies and herbs, sedge and ourisia. The park is also rich in birdlife, and species such as the paradise shelduck, bellbird, silvereye, fantail, kea and rifleman are often seen or heard. The area is home to a number of rare species, including the alpine rock wren, blue duck and great spotted kiwi.

A DRIVING TOUR
ARTHUR'S PASS

Length 160 km (100 miles) **Stopping-off points**
Arthur's Pass, Bealey **Terrain** Alpine route,
sometimes closed after snow

Arthur's Pass road is the highest and most
spectacular highway across the Southern Alps.
From Springfield, the road climbs steeply to
the 945-m (3,100-ft) Porters Pass before
travelling through wide, tussock-covered
basins hemmed by mountains and past
dramatic limestone outcrops.
Entering the eastern flank of Arthur's
Pass National Park, the road is
enveloped by mountain beech
forest. It then climbs to the
920 m (3,017 ft) Arthur's Pass
summit, before descending
steeply on the western side of
the Southern Alps.

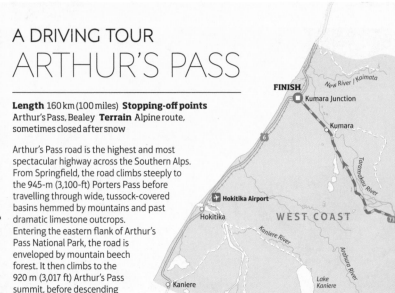

FINISH
Kumara Junction
New River | Kaimata
Kumara
6
Taramakau River
Hokitika Airport
Hokitika
WEST COAST
Kaniere River
73
Arahura River
Kaniere
Lake
Kaniere
Kokatahi River

← Eerie rock
formations at
Castle Hill, an
area once part
of the route used
by Māori to reach
the West Coast

→ Tall palm trees
overlooking
peaceful Lake
Lyndon, popular
with walkers and
fishing enthusiasts

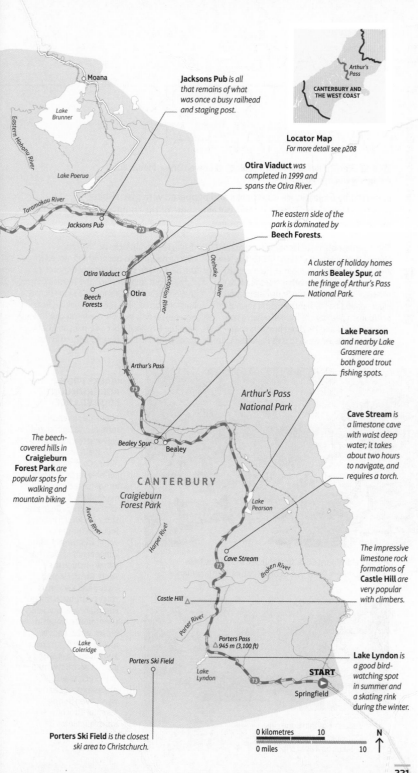

Jacksons Pub is all that remains of what was once a busy railhead and staging post.

Otira Viaduct was completed in 1999 and spans the Otira River.

The eastern side of the park is dominated by **Beech Forests**.

A cluster of holiday homes marks **Bealey Spur**, at the fringe of Arthur's Pass National Park.

Lake Pearson and nearby Lake Grasmere are both good trout fishing spots.

Cave Stream is a limestone cave with waist deep water; it takes about two hours to navigate, and requires a torch.

The beech-covered hills in **Craigieburn Forest Park** are popular spots for walking and mountain biking.

The impressive limestone rock formations of **Castle Hill** are very popular with climbers.

Lake Lyndon is a good bird-watching spot in summer and a skating rink during the winter.

Porters Ski Field is the closest ski area to Christchurch.

Locator Map
For more detail see p208

CANTERBURY AND THE WEST COAST

Arthur's Pass

Moana
Lake Brunner
Eastern Hohonu River
Lake Poerua
Taramakau River
Jacksons Pub
Otira Viaduct
Otira
Beech Forests
Deception River
Otehake River
Arthur's Pass
Arthur's Pass National Park
Bealey Spur
Bealey
CANTERBURY
Craigieburn Forest Park
Avoca River
Harper River
Lake Pearson
Broken River
Cave Stream
Castle Hill
Porter River
Porters Pass
△ 945 m (3,100 ft)
Lake Coleridge
Porters Ski Field
Lake Lyndon
START
Springfield

0 kilometres — 10
0 miles — 10

N

④ 🍴 🖵 🛍

AORAKI/ MOUNT COOK NATIONAL PARK

🔺 C6 ✈ 5 km (3 miles) S of Mount Cook 🚌 ℹ Bowen Drive, Mount Cook village; www.doc.govt.nz

Encircled by majestic, ice-clad peaks and peppered with glacial-blue rivers and lakes, this national park contains some of the country's most magical and awe-inspiring scenery.

The national park takes its name from Aoraki/ Mount Cook, which at 3,724 m (12,218 ft) is New Zealand's highest mountain and a premier mountaineering destination. It is sacred to the Ngai Tahu tribe of the South Island, and Māori legend has it that the mountain and its companion peaks were formed when a boy named Aoraki and his three brothers came down from the heavens to visit Papatuanuku (Earth Mother) in a canoe. The canoe overturned, and as the brothers moved to the back of the boat they turned to stone.

Stand out sights include the Tasman Glacier, the largest in New Zealand at 27 km (16 miles) long and up to 3 km (1.8 miles) wide. Other notable glaciers include Murchison, which along with the Mueller, Hooker, Tasman and Godley glaciers, dominate the valley pattern in the park.

↑ Aoraki/Mount Cook, first climbed in 1894 by New Zealanders Tom Fyfe, George Graham and Jack Clarke

Visitors navigate one of the park's ice-filled lakes on a boat trip ↑

WALKS FROM AORAKI/MOUNT COOK VILLAGE

There are several well formed and signposted walking tracks in the vicinity of Aoraki/ Mount Cook village, suitable for people who do not have climbing experience. Kea Point and Governors Bush are short walking trips that focus on the park's vegetation and birdlife. Longer walks from the village include the Sealy Tarns, Hooker Valley and Red Tarns tracks. Although these tracks are well marked, the ground is rough in places and it is advisable to wear stout shoes and to carry a walking stick. A warm sweater or jacket is needed for places exposed to the wind, even during summer. Brochures, are available at the visitor centre.

Did You Know?

Tasman Saddle Hut is one of 16 alpine shelters in the park for the use of hikers and climbers.

↑ Hikers exploring one of the many trails in Aoraki/ Mount Cook National Park

EXPERIENCE MORE

5

Port Hills

D6

The Port Hills separate Christchurch from Lyttelton Harbour, and were formed by the eruption of the now extinct Lyttelton volcano. Their tussock-covered slopes and volcanic outcrops flank the southern part of the city, and are popular with walkers, runners, rock climbers and mountain bikers. The Port Hills are also easily accessed by car, thanks to the work of early 20th-century conservationist and politician Harry Ell, who strove for the creation of a road across the hills.

Ell's vision included the construction of rest houses along the Port Hills, the most impressive of which is the 1949 Sign of the Takahe, now home to a restaurant.

6

Lyttelton

D6 ℹ 20 Oxford St; (03) 328 9093

Lyttelton was the landing place of the Canterbury

Pilgrims in 1850, and was named after Lord Lyttelton, the chairman of the Canterbury Association. In 1867, a rail tunnel was drilled through the volcanic rock of the Port Hills to provide a link between Lyttelton's port and Christchurch, and a road tunnel was completed in 1964.

The Lyttelton Museum has an interesting collection of local maritime history but is sadly closed while the building is rebuilt after suffering damage during the 2011 earthquake.

The Lyttelton Timeball Station stood sentry over the town from its construction in 1875 until 2011, when it was dismantled following irreparable damage during the earthquakes of 2010 and 2011. The large black ball hanging from its tower once signalled Greenwich Mean Time to the ships in the harbour. It is hoped that the timeball mechanism can be salvaged and reused in a possible reconstruction of the building, which had been one of only five working timeball stations in the world.

A ferry service to Quail and Rīpapa islands and the small township of Diamond Harbour runs from the Lyttelton docks.

RICHARD PEARSE

Canterbury-born inventor and farmer Richard Pearse (1877-1953) has been at the centre of debate about who was the first to achieve powered flight. Pearse constructed a monoplane of bamboo, aluminium, wire and canvas. His first flight is said to have covered 46-91 m (150-300 ft), ending with a crash. No records were kept but there is evidence that it occurred on 31 March 1903 - before the 13 December 1903 flight of Orville and Wilbur Wright, regarded as the first in the world.

7

Banks Peninsula

D6

Formed by numerous eruptions of the Lyttelton and Akaroa volcanoes, Banks Peninsula was, until some 25,000 years ago, an island. Reminders of this dramatic

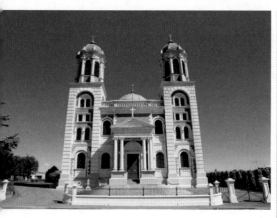

↑ Timaru's Sacred Heart Basilica, designed by the celebrated New Zealand architect, Francis Petre

geological past can be found everywhere, including rocky volcanic outcrops, craggy headlands, deep valleys and precipitous bluffs. The Summit Road allows fine views of this striking scenery.

The peninsula has been settled by Māori for almost 1,000 years, and until the 1820s was a place of prosperity for the Ngai Tahu tribe. That changed as a result of intertribal fighting, conflict that contributed indirectly to the decision taken by the British government to install a governor and sign the Treaty of Waitangi.

Among the peninsula's attractions are its beautiful bays and picturesque villages, including Pigeon Bay, Okains Bay, Laverick's Bay and Le Bons Bay. There are many walking tracks, including a 20-minute stroll through the Hay Scenic Reserve, which has one of the peninsula's best remaining strands of lowland podocarp forest; and the two-to four-day Banks Peninsula Track, which traverses private farmland and the coastline of the remote eastern bays.

←

The gondola that runs from Heathcote Valley to the rim of the crater at Port Hills

SHOP

Barry's Bay Traditional Cheese

Banks Peninsula has a long tradition of cheese making, kept alive at this factory.

 D6 5807 Christchurch Akaroa Rd barrysbay cheese.co.nz

⑧ Timaru

 C6 12 km (7 miles) N of city   2 George St; www.aoraki.tourism.co.nz

Built on rolling hills marking the edge of the Canterbury Plains, Timaru is the largest town in South Canterbury. Its name derives from Te Maru, meaning "a place of shelter", denoting its historical importance as a safe haven for Māori canoes travelling the coast. Today, many notable buildings grace the commercial heart of this regional capital. The Basilica of the Sacred Heart is arguably the most impressive, designed by Francis William Petre and built in 1910–11.

Timaru's artificial port was created in 1877; white sands have since accumulated beside the port to form Caroline Bay, a safe and popular swimming beach. The Piazza, a series of staircases and a lift, links the bay with the central city above.

The charming art museum **Aigantighe**, pronounced "egg and tie", has a permanent collection of works by New Zealand and British painters, as well as English and continental china. The octagonal-shaped **South Canterbury Museum** is the main regional museum. Its collections cover the natural history of the area, local Māori history, the early whaling industry and European settlement. A highlight is a replica of the aeroplane built by Temuka farmer Richard Pearse.

Opened in 1864, **Timaru Botanic Gardens** comprise 19 ha (50 acres) of undulating landforms and water features. Notable highlights include a cabbage tree believed to date from pre-European times and a 1911 band rotunda.

Aigantighe

 49 Wai-iti Rd 10am–4pm Tue–Fri, noon–4pm Sat & Sun aigantighe.co.nz

South Canterbury Museum

 4 Perth St 10am–4pm Tue–Fri, 1–4pm Sat & Sun museum-timari.govt.nz

Timaru Botanic Gardens

 Queen St (03) 687 7200 8am–dusk daily

 INSIDER TIP
Scenic Mail Run

At weekends, explore the spectacular bays of Banks Peninsula with postman Jeff on his red postal van tour. Ascend from volcano craters to remote farms, stopping for tea and strolls on the beach (www.akaroa. com/tours).

Timaru's rolling hills, on the edge of the Canterbury Plains

⑨ Lewis Pass

🅰 D5

Lewis Pass marks the crossing point on State Highway 7 over the South Island's Main Divide. The surrounding 183-sq-km (70-sq-mile) Lewis Pass National Reserve offers a range of unguided outdoor activities, including hiking, fishing and hunting. Just over the pass, **Maruia Springs Thermal Resort** has a small complex of outdoor hot pools in a natural setting, with views of the surrounding bush and mountain peaks. Snow can fall heavily in the area so check the weather forecast before exploring in the winter.

Maruia Springs Thermal Resort
◈ ⓦ 🄰 State Hwy 7
🄲 9am–9pm daily
ⓦ maruiahotsprings.nz

↑ Guests enjoying the hot thermal pools in an alpine-village style setting at Hanmer Springs

⑩ Hanmer Springs

🅰 D5 🚍 ℹ 42 Amuri Ave; (03) 315 0020

This small alpine village, 385 m (1,260 ft) above sea level, is best known for the vast **Hanmer Springs Thermal Pools & Spa**. Although hot springs were first discovered in the area in 1859, they were officially opened only in 1883. Today, the complex boasts 15 thermal and freshwater pools of varying temperatures, as well as private pools and a children's waterslide and activity area.

Surrounding the hot pools is a 168-sq-km (65-sq-mile) forest park, which offers activities such as mountain biking and walks, ranging from the short Conical Hill walk (one hour return trip) to the longer Mount Isobel walk (five to six hours return trip). At the Waiau Ferry Bridge, 5 km (3 miles) from the village, tourist operators offer bungee jumping, jet-boating and rafting down the Waiau River.

Hanmer Springs Thermal Pools & Spa
◈ ⓦ 🄰 42 Amuri Ave
🄲 10am–9pm daily
ⓦ hanmersprings.co.nz

⑪ Reefton

🅰 D5 🚍 ℹ 67-69 Broadway; www.reefton.co.nz

Founded in 1872, Reefton takes its name from the gold-bearing quartz reefs in the area. The town's gold-mining heritage is evident in the many historic remains of the 1870s boom dotted around the region, especially in the

JEAN FRANÇOIS LANGLOIS

The man primarily responsible for Akaroa's French heritage was whaler Jean François Langlois. In 1838, he conceived the idea of a French colony and tried to buy most of the peninsula from the local Ngai Tahu people. He then formed the Nanto-Bordelaise Company as the vehicle for his colonizing ambitions. But French ambitions were thwarted by the British who had signed the Treaty of Waitangi and, upon hearing of the settlers' impending arrival, rushed to appoint two magistrates to Akaroa. Despite the assertion of British sovereignty, the settlers stayed. The Nanto-Bordelaise Company was bought out in 1849, opening the way for large-scale British migration.

→

Daly's Wharf jutting out into the water at Akaroa harbour

> **Founded in 1872, Reefton takes its name from the gold-bearing quartz reefs in the area.**

beech forest-clad Victoria Forest Park. A network of tracks provides opportunity for exploration on foot or on mountain bike. A heritage walk around Reefton takes in many historic buildings, including the **School of Mines**, which operated from 1887 to 1970 as part of a network of similar schools around New Zealand. About two km (1 mile) from Reefton, the **Black's Point Museum** exhibits relics from the gold-mining era.

School of Mines
⊘⊛ ⬛22 Shiel St ☎(03) 732 8391 ⏱By arrangement

Black's Point Museum
⊘ ⬛Franklin St ☎(03) 732 8391 ⏱9am-4pm daily, 1-4pm Sat & Sun ⏳May-Sep

---

Akaroa

⬛D6 ⬛ ⓘ80 Rue Lavaud; www.akaroa.com

This attractive small town, nestled at the head of Akaroa Harbour, is the oldest town in Canterbury, and was founded by a small band of French settlers in 1840. The town features many French-influenced historic buildings, narrow streets and a beautiful harbourfront location. Among the many reminders of Akaroa's French heritage is Langlois-Eteveneaux House, believed to have been pre-fabricated in France and erected in Akaroa in 1841. It is part of the **Akaroa Museum** complex, which includes the town's old courthouse, opened in 1880. The museum exhibits cover natural and regional history and architecture. A self-guided walk through the town takes in 43 historic sites, including the 1880 **Akaroa Lighthouse**, which was moved to its present location in 1980.

A good swimming beach lies at the centre of the town. Harbour cruises operate from the main wharf, on which visitors may see Hector's dolphins, penguins and seal colonies. A number of walking tracks lead up to the surrounding volcanic saddles and peaks, affording panoramic views of the harbour. Akaroa also has an active art and crafts community, and many shops and galleries. Akaroa has become popular with cruise ships so it's best to avoid visiting on the days that they are in port.

Akaroa Museum

⊘⊛⬛ ⬛71 Rue Lavaud ☎(03) 304 1013 ⏱10:30am-4:30pm daily

Akaroa Lighthouse

⊘⊛ ☎(03) 304 7325 ⏱11am-2pm Sun & cruise ship days

EAT

Ma Maison
Seafood fresh from Akaroa Harbour is a speciality, but the *filet de boeuf* is equally tempting.

⬛D6 ⬛2 Rue Jolie, Banks Peninsula, Akaroa ⏳Tue & Wed ⬛mamaison.co.nz

$$ⓈⓈ⑤

The Oxford
This Timaru brasserie is serious about local wines, and offers tasty, French-style cuisine.

⬛C6 ⬛152 Stafford St, Timaru ⏳Tue ⬛theoxford.co.nz

$$ⓈⓈ⑤

⓭ Karamea

 D4 🚌 ℹ️ Market Cross;
www.karameainfo.co.nz

Settled by Europeans in 1874, Karamea is an isolated farming community at the northern end of the West Coast's State Highway 67. Nestled in a basin dominated by dairy farming and fringed by Kahurangi National Park, Karamea is best known as the exit point for the Heaphy Track (p192), which after following the coast from the Heaphy River ends 15 km (9 miles) to the north. Short walking tracks are based around the Heaphy exit point, including the 40-minute Nikau Loop and the 90-minute Scotts Beach walk.

About 26 km (16 miles) to the northeast of Karamea is the **Oparara Basin**, featuring impressive limestone formations and a 15-km (9-mile) system of caves enveloped by dense forest. Much of the gravel road to the basin is narrow and winding, but can be undertaken in a two-wheel-drive vehicle. The fragile Honeycomb Caves system, first explored in 1980, is accessible only with a government-accredited guide, and contains the remains of about 50 species, including the extinct moa and New Zealand eagle. Areas that can

be explored without a guide are the Oparara Arch, 43 m (141 ft) high and 219 m (719 ft) long, reached after a 20-minute walk on a good track through the forest, and the Box Canyon and Crazy Paving caves. It is essential to carry a good torch. For the adventurous, local tourist operators run grades four and five white-water rafting trips down the Karamea River.

Karamea is also a base for walkers using the popular three- to five-day Wangapeka Track. The Fenian Track is a historic gold-miners' route, and the four-hour return walk leads to the former mining settlement of Adams Flat.

Oparara Basin

♿🚫 📍 State Hwy 67
🌐 oparara.co.nz

⓮ Westport

📍 C5 ✈️ 5 km (3 miles) N of town 🚌 ℹ️ 123 Palmerston St; www.buller.co.nz

Westport's origins lie in the gold rush of the 1860s but coal has been its lifeline for much of its history. Until 1954, coal from mines in the surrounding mountains was shipped out through the town's once-busy port at the head of the Buller River; today the bulk is taken

by train to Lyttelton on the east coast. The **Coal Town Museum** has exhibits reconstructing aspects of the region's coal-mining heritage.

Westport is a base for outdoor activities, including jet-boating and jet-skiing on the river. Among the most popular activities is underground rafting in the Nile River Canyon area. This can be done only with a guide and involves floating in inner tubes through grottos and caverns before emerging into the open to float down the Waitakere River rapids and Nile River Canyon.

Westport's North Beach and Carter's Beach are popular swimming and surfing spots, as is Tauranga Bay. On the Cape Foulwind Walkway at the edge of Tauranga Bay is a breeding colony of fur seals. The walkway, which takes three hours there and back, crosses rocky bluffs, grassy downs, swampy streams and sandy beaches.

Coal Town Museum

♿ 📍 123 Palmerston St
🕙 10am–4pm daily
🌐 coaltown.co.nz

←
A dramatic limestone arch, part of the Oparara Basin cave system

↑ Deserted tracks of Stockton Mine, once a thriving coalfield

COAL-MINING HERITAGE

Coal was first discovered on the West Coast by explorer Thomas Brunner in 1848. The largest of the early mines were on the Denniston and Stockton plateaus, north-east of Westport, where large-scale exploitation began in 1878.

The task of extracting coal from this region's rugged terrain was hazardous, and required feats of engineering. The most famous was the Denniston Incline, a gravity-powered rail system under which laden coal trucks were lowered 520 m (1,700 ft) down the mountain. The incline closed in 1967, but during its 87 years of operation 13 million tonnes of coal were extracted. The industry continues to support the West Coast economy, with over 2 million tonnes exported from the coalfields each year.

EARLY MINING TOWNS

Mining settlements sprang up in the 19th century to support the coal industry, but they are little more than ghost towns today. The 120-km (75-mile) self-guided Buller Coalfields Heritage Trail leads through many mining relics, including the once thriving towns of Brunner, Denniston, Stockton and Millerton where miners and their families lived in remote tight-knit communities. Information on the trail is available at the i-SITE Visitor Centre in Westport (www.doc.govt.nz).

←
A model of a wagon rolling down the steep Denniston Incline at Westport's Coal Town Museum

→

Pancake Rocks at Dolomite Point in Punakaiki, Paparoa National Park

 15

Paparoa National Park

🅰C5 🚌 ℹ️ State Hwy 6, Punakaiki; (03) 731 1895

Established in 1987, this 300-sq-km (115-sq-mile) park contains varied and dramatic scenery, most famously the Pancake Rocks and blowholes near the small coastal settlement of Punakaiki. Bands of limestone, separated by thin bands of softer mudstone, which has been worn away by thousands of years of rain, wind and sea spray, have created the layered formations of the Pancake Rocks. Over hundreds of thousands of years, caverns have formed as carbon dioxide-bearing rainwater has gradually eaten into cracks in the limestone. During high seas, these subterranean caverns become blowholes as the waves surge in under huge pressure and explode in a plume of spray. The Pancake Rocks and blowholes are easily accessible from the highway via the short Dolomite Point walk. Wheelchair access, if assisted, is also possible.

Other short walks as well as longer hikes are available in the park, including the 15-minute Truman Track through

subtropical forest to a wild coastline featuring caverns, a blowhole and waterfall, and the two-hour walk to a huge limestone structure known as "the ballroom overhang". A two- to three-day hike through the heart of the park follows a pack track, built in 1867 to avoid dangerous travel along the isolated and rugged coastline.

 16

Greymouth

🅰C5 🚆🚌 ℹ️ 164 Mackay St; www.westcoast.co.nz

The largest town on the West Coast, Greymouth occupies the site of what was once Mawhera Pa. Although colonial government agents purchased the majority of the West Coast in 1860 for £300, the land under modern Greymouth remained a Māori reserve. Greymouth was laid out in 1865. Around this time, gold was being found in large quantities in the area, and coal had been discovered 17 years earlier. When the gold boom ended, coal mining ensured the district's continued survival. However, the Grey River mouth, which has served the town as a port,

has also delivered misfortune. Repeatedly throughout its history, Greymouth has been submerged by flood waters, including twice in 1988. Since then a flood wall has been erected, popularly called "the great wall of Greymouth".

The **Left Bank Art Gallery**, housed in an imposing old bank building, features an important greenstone collection, crafted in both contemporary and traditional designs

Like other West Coast towns, Greymouth offers a range of adventure tourism activities,

---

GREENSTONE

Emerald green nephrite jade *(pounamu)*, also known as greenstone, is a hard stone formed in New Zealand's alpine fault lines. The stone holds great spiritual significance for Māori and is used for making tools and jewellery. In 1997, ownership of the greenstone resource on the West Coast was handed back to the South Island Ngai Tahu tribe as part of a major Treaty of Waitangi settlement *(p56)*.

including floating through the Taniwha Caves on inflated tubes and dolphin watching. The Grey River system is known for good fishing.

Greymouth is also famous for the West Coast Wilderness Trail. With easy access, the track is well-surfaced for most of the 135-km (84-m) route from Greymouth to Ross. It follows old railway lines and views of the Southern Alps vie with visions of the Tasman Sea as the trail traverses several goldmining towns.

Left Bank Art Gallery
⊕⊗⊙ 🄰1 Tainui St
🕒10am–4pm daily 🗓1 Jan, 25 Dec 🅆bankarts.com

---

⑰
Hokitika

🄰C5 ⊡2 km (1.2 miles) N of town 🚌 🄸36 Weld St; www.hokitika.org

With its wide streets, notable historic buildings and excellent local craft studios, Hokitika is perhaps the West Coast's most attractive town. Little more than a shanty town in 1864, by 1866 Hokitika had become a thriving commercial centre thanks to gold. The town's river port bustled with ships bearing miners flocking from the goldfields of Australia, but it was a treacherous harbour where a ship went down every ten weeks in the years 1865 and 1866. The wreck of one such ship is on the self-guided Hokitika Heritage Trail, which includes 22 historic buildings and sights. The most impressive of these is the 1908 Carnegie Library, now the home of the town's information centre.

The **National Kiwi Centre** is a small wildlife centre specializing in kiwi, tuatara, giant longfinned eels and the tiny whitebait and koura or "crawlies" for which the West Coast's rivers are renowned. The centre's freshwater eel specimens are particularly astonishing, with some reaching 2 m (6.5 ft) in length, and up to 110 years in age. The tuatara, New Zealand's unique reptile, and the nocturnal kiwi bird are also presented in their natural habitats. All the animals have public feeding times, twice daily.

Hokitika's remarkable Glowworm Dell, on the northern edge of the town, is worth a visit after dark. The best time to view the lights exuded by these carnivorous larvae is on a wet night.

There are a number of stunning scenic areas around Hokitika. Lake Mahinapua, 10 km (6 miles) south, and Lake Kaniere, 20 km (12 miles) east of the town, are peaceful retreats, popular for boating, fishing, swimming and bush walking. The Lake Kaniere Walkway is 13 km (8 miles) and takes about four hours. Ross township, 28 km (17 m) south of Hokitika, has a small local museum devoted to its gold-mining history. Walks take visitors past old mine workings. New Zealand's biggest gold nugget was discovered in Ross in 1909, and the area – said still to contain millions of dollars' worth of gold – is again being mined.

National Kiwi Centre
⊕⊗ 🄰64 Tancred St
🕒9am–5pm daily 🗓1 Jan, 25 Dec 🅆thenational kiwicentre.co.nz

→
Hokitika's memorial clock tower, unveiled in 1903

18 Arthur's Pass

C5 🚐💺 ℹ️ Dept of Conservation, State Hwy 73, Arthur's Pass; (03) 318 9211

The tiny village of Arthur's Pass is nestled in a scenic valley east of the summit of Arthur's Pass mountain way. In 1908, workers began construction of the 8-km (5-mile) Otira rail tunnel which would run under the Southern Alps from Arthur's Pass to Otira. It took ten years for the two ends of the tunnel to meet, and another five years before the first train travelled through. A number of tunnellers' cottages remain in the village, now used as private holiday homes.

Since the 1920s, the village has been a base for day-trippers from Christchurch and Greymouth, walkers, hikers and mountaineers, and skiers who enjoy the splendid views and low-key atmosphere of the nearby Temple Basin ski field. It is also the headquarters of Arthur's Pass National Park (*p218*).

19 Mount Hutt

C6 🚐 ℹ️ 121 Main St, Methven; (03) 302 8955

Mount Hutt, in the foot hills of the Southern Alps above the upper reaches of the Rakaia River, is Canterbury's largest ski field, and claims to have the longest ski season in Australasia (early June to mid-October). The ski field is served by nine lifts and tows, as well as artificial snow-making facilities. From the 2,075-m (6,808-ft) mountain, there are excellent views over the Canterbury Plains.

The town of Methven serves as Mount Hutt's après-ski centre in winter, and reverts in summer to a typical New Zealand farming town. The 42-sq-km (16-sq-mile) Mount Hutt Conservation Area, 14 km (9 miles) west of the town, has a number of short walking tracks through native forest dominated by mountain beech. The Rakaia Gorge, about 16 km (10 miles) north of Methven, is popular for jet-boating. A 5-km (3-mile) walkway traverses the edge of the Rakaia Gorge through forests and past spectacular geological features.

20 Ashburton

C6 🚐💺 ℹ️ The Green, East St; (03) 308 1050

Ashburton straddles the Ashburton River and is the principal town in the farming district of mid-Canterbury. The town was named after Lord Ashburton, a member of the Canterbury Association, which settled the province in the 1850s. Although originally dry and tussock covered, irrigation has allowed agriculture to flourish. The well-laid-out town has historic brick buildings and many mature trees, including some in the Ashburton Domain. **Ashford Village** is a collection of shops and work-shops. There is also a museum housing spinning wheels.

Ashford Village

🕙😊🅿️ 🏠 427 West St
🕙 9am–5pm daily 🚫 1 & 2 Jan, Good Fri, Easter Mon, 25 & 26 Dec 🌐 ashford.co.nz

----

21 Geraldine

C6 🚐 ℹ️ Kiwi Country, 38 Waihi Tce; www.aoraki.tourism.co.nz

This attractive small farming town is a popular stopover for travellers heading south to the Mackenzie Country. First known as Talbot Forest, in 1866, it began as a sheep run and base for sawmillers. Talbot Forest now refers to the lowland podocarp forest that provides a backdrop to Geraldine. The town still has many historic buildings, such as the 1908 Post Office, which can be seen on a self-guided walking trail.

Locally produced juices and condiments can be sampled at **Four Peaks Plaza**.

←

Skiers and snowboarders speeding down the slopes of Mount Hutt

↑ Lupins and the Church of the Good Shepherd *(inset)* on Lake Tekapo

The fascinating **Vintage Car and Machinery Museum** has a great collection of cars dating from 1907 to 1953 and tractors from 1874 as well as early agricultural machinery.

Four Peaks Plaza
🏛 🏠 76 Talbot St 📞 (03) 693 9727 🕐 9am–8pm daily

Vintage Car and Machinery Museum
♿ ⛔ 🏠 178 Talbot St 📞 (03) 693 8756 🕐 9:30am–5pm daily 🚫 1 Jan, 25 & 26 Dec

---

㉒
Lake Tekapo

🏛 C6 🚌 ℹ Pukaki, State Hwy 8; www.mt cooknz.com

Lake Tekapo is a place of exceptional beauty. The remarkable blue of the lake is caused by "rock flour" – fine particles of rock brought down by the glaciers at the head of the lake and held in suspension in the melt water. The lake is a popular venue for fishing, boating, kayaking, swimming and hang-gliding.

On the lake front stands the Church of the Good Shepherd. The foundation stone of this stone-and-oak church was laid in 1935 by the Duke of Gloucester. The front window of the church creates a perfect frame for a view of the lake. Next to the church is a bronze statue of a sheepdog, erected in 1968 as a tribute to the important role played by these animals in the development of high country farming.

Because of the purity of the atmosphere above Lake Tekapo, the University of Canterbury has an observatory atop Mount John to the west of the township.

Lake Tekapo village is a good base for skiing at Mount Dobson, Roundhill and Ohau, about 30 km (18 miles) away, while the town's small tourist airport is also a base for scenic flights over Mount Cook. Lake Alexandrina, 10 km (6 miles) from Tekapo, is renowned for its trout fishing.

HIGH-COUNTRY FARMING

When the "Canterbury Pilgrims" arrived in 1850 to establish their new settlement, they saw the potential of pastoral farming, and the runholders - the farmers who grazed the land - became a powerful economic and political force. Although land reform in the late 19th century saw the great estates broken up, large high country stations remain a feature of farming in New Zealand, particularly in Canterbury. Good roads and modern communications have reduced the isolation and harshness of station life, but it remains a unique existence.

㉓
Twizel

⚠C6 ⬛ ℹ️15 Wairepo Rd; (030) 435 0802

Twizel was built in 1969 as a construction town for the Upper Waitaki hydroelectric development scheme. Once the hydro scheme was completed, the local people successfully fought to retain the town, and began to exploit its proximity to excellent fishing and boating lakes, and to Mount Cook 61 km (37 miles) away. Lake Ruataniwha, a manmade lake just south of Twizel, is popular for watersports. It has an international-standard rowing course and is the site of national rowing events every year. From Lake Ruataniwha, a sealed back road leads to Lake Benmore, a 75-sq-km (29-sq-mile) hydroelectric dam that has also become a favourite boating destination.

South of Twizel, on State Highway 8, lies the small town of Omarama. The town has a worldwide reputation for gliding because of its strong northwest thermal updraughts and many gliding records have been set here.

About 10 km (6 miles) west of the town are the **Clay Cliffs**, a set of steep, high pinnacles separated by deep, narrow ravines. The cliffs are said to have been frequented by early Māori travelling into the Mackenzie Country to hunt. Although privately owned, the cliffs are protected by covenant, and are accessible to the public. Access is by a rough dirt road, and sunset is the most impressive time to visit. Payment is by donation in an honesty jar.

Clay Cliffs
🏛 🅐Henburn Rd 📞(03) 438 9780 ⏲No restriction

↑ A road twisting and turning through Mount Cook National Park with views of glacial Lake Pukaki

㉔
Lake Pukaki

⚠C6 ℹ️State Hwy 8; www.mountcooknz.com

Majestic Pukaki, Ohau and Tepako lakes lie within the great Mackenzie Basin. State Highway 8 hugs the southern tip of Pukaki, and a large and popular lay-by and picnic area allows stunning views of Mount Cook as well as the Southern Alps. The lake is fed by the waters of the Tasman River, which flows off the Tasman Glacier. It has been artificially raised as part of the Upper Waitaki hydro-electricity network and is also linked by canals to Lake Tekapo and Lake Ohau.

← Metal sculpture of the kakī (black stilt) bird in the market place at Twizel

On a clear day, Mount Cook is reflected in the waters of the lake.

Scenic **Glentanner Park Centre**, located about 20 km (12 miles) south of Mount Cook village, on the beautiful shores of Lake Pukaki, is a campsite – the closest accommodation for Mount Cook. The centre is set amid the family-run Glentanner Station, a 182-sq-km- (70-sq-mile-) high country farm. Occasional short tours of the farm allow visitors to see sheep shearing and sheepdog demonstrations.

Glentanner Park Centre
🏛 🅐State Hwy 80
🌐glentanner.co.nz

25

Waipara Vineyards

 D5

The Waipara district's first vineyards were planted in the 1980s, and the area quickly emerged as a premium wine-growing region, with its favourable growing climate of warm summers, abundant sunshine and low annual rainfall. Today many of the 80-plus vineyards here are award-winners, celebrated for their Pinot Noir, Riesling, Sauvignon Blanc and Chardonnay wines.

Many Waipara wineries offer tours and tastings. The family-owned **Pegasus Bay** has a charming restaurant and garden overlooking the surrounding countryside, while **Waipara Springs** has a lovely café that serves produce from local farms. First planted in 1993, **Black Estate** crafts organic, biodynamic wines, with its three vineyards, a tasting room, boutique accommodation and a delightful eatery at its "Home" site.

Pegasus Bay

Ⓧ Ⓨ Ⓩ 🅰 Stockgrove Rd, Waipara, 🕙 10am–5pm daily 🅦 pegasusbay.com

Waipara Springs

Ⓔ 🅰 409 Omihi Rd, Waipara 🕙 10am–5pm daily (to 8pm Thu & Fri) 🅦 waiparasprings.co.nz

Black Estate

Ⓟ 🅰 614 Omihi Rd, Waipara 🕙 10am–5pm daily 🅦 blackestate.co.nz

---

26

Rakaia

 C6 🚐

On the southern bank of the Rakaia River, the small farming settlement of Rakaia claims to be "the salmon capital of New Zealand". A large fibreglass fish in the middle of the township celebrates the excellent salmon and trout fishing to be had at various spots along the river.

27

Lake Ohau

B6

About 30 km (18 miles) to the west of Twizel, Lake Ohau is a popular swimming, fishing, skiing and boating spot. The six native forests that surround the lake – the Ohau, Temple, Dobson, Huxley,

HYDROELECTRIC DEVELOPMENT

The power stations of the Upper Waitaki and Mackenzie Basin provide about one-third of New Zealand's hydroelectricity. The idea of harnessing the water resources of the region was first mooted in 1904, and today the vast scheme includes the Tekapo A and B power stations, Ohau A, B and C stations, and Benmore, Aviemore and Waitaki stations. An important feature of the scheme is 58 km (36 miles) of manmade canals, which pool the resources of Lakes Tekapo, Pukaki and Ohau, along which there is an attractive scenic drive. The lakes created by the hydro scheme have become very popular venues for watersports.

Hopkins and Ahuriri – also provide excellent hiking and walking opportunities. Many huts are scattered in the forests for the use of more experienced hikers.

Overlooking the western side of the lake, the Ohau ski-field in the foothills of the Southern Alps offers off-piste runs accessible from platter and chair ski lifts.

← Vineyards of Waipara carpeting the beautiful Canterbury landscape

**PENGUINS
CROSSING**

SLOW

OTAGO AND SOUTHLAND

This region was initially settled by the Māori, who fished along the coast, as well as hunting and collecting greenstone (pounamu) in the area's rugged interior. The first Europeans looked to coastal areas for their new settlements, with Members of the Free Church of Scotland the first to inhabit the area in an organized way; they made Dunedin the centre of their new land. Hopes of an idyllic enclave were dashed in the early 1860s with the discovery of gold. Gold miners from flagging goldfields of California and Australia poured into the inhospitable lands of what is now known as Central Otago, in search of a "flash in the pan". Fortunes from gold saw the region prosper, and for a time Dunedin became New Zealand's commercial capital. The legacy of the gold mining era lives on in the humblest of stone cottages on remote and rugged landscapes as well as in the splendid buildings that adorn the streets of Dunedin.

Old miners' cottages still pepper the dry grasslands of Central Otago around bustling Queenstown, where stunning landscapes set the scene for a burgeoning tourist scene to flourish in the 1960s. During the 1970s, the town emerged as a world centre for adventure sports; it was here that extreme sports such as paragliding and bungy jumping were first developed. Today Queenstown continues to thrive as a premier destination for thrillseekers, and make a perfect springboard from which to explore the spectacular landscapes of Mount Aspiring and Fiordland national parks.

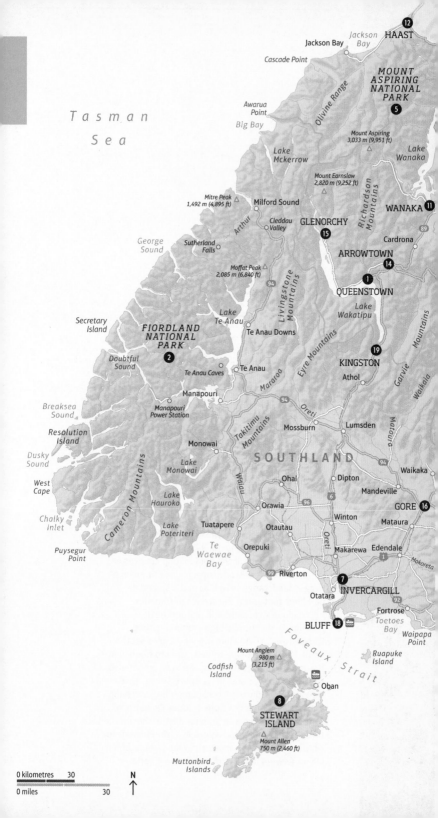

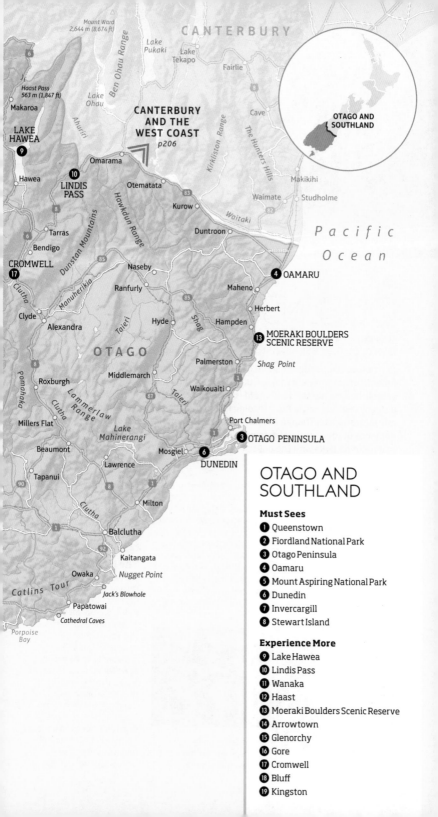

CANTERBURY

Mount Ward
2,644 m (8,674 ft)

Lake
Pukaki

Lake
Tekapo

Fairlie

Ben Ohau Range

Lake
Ohau

Cave

Haast Pass
563 m (1,847 ft)

Makaroa

**LAKE
HAWEA**
9

Hawea

**10
LINDIS
PASS**

**CANTERBURY
AND THE
WEST COAST**
p206

Omarama

Otematata

Kurow

Makikihi

Waimate

Studholme

Ahuriri

Hawkdun Range

Kirkliston Range

The Hunters Hills

Tarras

Bendigo

CROMWELL
17

Clyde

Alexandra

Dunstan Mountains

85

Manuherikia

Naseby

Ranfurly

Hyde

OTAGO

Taieri

Duntroon

Waitaki

Pacific

Ocean

4 OAMARU

Maheno

Herbert

Hampden

13 MOERAKI BOULDERS
SCENIC RESERVE

Palmerston

Shag Point

Clutha

Roxburgh

Millers Flat

Beaumont

Tapanui

90

Pomahaka

Lawrence

8

Clutha

Milton

Balclutha

92

Kaitangata

Owaka

Catlins Tour

Papatowai

Cathedral Caves

*Porpoise
Bay*

Lammerlaw Range

Lake
Mahinerangi

Middlemarch

Taieri

Shag

Mosgiel

6
DUNEDIN

Waikouaiti

Port Chalmers

3 OTAGO PENINSULA

Nugget Point

Jack's Blowhole

OTAGO AND
SOUTHLAND

OTAGO AND
SOUTHLAND

Must Sees

1 Queenstown
2 Fiordland National Park
3 Otago Peninsula
4 Oamaru
5 Mount Aspiring National Park
6 Dunedin
7 Invercargill
8 Stewart Island

Experience More

9 Lake Hawea
10 Lindis Pass
11 Wanaka
12 Haast
13 Moeraki Boulders Scenic Reserve
14 Arrowtown
15 Glenorchy
16 Gore
17 Cromwell
18 Bluff
19 Kingston

❶ QUEENSTOWN

B6 🚗 6 km (4 miles) E of town 🚢 Steamer Wharf
ℹ i-SITE, Cnr Camp & Shotover sts; www.queenstownnz.co.nz

Perched on the northeast shore of Lake Wakatipu and presided over by the Remarkables mountain range, Queenstown is set amid spectacular scenery. First established during the 1860s gold rushes, since the 1970s it has developed from a sleepy lakeside town into a leading international resort and world centre for adventure sports. Though the pace of development has been dictated by the demands of tourism, Queenstown still has the feel of a small town, and proudly maintains its links with the days of the gold boom.

① Queenstown Gardens

Park St 🕒 Daily

Set on a glacial moraine peninsula, the 150-year-old Queenstown Gardens are within walking distance of the town centre. The gardens are surrounded by stands of large fir trees and encompass broad lawns, a pergola, pond and rose beds, along with informal plantings of native and exotic trees. The gardens are a quiet oasis in an otherwise incredibly busy tourist town, and are particularly attractive in autumn, when Japanese maples flush with colour. An ice skating rink, sporting greens, frisbee golf course, skate park and tennis courts are other attractions.

②   The Mall

The best way to get to know Queenstown is on foot and the best place to start is at the Mall. A popular meeting place, it has a food court for visitors and a pedestrian-only street dominated by a variety of restaurants, cafés and pubs, as well as numerous souvenir shops. The Mall leads from the Village Green directly down to the Maintown pier, from which boats regularly depart for cruises on the lake. A number of interesting old colonial buildings, such as the former bank, remain here.

↑ Strolling along Queenstown's pleasant pedestrianized Mall

Did You Know?

Queenstown was first discovered around AD 1200 by Māori searching for green-stone and moa.

↑ Queenstown, nestled on the shore of the majestic Lake Wakatipu

FOLLOW THE PATH

Eagle-eyed fans of Peter Jackson's world-famous *Lord of the Rings* trilogy will recognize scenes from Middle-Earth in the wonderfully majestic landscape surrounding Queenstown. Isengaard (Paradise), Rivendale (Earnslaw Burn) and Rohan (Deer Heights Park) are within reach of the town, and can be experienced on both self-led or organized tours. Follow in the footsteps of the heroic Fellowship and cross the "Anduin" river at Karawau Gorge suspension bridge, part of the Arrow River cycling route *(doc.govt.nz)*. Or take a four-wheel-drive tour through Wakatipu Basin to see Minas Tirith and the Misty Mountains *(www.nomadsafaris.co.nz)*.

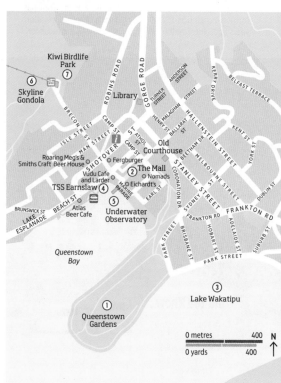

Tramp the Ben Lomond Track

Head off on a hike up Ben Lomond, a 1,748-m- (5,735-ft-) high mountain overlooking Queenstown. This trail is well-trodden, but challenging; it takes 3 to 4 hours to reach the mountain's saddle, and 6 to 8 to reach the summit. Along the way, traverse tussocky shrubland and stands of Douglas Fir. When you reach the top, you'll be rewarded with epic panoramas of Lake Wakatipu and the mountains beyond. (doc.govt.nz).

③

Lake Wakatipu

This vast glacial lake was formed as many as 15,000 years ago, when meltwater from mountain glaciers filled the basin. Wakatipu can be translated as "Hollow of the Giant"; Māori legend has it that the lake was formed by the imprint of a sleeping giant burned to death by a beautiful Māori woman's vengeful lover. The giant's heart did not perish and still beats, so today the level of the lake rises and falls as much as 7 cm (3 inches) every five minutes – a phenomenon known as seiche.

The second largest of the southern glacial lakes, after Te Anau, Wakatipu is up to 380 m (1,246 ft) deep in places. The waters are home to many fish, including trout, salmon and longfin eel. The rugged slopes of the Remarkables drop steeply down to the water's edge, leaving downtown Queenstown nestled on one of the few pieces of flat land in the area.

During the mining boom, the lake was the principal means of communication, but today it is a focus for recreational activities such as paddle boarding, parasailing and jetskiing.

④

TSS Earnslaw

🏠Steamer Wharf 🔵tss earnslaw.co.nz

The TSS (Twin Screw Steamer) *Earnslaw* is a relic of the mining boom, when paddle steamers plied Lake Wakatipu as the principal means of transport. Launched in 1912, the 51 m (168 ft) vessel, affectionately known as "the lady of the lake", is still powered by original twin 500-hp coal-fired steam engines. Its interior is finished with wood and brass.

Cruises depart daily from Queenstown all year round, with 90-minute to 4-hour dinner trips in the warmer months. Visitors can also take daytime or evening excursions across the lake to the Walter Peak High Country Farm for a farmyard tour and tea.

Did You Know

Lake Wakatipu stood in as Scotland's Loch Ness in the 2005 film *Mysteries of the Deep*.

↑ Spotting trout and salmon under the waters of Lake Wakatipu at the Underwater Observatory

Underwater Observatory

🏠 Main Town Pier ⏱ 8am to dusk daily 🌐 kjet.co.nz

Built beneath the Main Town Pier, Underwater Observatory provides a unique opportunity to see life below the surface of the lake. From a viewing lounge 5 m (16 ft) under the water, visitors can observe brown and rainbow trout peacefully swimming alongside enormous New Zealand long-finned eels, which can weigh up to 16 kg (35 lbs). Fish are often joined by diving black teal ducks.

Informative exhibitions explore the Māori mythology surrounding the lake.

← Boarding historic pleasure steamer TSS *Earnshaw* at Lake Wakatipu's port

EAT & DRINK

Fergburger
Billed as the best burger joint in the world, this Queenstown stalwart is always buzzing.

🏠 42 Shotover St 🌐 fergburger.com

💲💲💲

Vudu Cafe and Larder
This waterside spot offers fresh, modern dishes, zingy juices and delicious coffees.

🏠 16 Rees St 🌐 vudu.co.nz

💲💲💲

Roaring Meg's Restaurant
Taste award-winning lamb dishes in a candlelit dining room.

🏠 53 Shotover Street 🌐 roaringmegs.co.nz

💲💲💲

Smiths Craft Beer House
In the same building as Roaring Meg's, this bar serves cutting-edge craft beers and generous New Orleans po'boy sandwiches.

🏠 53 Shotover Street 🌐 smithscraftbeer.co.nz

💲💲💲

Atlas Beer Cafe
Hearty breakfasts and lunches, with tapas in the evenings, and 22 craft beers on tap.

🏠 88 Beach Street 🌐 atlasbeercafe.com

💲💲💲

↑ Epic views from the Skyline Gondola *(inset)* at Bob's Peak

STAY

⑥

Skyline Gondola

⌂ Brecon St ⌚ 9am-9pm daily ⓦ skyline.co.nz

For an essential Queenstown experience, ride the Skyline gondola up to Bob's Peak, and enjoy breathtaking views along the way. The gondola rises 450 m (1,476 ft) in just 730 m (2,400 ft) and affords panoramic vistas of the Remarkables, Lake Wakatipu and Queenstown from the observation deck at the top. At the summit there is a restaurant and café from which visitors can watch parapenters floating down from Bob's Peak. Mountain-bike trails can be accessed from the gondola, and adventurers can make the trip back downhill to town on an exhilarating ride on the luge – a short, raised toboggan.

⑦

Kiwi Birdlife Park

⌂ Brecon St ⌚ Times vary, check website for details ⓦ kiwibird.co.nz

Set just below the gondola terminal, the Kiwi Birdlife Park is home to several kinds of kiwi and other endangered native birds such as large alpine parrots known as kea, parakeets and the black stilt – a rare wader, as well as native Tuatara reptiles. Birds are housed here as part of national breeding programmes for release into the wild, or are being rehabilitated after injury.

At the park's nocturnal Kiwi House visitors can watch the elusive kiwis and other species, including native owls, in naturalistic night time surroundings with the aid of infra-red cameras and special low lighting.

ADVENTURE SPORTS PARADISE

Named the "Adventure Capital of the World", Queenstown's stunning landscape sets the scene for a plethora of adrenaline-pumping sports.

As tourism boomed in the 20th century, entrepreneurs found innovative ways for visitors to experience Queenstown's spectacular natural playground. This is the birthplace of jet boating, but the town's reputation rests on its thrilling aerial pursuits, such as paragliding. Made famous by New Zealander A J Hackett, who dived from the Eiffel Tower in 1986 suspended by a rubber cord strapped to his ankles, bungy was first launched as a commercial activity in 1988 at Kawarau bridge. Today, daredevil New Zealanders pioneer ever more thrilling sports for the enjoyment of visitors.

TOP 5 ADRENALINE SPORTS

Bungy Jumping
Plummet from a height tethered by an elastic bungy cord that recoils when stretched. At Kawarau Bridge the drop dips jumpers into the water.

Tandem-Parapeting
Tandem parapeting (or paragliding) entails plunging off a hill with a guide, strapped to a rectangular parachute.

Jet Boating
Power boats propel adventurers at breakneck speed down narrow river gorges, skimming across the surface of the water.

Skiing and Snowboarding
In winter, two ranges within 30 km (19 miles) of Queenstown – the Remarkables and Coronet Peak – provide perfect conditions for winter sports.

White-Water Rafting
Speed through narrow gorges and canyons on the thundering rapids of the Kawarau and Shotover rivers.

↑ Paradligers lifting off from Bob's Peak above Lake Wakatipu

→ Snowboarding on fresh powder, at Coronet Peak

White-water rafting over the rushing rapids of Shotover River ↑

FIORDLAND NATIONAL PARK

🅰 A6 🚌 Queenstown 160 km (100 miles) from park 🚐 Queenstown
ℹ Visitor Centre, Te Anau; www.fiordland.org.nz

Dominated by towering peaks, lush forests and reflective water, the Fiordland National Park is truly sublime. It's an area that can only be described with superlatives – its scale is vast, its moutains are sky-grazing and its fiords will take your breath away. Get your camera ready to capture some of New Zealand's most epic scenery.

The largest of New Zealand's national parks, the Fiordland encompasses an area of 12,500 sq km (4,826 sq miles) and features unique flora and fauna, including the Fiordland-crested penguin, earning it a place in the Te Wāhipounamu – Southwest New Zealand World Heritage Area.

The park takes its name from its many mirror-like fiords. Despite their monikers, the Milford Sound/Piopiotahi *(p251)*, Doubtful Sound/Patea *(p252)* and the other sounds are, in fact, fiords. Whereas sounds are flooded river valleys, fiords are valleys carved by the tremendous pressure and power of glaciers during successive Ice Ages, then later flooded by the sea as the ice melts and sea levels rise. This geologic past has gifted the area with an enthralling landscape. Sheer rock walls climb 1,200 m (3,940 ft) from the park's deep fiords, while waterfalls tumble 160 m (530 ft) below.

Until 1953, when State Highway 94 (the Milford Road) was completed, the park was uncharted, and the only way to the Milford Sound was by boat or via the Milford Track. Today, visitors arrive by the busload, but the park's 14 fiords and 5 major lakes flanked by

Did You Know?

Mitre Peak is so-called because of its resemblance to a bishop's hat.

↑ The beautiful view from Luxmore Hut on the Kepler Track

steep mountains, rising 2,750 m (9,020 ft) and clad with thick, temperate rainforest, still make the interior virtually impenetrable except along its 500 km (310 miles) of walking trails. It'll come as no surprise then that the Fiordland National Park is considered by many to be the best place in New Zealand for hikers, and it boasts three major tracks – the Milford, Routeburn and Kepler *(p251)*. As well as treading these snaking walking trails, you can also experience the park by taking a boat ride on one of the peaceful fiords or flying overhead in a whirring light aircraft or helicopter.

↑ A hiker navigating the dramatic Clinton Valley on the Milford Track through the Fiordland National Park

↑ Admiring Mitre Peak reflected in the waters of Milford Sound

Forming the Fiords

10 million years ago

Intense pressure in the earth's crust caused the most recent geologic uplift in the area, forming both the rounded peaks and dramatic V-shaped valleys that became the basis of the Fiordland National Park.

2 million years ago

The rounded mountains were covered by glaciers and, as a result, the ridges and peaks were sharpened into horns, while the valleys became U-shaped.

20,000–12,000 years ago

As the Ice Age came to an end the glaciers retreated, leaving multiple hanging valleys above the main valley; water flowed down from these higher valleys as waterfalls.

6,000 years ago

At the end of the last Ice Age, the sea reached its present levels, flooding the valleys and leaving the peaks exposed, resulting in the present landscape.

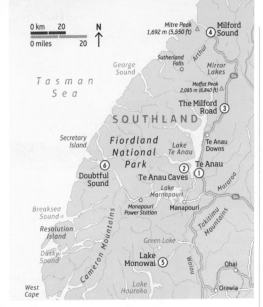

cascading alpine rivers and picturesque walks, the 121 km (75 mile) road to Milford Sound from Te Anau has earned World Heritage Highway status for its beauty and scenic variety. Although Milford Sound can be reached by road in two hours, there are many side trips possible along the way to make the drive more memorable.

Te Anau Downs, 30 km (19 miles) from Te Anau, is the departure point for the boat to the Milford Track. From here there is a 45-minute forest walk to Lake Mistletoe. Further on, the Mirror Lakes are a short five-minute walk from the road across a board-walk, and at Lake Gunn, about 46 km (29 miles) from Te Anau Downs, an easy 45-minute loop through beech forest is suitable for all ages and for people in wheelchairs. The Divide, a short distance away, marks the start of the Routeburn Track, which winds through spectacular subalpine

EXPLORING FIORDLAND

①

Te Anau

🏠 **Miro St Lakefront Drive**
📞 **(03) 249 2924**

The picturesque town of Te Anau, on the southeastern shore of Lake Te Anau, is the largest town in Fiordland and a good base for exploring Fiordland National Park. The lake, the largest in the South Island, is 61 km (38 miles) long and 417 m (1,370 ft) deep, the result of glacial action. It is a popular venue for boating and fishing.

②

Te Anau Caves

🏠 **Real Journeys Visitor Centre: 85 Lakefront Drive, Te Anau** 🌐 **realjourneys. co.nz**

At the Te Anau Caves, reached by a boat trip across Lake Te Anau, a combination of carefully formed walkways and small boats allow visitors to explore a series of magical limestone grottos. The caves

are home to thousands of tiny New Zealand glowworms, which use their light – the result of a chemical reaction – to attract insects for food. Return trips, which depart several times a day, take two and a half hours.

③

The Milford Road

Encompassing lush lakeside forest, rugged mountains,

Did You Know?

The building of the Homer Tunnel was twice delayed: first by World War II, then by an avalance.

Kayakers navigating the calm clear waters of Milford Sound in Fiordland

GREAT WALKS IN FIORDLAND NATIONAL PARK

GREAT WALKS IN FIORDLAND NATIONAL PARK

Fiordland National Park is one of New Zealand's best spots for experienced hikers. Its three major walking tracks – the Milford, Routeburn and Kepler trails can be walked independently, or in a guided group, all year round. Advance booking and hut or campsite passes can be obtained from the DOC (doc.govt.nz). All three walks are suitable only for experienced, well equipped parties.

terrain, with the peak of Key Summit to the west, before crossing the Harris Saddle. The nearby Hollyford Valley also makes a scenic trip.

Nineteen kilometres (12 miles) east of Milford Sound is the impressive 1,200-m- (3,940-ft-) long Homer Tunnel, completed in 1954. Leaving the tunnel, the road slopes very steeply downhill to the Milford side where there are views of the Cleddau Valley. The Chasm, a few kilometres from the tunnel, is reached by a 20-minute walk to where the Cleddau River drops 22 m (72 ft) through a series of rock formations.

④

Milford Sound

Milford Sound, a 16 km (10 mile) long fiord, is the national park's best-known attraction. Its most famous landmark is Mitre Peak, a pyramid-shaped mountain rising 1,692 m (5,550 ft) straight from the deep fiord.

Although scenic flights are available, the grandeur of Milford Sound is best appreciated by boat. Trips pass unusual geological features, such as Lion Mountain, the Elephant and Copper Point, as well as waterfalls: the Bowen Falls drop 160 m (530 ft) into the water and the Stirling Falls 146 m (480 ft). Fur seals, dolphins and the occasional Fiordland crested penguin can be seen along the way. An Underwater Observatory at Milford Sound allows visitors to see the unusual black coral, red coral, anemones, starfish and fish that live in the fiord. Apart from day trips in the Milford Sound, full-day and overnight cruises take visitors out of the sound to the open Tasman Sea, with stops at other sounds.

⑤

Lake Monowai

In the south of Fiordland, this pretty lake is surrounded by pristine native bush, making it the perfect setting for cycling, boating and fishing. With family camping grounds and good short walks, such as the Borland Nature Walk, this is a pleasant place to bring the kids. Nearby to the north is the Green Lake, while to the south lies the deepest lake in the country, Lake Hauroko, reached from Clifden.

Surveying the sights from Key Summit, on the Routeburn walking track

Did You Know?

In Māori, tranquil Doubtful Sound is known as Patea, or "the place of silence".

⑥

DOUBTFUL SOUND

🅰A6 🚢From Pearl Harbour, Manapouri, then coach 🌐doc.govt.nz

Only the growls of lazing fur seals, the splash of leaping bottlenose dolphins, and the lapping of the water against your boat or kayak will interupt the tranquility of the Doubtful Sound. With its abundant wildlife and dramatic scenery, Patea is bound to leave you as speechless as its Māori name suggests.

In 1770, when Captain James Cook, on his voyage to New Zealand, looked out at the narrow entrance to this fiord, he was doubtful that he could safely get his vessel in and out. Since then, this stretch of water has been called the Doubtful Sound, although its Māori name is perhaps more appropriate given the meditative state that the fiord inspires.

The 40-km- (25-mile-) long fiord is Fiordland's second largest and, at 421 m (1,380 ft), the deepest. It is a remote, unspoiled wilderness that supports a rich array of bird and marine life, including crested penguins, fur seals and bottlenose dolphins. Getting there is an adventure in itself, involving two boat trips and a coach ride over a mountain pass.

TIPS FOR VISITORS

The trip from Manapouri to the mouth of the fiord takes eight hours and can only be undertaken with a commercial tour operator. There are several operators to choose from, including Real Journeys *(real journeys.co.nz)* and Deep Cove Charters *(doubtfulsoundcruise. nz)*, which offer overnight cruises with the option to explore by sea kayak. Visitors can order a picnic lunch or snackpack when booking but are advised to take additional food, as well as insect repellent, warm clothing and a waterproof jacket. Choose to visit in winter for clear views, little rain and fewer boats.

←
An aerial view of Hall Arm, a branch of the enchanting Doubtful Sound

① Boat cruises take visitors from Deep Cove to the mouth of the Doubtful Sound, taking in awe-inspiring scenery en route.

② Real Journey's *Fiordland Navigator* is designed to look like a traditional scow.

③ A pod of bottlenose dolphins may be seen playing in the waters at Malaspina Reach.

3

OTAGO PENINSULA

⚠C7 **ℹ Visitor Centre, 26 Princes St, Dunedin;**
www.otago-peninsula.co.nz

The 24-km- (15-mile-) long Otago Peninsula offers a wide variety of attractions, including rare and unusual wildlife, historic buildings, beautiful woodland gardens, secluded bays and vast swathes of coastal scenery.

Royal Albatross Centre

🏠 Taiaroa Head
🕐 10:15am–dusk daily
🌐 albatross.org.nz

Located at the mouth of Otago Harbour, the prominent Taiaroa headland is home to the only mainland royal albatross colony in the world. Opened in 1989, the centre contains excellent displays about these magnificent birds, whose wingspan can reach 3 m (10 ft). The centre offers guided tours to an observatory where the albatrosses can be seen. Prebooking is recommended, and viewing areas should not

be visited unaccompanied. A colony of Stewart Island shags is also visible from the observatory. Blue penguin viewing tours are available each evening; these delightful little creatures can be watched scurrying up the beach to their burrows after a day out foraging at sea.

Taiaroa Head's other main attraction is the Armstrong disappearing gun, a 15-cm (6-inch) diameter naval defence gun installed in 1886 during the "Russian scare". Designed to pop out of the ground, fire and then recoil back into its pit, it is the only one of its kind in the world still in working order and in its original position.

2

Larnach Castle

🏠 145 Camp Rd **🕐 9am–5pm**
daily **🌐 larnachcastle.co.nz**

Some 14 km (9 miles) from central Dunedin along the "high" road, Lanarch Castle is New Zealand's only castle and has been designated a Garden of International Significance. Built between 1871 and 1885 by financier, businessman and politician William J M Larnach for his wife Eliza, the grand stone mansion has many fine features, including elaborately carved and decorated ceilings and a large, hanging staircase. A ballroom was added as a

↑ Splendid Larnach Castle, built in fine Scottish Baronial style

↑ Sunset over Sandfly Bay on the unspoilt Otago Peninsula

complete wing for Larnach's daughter. Visitors can climb up narrow stone steps for views from the top of the tower.

In 1967 the Barker family bought the castle which was by then derelict and spent many years restoring it. Margaret Barker has worked especially hard to restore the gardens and grounds, and they now contain a fine show of native and exotic plants.

The castle is a stopping point on a circular driving tour of the peninsula. On the way out follow the "high" Highcliff Road running over the top of the peninsula, returning via the "low" Portobello Road along the coast. The loop offers stunning views over the rolling peninsula.

 ③ 🏵️ Ⓜ️ 🖥️

Glenfalloch Woodland Gardens

🏠 430 Portobello Rd
🕐 Dawn to dusk daily
🌐 glenfalloch.co.nz

Situated on Portobello Road, 10 km (6 miles) from Dunedin, the Glenfalloch Woodland Gardens have been attracting visitors since the 1870s. An elegant homestead, built in 1871, summer tearooms and

a pottery, its wares for sale, are sheltered in grounds containing mature trees, shrubs and a stream. The gardens are ablaze with rhododendrons and azaleas in spring, and in summer there are glorious displays of fuchsias and roses.

 ④

Sandfly Bay Recreation Reserve

🏠 Seal Point Rd 📞 (03) 477 0677

Known for its native fauna and flora, this reserve offers brilliant views of the peninsula's coastline and cliff tops. Among the many outstanding attractions, the most striking are the yellow-eyed penguins. The best time to see them is late afternoon/early evening; a marked track leads up to a public hide near the southern end of the beach.

⑤

Otakou

🏠 Tamatea Rd, off Harrington Point Rd
🕐 Daily, by appointment
🌐 otakourunaka.co.nz

Otakou is the site of one of the earliest Māori settlements in the area, and it was this word that was anglicized

PENGUIN PARADE

The yellow-eyed penguin is found only on the Otago Peninsula and isolated east coast areas of Otago and Southland. During the nesting season, you can view them at close range from hides at the award-winning Penguin Place, on the road to Taiaroa Head (penguinplace.co.nz).

to "Otago" to give the surrounding province its name. The local church and meeting house were built in 1840 to commemorate the centenary of the signing of the historic Treaty of Waitangi (p56). What at first sight appear to be carvings in the stonework are actually moulded concrete.

4

OAMARU

🗺 C6 🚌 Humber St 🚌 Cnr Eden & Thames sts
ℹ️ 1 Thames St; www.visitoamaru.co.nz

The main town of North Otago and service centre for a rich agricultural hinterland, Oamaru is a pretty town with wide, treelined streets, fine historic buildings, well-kept gardens, galleries, beaches and colonies of rare penguins. The buildings were fashioned in the 1880s from Oamaru stone, a local cream-coloured limestone which is easily cut, carved and moulded. Oamaru was the childhood home of the internationally reputed novelist Janet Frame, and today is also famous as the "Steampunk capital" of New Zealand.

①

Oamaru Blue Penguin Colony

📍 2 Waterfront Rd 🕙 10am-8pm daily 🚫 25 Apr, 25 & 26 Dec 🌐 penguins.co.nz

At Friendly Bay, in an old quarry at the end of Oamaru's harbour, visitors can see tiny blue penguins going out to sea to feed, and returning at dusk. From another viewing area, the penguins can be observed in their nesting boxes (note that flash photography is not permitted).

Just around the headland is Bushy Beach, where yellow-eyed penguins can be seen from a viewing hide.

---

②

Oamaru Public Gardens

📍 Chelmer St 🕙 Daily, until sunset

Established in 1876, these gardens contain traditional features such as rose gardens, ponds, an azalea lawn and rhododendron dell. A band

→

Oamaru's waterfront, where small sailcraft take shelter in the harbour

rotunda, summerhouse, aviary, peacock house and marble fountain are other attractions.

---

③

Totara Estate

📍 State Hwy 1 ℹ️ (03) 433 1269 🕙 10am-4pm daily 🚫 Jun-Aug

About 8 km (5 miles) south of Oamaru, this is where New Zealand's first shipment of frozen mutton to England in

| 0 metres | 500 |
| 0 yards | 500 |

N ↑

Oamaru Public Gardens ②

Totara Estate 7 km (4 miles)

North Otago Museum

Oamaru Station

④ Victorian Precinct

Whitestone City

Oamaru Farmers Market

King George Park

Oamaru Old Cemetery

Oamaru Blue Penguin Colony ①

Oamaru Lookout Point

Streets: DEE ST, RIBBLE STREET, THAMES STREET, FRANCE ST, EDEN STREET, REED STREET, ALN STREET, YARE ST, CROSS ST, RECOQUET STREET, CHELMER ST, ISIS STREET, STOUR ST, ROTHER ST, SEVERN STREET, ITCHEN STREET, WANSBECK STREET, URE STREET, TYNE STREET, ARUN STREET, ESPLANADE, LUNE ST, GRETA ST, HULL ST, TWEED ST, WHARFE ST, TEES ST, TEST STREET, PERTH STREET, UPPER URE ST, TAMAR STREET, AVON STREET, WATERFRONT ROAD, TILL ST

Totara Estate 7 km (4 miles)

SHOP

Oamaru Farmers Market
On Sunday mornings, hunt for local produce and baked goods to the sounds of live music in the Victorian Precinct.

📍 1 Wansbeck St
🌐 oamarufarmers market.co.nz

1882 was processed, heralding the beginning of its most important industry. Limestone buildings house displays on the industry's history.

④
Victorian Precinct

📍 2 Harbour Street
🌐 victorianoamaru.co.nz

In this pedestrian zone, which contains some of the town's finest heritage streetscapes, the past is brought alive in art galleries, antique and book shops, and craft workshops. There's a steam train to ride, and ice cream shops, cafés, bakeries and craft breweries to provide refreshment. **Whitestone City**, set in an old feed store, offers a taste of life in the Victorian era: kids can dress up, play games and ride high-wheeled bicycles in the recreated streets and shops. Each November, elaborately costumed ladies and gents reimagine the 19th century at the annual Victorian Fete.

Whitestone City
📍 12 Harbour St 🕐 10am-6:30pm daily 🌐 white stonecity.com

STEAMPUNK CAPITAL

Steampunk is a cultural genre that mixes science fiction with the steam-powered technology of the 19th century. The movement has been officially recognized by Oxford University's Museum of the History of Science. Nowhere in the world, however, has embraced this ethos like Oamaru. Suitably sited in the Victorian Precinct is Steampunk HQ, where the whistling steam engines and bizarre sculptures are strangely fascinating (*www.steampunk oamaru.co.nz*).

 Historic limestone buildings lining the streets of Oamaru's Victorian Precinct

⑤

MOUNT ASPIRING NATIONAL PARK

🅰 B6 🚌 Ardmore St ⓘ Wanaka: Ardmore St, (03) 443 7660; Queenstown: 50 Stanley St, (03) 442 7935 🅦 doc.govt.nz

Encompassed within this national park's 3,555 sq km (1,373 sq mile) area, the diverse scenery encompasses snow- and glacier-clad mountains, remote wilderness, rugged rock faces, spectacular forested river valleys and picturesque river flats.

Mount Aspiring National Park enjoys World Heritage status as part of the Te Wāhipounamu/ Southwest New Zealand World Heritage Area, which stretches from Aoraki/Mount Cook to the southern tip of Fiordland. In the west, the Olivine Wilderness Area is maintained in an undeveloped state, without tracks or huts, for wilderness recreation. In the east, a forest track from State Highway 6 leads to the 30 m (98 ft) Thunder Creek Falls, which drop from a notch in a rock. Also accessible from State Highway 6, Mount Brewster is a popular climbing and camping spot. Nearby, at the Gates of Haast bridge, the Haast River roars down a steep-sided gorge. Exploring the park on foot is varied, ranging from short walks from the road to country circuits for fit hikers.

↑ Glacial streams from the mountains beyond wend through the lush green Matukituki Valley

INSIDER TIP
The Blue Pools Walk

This soul-satisfying nature walk is only a gentle 1.5 km (1 mile) in length. The track begins at the Blue Pools car park on Haast Pass-Makarora Road. The route takes in azure pools of crystal-clear water teeming with trout, native beech forests and a wooden suspension bridge.

① Hikers cross a babbling brook surrounded by astonishing mountain scenery.

② An isolated mountain hut sitting above the clouds over the national park.

③ Pristine azure waters of the Makarora River's Blue Pools.

← The icy pyramidal peak of Mount Aspiring, the "Matterhorn of the South"

BIRDLIFE IN MOUNT ASPIRING NATIONAL PARK

Some 59 species, 38 of them native, inhabit the national park. Especially symbolic are the kea, rock wren and blue duck. The kea is an inquisitive bird well known for its interest in hikers' food. The hardy rock wren lives high in the hills in one of the harshest environments in the park, while pairs of blue ducks can be seen feeding on vegetation and insects in the swift mountain streams, especially in the hanging valleys.

THE KEA BIRD

Did You Know?

Mount Aspiring's Māori name is Tititea, which translates as "steep peak of glistening white".

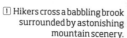

6

DUNEDIN

C7 ✈ **25 km (16 miles) S of city centre** 🚌 **Anzac Ave** 🚍 **Intercity, 7 Halsey St / Dunedin Railway Station** ℹ **26 Princes St, www.dunedinnz.com**

The joy of exploring Dunedin is that it's both compact and full of interest, with some of the most distinctive and architecturally diverse buildings in the country.

①

The Octagon

When the site of Dunedin, or "New Edinburgh", was first assessed in 1846 by its Edinburgh-based surveyors, the Octagon was planned as the focal point. More than 150 years later, the Octagon continues to fulfil that role. It has watched over a passing parade of festivals, protests, parties and royal visits, as well as waving off and welcoming sporting heroes.

This small oasis in the heart of the city – a popular lunchtime spot – is surrounded by a number of fine buildings. A large bronze statue of Scottish poet Robert Burns, erected in 1887, has a prominent place in front of St Paul's Cathedral. Burns' nephew, the Reverend Thomas Burns, was the spiritual leader for the first group of Scottish settlers to arrive in Dunedin in 1848.

②

Municipal Chambers

🏛 **48 The Octagon** 🕐 **8:30am-5pm daily (to 6pm Nov-Mar)** ❌ **Public hols** 🌐 **dunedin.govt.nz**

Completed in 1880, the Municipal Chambers is an excellent example of the use of Oamaru stone (p256). It has undergone considerable restoration and refurbishment both inside and out. It is home to the Council Chambers, where city councillors meet, and features a number of reception and meeting rooms.

The size of the chambers is massive, as it is able to incorporate both the 450-seat Glenroy Auditorium and the 2,100-seat Town Hall.

③

Dunedin Public Art Gallery

🏛 **30 The Octagon** 🕐 **10am-5pm daily** 🌐 **dunedin.art.museum**

This modern gallery, designed to work in harmony with the Octagon's historic buildings, has one of the best collections

↑ Gainsborough's *Charlotte, Princess Talbot*, Dunedin Public Art Gallery

 Must See

 GREAT VIEW
Signal Hill

From Opohoi Road to the north of the city, the road up Signal Hill leads to a monument built in 1940 to mark 100 years of British sovereignty. It has superb views of the city, upper harbour and Otago Peninsula.

↑ Dunedin and its harbour seen from the green hills that overlook the bay

of European art in the country, including works by Turner and Monet. It features exhibitions of traditional and contemporary art, and a special gallery dedicated to the works of renowned Dunedin artist Frances Hodgkins. There is sometimes an entrance charge for special exhibitions.

---

④
First Church

🏠 415 Moray Place 📞 (03) 477 7118 🕐 8am–6pm daily

The flagship of the Presbyterian Church in Otago, First Church, consecrated in 1873, is considered to be architect Robert Lawson's greatest contribution to Dunedin's rich architectural heritage (p263). Of note are its beautiful rose window, wooden ceiling and 56-m- (184-ft-) high spire.

The church has undergone considerable restoration work to repair its exterior. Its history is told at the church's heritage centre. Bell Hill, on which First Church stands, was lowered by about 12 m (40 ft) to improve the city's traffic.

Services are held on Sundays, in English, Cook Islands Māori and Samoan.

⑤
St Paul's Cathedral

🏠 The Octagon 🕐 7am–7pm daily 🌐 stpauls.net.nz

Consecrated in 1919, the Anglican St Paul's stands high above the Octagon on an elevated site, with a broad staircase leading to its doors. It owes its prominent position in a predominantly Presbyterian settlement to the generosity of Johnny Jones, an early whaler and trader. The cathedral, which replaced a smaller church built on the site in 1863, has many fine architectural details, including a vaulted stone ceiling.

The cathedral has a world-renowned choir and hosts regular music events.

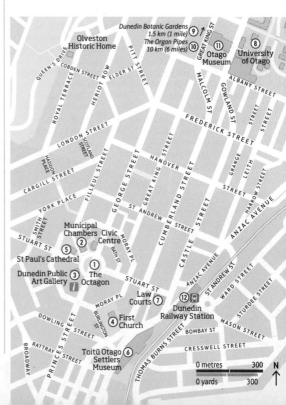

PICTURE PERFECT
Tunnel vision

Tunnel Beach, 7 km (4 miles) south of the city, is home to wind-and-sea sculpted cliffs. Before descending to the beach, snap a shot of the spectacular sandstone arch that juts dramatically out into the ocean.

⑥

Toitū Otago Settlers Museum

🏠 31 Queens Gardens 🕐 10am–5pm daily 🚫 Good Fri, 25 Dec 🌐 toituosm.com

New Zealand's oldest social history museum occupies its original Edwardian galleries, with the addition of a dazzling modern entrance lobby. The museum focuses on the lives of the province's settlers from Southern Māori to Scottish pioneers to Chinese gold miners (Chinese New Year is enthusiastically celebrated in the city). The displays range from early photographs and household goods to implements and vehicles, including two large steam locomotives, one of which dates back to the 1870s. The Smith Portrait Gallery showcases old photographs and paintings of the early settlers and the ICT section displays the region's first digital technology. A public archive and exhibition space are also accessible.

⑦
Law Courts

🏠 41 Stuart St

The courts were completed in 1902 to a design by government architect John Campbell. The building is distinguished by its combination of local Port Chalmers bluestone and lighter Oamaru stone.

Standing just around the corner, in total contrast, is the red-brick former Dunedin Prison, built to another Campbell design which mimics many aspects of London's New Scotland Yard, although on a smaller scale. Completed in 1895, it also served as the Dunedin Police Station until a new building was built in the mid-1990s.

⑧
University of Otago

🏠 Leith St 🕐 Grounds and public areas only 🚫 Public hols 🌐 otago.ac.nz

Founded in 1869, the University of Otago – New Zealand's oldest university – plays a crucial role in the life of the city. The clock tower registry building dates from 1878, while the semi-detached houses close to its northern end were built in 1879. The grounds are a pleasant place to wander.

→
Otago university's registry building with clock tower

⑨
Dunedin Botanic Gardens

🏠 Opoho Rd 🕐 Dawn to dusk daily; glasshouses 10am–4pm 🌐 dunedin botanicgarden.co.nz

Dunedin's extensive Botanic Gardens were the first to be established in New Zealand, in 1868. The area's

highly varied topography and microclimates are used to grow a diverse range of plants. The flat lower gardens are home to the more formal displays – lawns interspersed with trees and native bush, and formal flower gardens – and to the Edwardian Winter Garden, first opened in 1908. On the hill, the upper gardens include more than 3,000 rhododendron varieties in the renowned Rhododendron Dell. These provide a springtime feast for the eyes. The gardens are the first in New Zealand to be rated as a Garden of International Significance.

The Organ Pipes

🏠 Mount Cargill Rd

Strange multi-sided basalt columns, known as "the organ pipes", are a reminder of

←

The prow-like entrance lobby to the Toitū Otago Settlers Museum

Dunedin's volcanic past. Reaching them requires a walk of at least an hour from a signpost on Mount Cargill Road, north of the city. The panoramic views are a bonus.

Otago Museum

🏠 419 Great King St
🕙 10am–5pm daily
🌐 otagomuseum.nz

The displays in the large, Classical-style Otago Museum, opened in 1877, introduce visitors to the region's human, cultural and natural history. There are halls dealing with pre-European Māori life, Pacific culture, marine life, and archaeology of the ancient world. The museum also houses one of New Zealand's leading maritime exhibitions, treasures of Māori life, a Victorian-inspired "Animal Attic" and a 3D planetarium (for which there is an entrance charge). The interactive Discovery World science centre includes a tropical forest with exotic butterflies.

ROBERT LAWSON

Many of Dunedin's finest Victorian and Scottish Edwardian-style buildings are attributed to Scottish-born architect Robert Lawson (1833–1902). He moved to Dunedin from Melbourne – where his career had not taken off – after winning a competition to design the First Church (p261). He went on to design buildings such as the Municipal Chambers, Otago Boys High School and Knox Church in George Street.

DUNEDIN RAILWAY STATION

🏠 Anzac Ave 🕐 8am–5pm Mon–Fri, 8:30am–3pm Sat, Sun & public hols

A five-minute walk from the Ocatagon, Dunedin's Railway Station is one of New Zealand's finest historic buildings and one of the best examples of railway architecture in the southern hemisphere.

Although it is rather small by international standards, the Railway Station's delightful proportions lend it an air of grandeur. Opened in 1906, the Flemish Renaissance-style building was designed by New Zealand Railways architect George Troup, whose elaborate detailing on the façade of the building earned him the nickname "Gingerbread George". The tiled booking hall within is magnificent, reflecting the splendour of Dunedin's most prosperous era. While there is no longer an intercity passenger service to Dunedin, the station is now the departure point for local scenic rail tours.

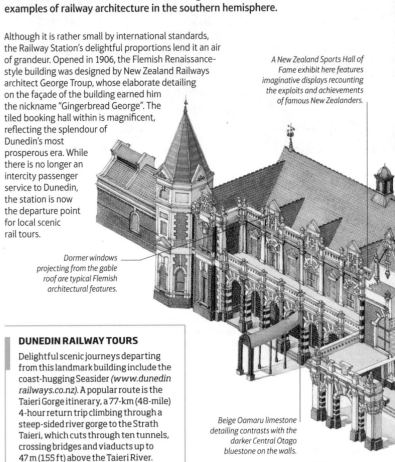

A New Zealand Sports Hall of Fame exhibit here features imaginative displays recounting the exploits and achievements of famous New Zealanders.

Dormer windows projecting from the gable roof are typical Flemish architectural features.

Beige Oamaru limestone detailing contrasts with the darker Central Otago bluestone on the walls.

DUNEDIN RAILWAY TOURS

Delightful scenic journeys departing from this landmark building include the coast-hugging Seasider *(www.dunedin railways.co.nz)*. A popular route is the Taieri Gorge itinerary, a 77-km (48-mile) 4-hour return trip climbing through a steep-sided river gorge to the Strath Taieri, which cuts through ten tunnels, crossing bridges and viaducts up to 47 m (155 ft) above the Taieri River.

Did You Know?

The station's mile-long platform becomes a catwalk during the annual iD Dunedin Fashion Week.

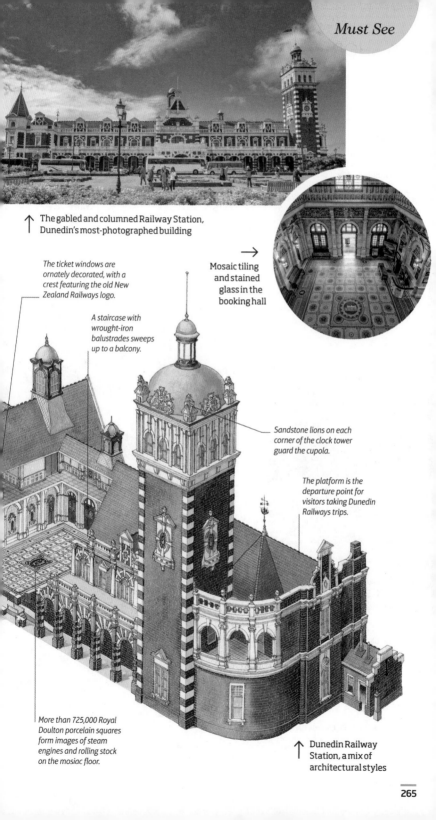

↑ The gabled and columned Railway Station, Dunedin's most-photographed building

→ Mosaic tiling and stained glass in the booking hall

The ticket windows are ornately decorated, with a crest featuring the old New Zealand Railways logo.

A staircase with wrought-iron balustrades sweeps up to a balcony.

Sandstone lions on each corner of the clock tower guard the cupola.

The platform is the departure point for visitors taking Dunedin Railways trips.

More than 725,000 Royal Doulton porcelain squares form images of steam engines and rolling stock on the mosaic floor.

↑ Dunedin Railway Station, a mix of architectural styles

A SHORT WALK
CENTRAL DUNEDIN

Distance 1.5 km (1 mile) **Nearest bus stop** Intercity, Halsey St **Time** 25 minutes

Dunedin has close historical links with the Scottish city of Edinburgh. Not only is Dunedin the old Gaelic name for Edinburgh, but many of its street names are Scottish and several Scottish traditions have been preserved since the first Presbyterian settlers arrived in 1848. The Octagon, so-called because of its eight sides, gives the city a central focus. A stroll around it and beyond takes in a number of Victorian and Edwardian public buildings, among the finest in the country; its many cafés and restaurants are perfect for a rest stop.

St Paul's Cathedral has the only vaulted stone ceiling in New Zealand (p261).

START

Built around 1900 as residences for country folk, the **Stuart Street terraces** now house shops and restaurants.

Dunedin Public Art Gallery (p261)

First Church (p261)

MORAY PLACE

BURLINGTON STREET

RATTRAY ST

CUMBERLAND

↑ The Dunedin Chinese Garden, celebrating Otago's Chinese heritage

Queens Gardens

The **Dunedin Chinese Garden** is an authentic example of a late Ming/early Ching Dynasty Scholar's garden.

The **Toitū Otago Settlers Museum** tells the story of Otago and its settlers. One wing is dedicated to old forms of transport (p262).

← Robert Burns statue in front of the Municipal Chambers and St Paul's Cathedral

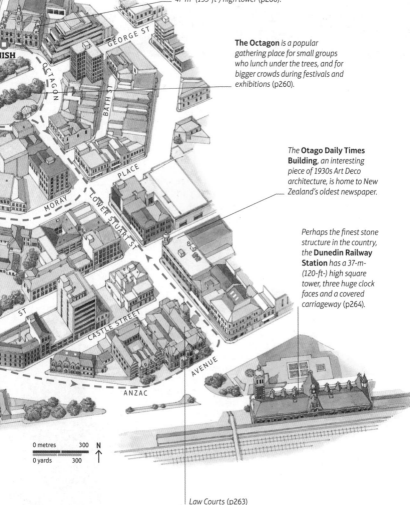

Built in 1880, the **Municipal Chambers building** *is topped by a 47-m- (155-ft-) high tower (p260).*

The Octagon *is a popular gathering place for small groups who lunch under the trees, and for bigger crowds during festivals and exhibitions (p260).*

The **Otago Daily Times Building**, *an interesting piece of 1930s Art Deco architecture, is home to New Zealand's oldest newspaper.*

Perhaps the finest stone structure in the country, the **Dunedin Railway Station** *has a 37-m- (120-ft-) high square tower, three huge clock faces and a covered carriageway (p264).*

GEORGE ST

OCTAGON

NISH

BATH ST

MORAY

PLACE

LOWER STUART ST

ST

CASTLE STREET

ANZAC

AVENUE

0 metres 300
0 yards 300

N ↑

Law Courts (p263)

INVERCARGILL

 B7 ✈ 2 km (1.2 miles) W of city 🚌 ℹ Wachner Place; www.invercargillnz.com

New Zealand's southernmost city has wide, tree-lined streets and many parks. Settled in the 1850s and 1860s by Scottish immigrants, its cultural links with Scotland are reflected in the streets named after Scottish rivers and in its many historic buildings. To the west of the city are sheltered beaches and walking tracks.

① Dee and Tay Streets

Invercargill's early prosperity resulted in the construction of many fine commercial buildings. At the northern end of Dee Street lies the former Dee Street Hospital, the oldest public hospital buildings in New Zealand, and the quaint former Porter's Lodge, built around 1866 and reputed to be the oldest house in Invercargill. Nearby is St Paul's Presbyterian Church, whose square tower houses bells manufactured in Italy from captured guns. Further down, the 1901 red-brick Alexander Building is noted for its eclectic style, while the Grand Hotel opposite has fine iron balconies. At the intersection of Dee Street and Tay Street (Invercargill's main street) stands the impressive Troopers' Memorial flanked by three elegant bank buildings, erected between 1876 and 1926. In Tay Street is the imposing Renaissance-style Civic Theatre, completed in 1906, and St John's Anglican Church, noted for its stained-glass windows and timber barrel-vaulted ceiling. The Lombardy-style Romanesque First Presbyterian Church, also in Tay Street, features an unusual, square 32-m- (105-ft-) high tower.

② Water Tower

🏠 101 Doon St ⏱ 1.30– 4.30 pm Sun

A distinctive landmark in the city, the 42-m- (138-ft-) high red brick water tower was completed in 1889. A fine example of Neo-Romanesque industrial

→ Invercargill's distinctive red brick Water Tower

← Strolling the wide beech-lined promenade of Queen's Park

STRIKING STREET ART

Invercargill is known for the many bold sculptures that decorate its boulevards. Most impressive is the *Blade of Grass*, a steel kinetic block on Esk Street. Don Street's *Umbrella* is a steel sundial and star map bearing all the names of local residents at the time of the millennium. *The Cube of Learning* on Tay Street references the building blocks of knowledge. Local fauna is represented by the *Weka Statue* on Esk Street, denoting the native bird sometimes called a bush hen, and by the massive *Whale Tail* on Russell Square.

Did You Know?

Motorbike speed demon and Invercargill resident Burt Munro set his first speed record in 1938.

design of the time, the tower's ornate brickwork is crowned by a decorative cupola.

Fastest Indian starring Antony Hopkins as Burt Munro, a local motorbike riding folk hero. The town is a go-to destination for fans of motorbikes and classic cars, with this automotive museum chronicling motoring history with its vast collection of classic vehicles.

③

Queen's Park

🅰 Gala St ⏰ Daily

The best-known reserve in the city centre is Queen's Park, a generous botanical reserve featuring formal gardens, rose gardens and the Steans Memorial Winter Garden. There is also a small wildlife park with deer and wallabies, an aviary and a challenging 18-hole golf course.

④

Bill Richardson Transport World

🅰 491 Tay St ⏰ 10am–5pm daily 🌐 transportworld.co.nz

Invercargill was made famous by the 2005 film *The World's*

8

STEWART ISLAND

🅐A7 ✈From Invercargill (20 mins) ⛴From Bluff (60 mins)
ℹRakiura National Park Visitor Centre, 15 Main Rd; www.
stewartisland.co.nz

Separated from South Island by the 32-km (20-mile)
Foveaux Strait, Stewart Island's unspoiled inlets and
beaches, bush-clad hills, rugged coastline and native
birdlife combine to make it a naturalist's paradise.

①
Oban

Oban, Stewart Island's only settlement, sits snugly around the picturesque shores of Halfmoon Bay. Easily explored on foot, this tiny town boasts a number of good seafood restaurants. It's also home to the **Rakiura Museum**, which provides a fascinating insight into the island's past. Exhibits cover such topics as: Māori settlement; seafaring (with a focus on whaling and sealing); tin mining; and timber milling. From Oban many short tracks lead through beautiful bush to places of scenic or historic interest, and to lookouts with stunning views, including Observation Rock, which provides splendid views over Paterson Inlet towards Ulva Island. On a clear, summer evening it is easy to see why the Māori name for Stewart Island means "the land of the glowing skies". Beautiful beaches also lie within walking distance to the north and east of the town. A three-hour return walk through coastal forest to Ackers Point Lighthouse goes past one of New Zealand's oldest buildings, Ackers Cottage,

Sheltered Oban harbour, sprinkled with yachts and fishing boats

built in 1835. The Ryan's Creek Track is a three- to four-hour loop through coastal forest above Paterson Inlet.

Boat charters available from Oban cater for a range of interests, including fishing, sightseeing and wildlife spotting, or, for the more active, diving, kayak hire and guided sea kayak excursions.

Rakiura Museum
🅐Ayr St 🕐10am–1:30pm
Mon–Sat, noon–2pm Sun
🌐rakiuramuseum.co.nz

Black Rock Point
Foveaux Strait
Codfish Island
Mount Anglem 980 m (1070 yd)
Bluff 40 km (25 miles) ↗
Stewart Island
Titī Islands
Oban ⓵ ⑥
Ernest Islands
Mason Bay
Paterson Inlet ②
③ Ulva Island
④ Ocean Beach
⑤
Big Glory Bay
Doughboy Bay
Rakeahua River
Mount Allen 750 m (820 yd)
Lords River
Tin Range
Kopeka River

Pearl Island

0 kilometres 15
0 miles 15

N ↑

South Cape

Did You Know?

Stewart Island was first settled by Māori in the 13th century; Europeans arrived in the 1820s.

Paterson Inlet

Over the hill from Halfmoon Bay is Paterson Inlet, which extends deep into the hinterland. Charter boats and a water taxi can be hired in Oban and Golden Bay for sightseers, divers and those wanting to catch their own fish. Look out for yellow-eyed and little blue penguins, as well as seals and dolphins. The remains of an old sawmill and whaling station are also accessible from the inlet.

③

Ulva Island

Located in the centre of Paterson Inlet, Ulva Island is a 10-minute trip by water taxi from the wharf at Golden Bay. The island is predator free, creating a sanctuary where visitors can get a close look at native New Zealand birds.

Ocean Beach

"Kiwi spotting" is an experience unique to Stewart Island. Licensed tour operators take small groups by boat to the Neck in Little Glory Bay, then on foot through the bush to Ocean Beach where the Stewart Island brown kiwi can be seen feeding as darkness falls.

Big Glory Bay

Salmon and mussel farming have become important industries in Paterson Inlet. A boat trip takes visitors to a salmon farm at Big Glory Bay, past seal colonies and shag rookeries, with a stopover at Ulva Island on the way.

Titī Islands

Muttonbirds, or sooty shear-waters, breed on Stewart Island's many offshore islands after a round-the-world migration. Young birds are harvested for food by descendants of the Rakiura Māori. By day, Ackers Point lighthouse gives panoramic views of the islands, and at night, from October to April, visitors can hear the mutton-birds returning to land. Some tour operators are licensed to take visitors to the islands to view the birds from the boat.

TRAMPING THE ISLAND TRACKS

Stewart Island's long-distance trails take visitors into some of New Zealand's most beautiful bush. The Rakiura Track is a popular three-day circuit that climbs a high, forested ridge and traverses the sheltered Paterson Inlet. There are also 10- to 14-day North-West and Southern Circuits. Route maps and hut and camp passes can be obtained from the visitor centre in Oban.

A hiker gazing out over Lake Hawea and the mountains in the distance ↑

EXPERIENCE MORE

Lake Hawea

🅰B6

Tucked among hills and mountains, the bright blue waters of Lake Hawea make it one of the most beautiful of the southern lakes. The lake, which is 410 m (1,345 ft) deep in places, is separated from the equally beautiful Lake Wanaka by a narrow 35-km (22-mile) isthmus, known as "the neck".

Lake Hawea is a popular holiday haven. It is also well known for its good trout and landlocked salmon fishing and for various boating activities. The small town of Hawea on the lake's southern shores is the main base for outdoor activities.

Lindis Pass

🅰B6

The main inland link between Otago and the Waitaki Basin, the Lindis Pass climbs through dramatic rocky gorges before reaching the tussock-covered hills of a Department of Conservation reserve near the summit. First used by early Māori as a route to get to Lakes Wanaka and Hawea in summer, it is now walked by holiday-makers.

In 1858, John McLean established the 2,000 sq km (772 sq mile) Morven Hills Station. Many of the original buildings can still be seen about 15 km (9 miles) south of the summit. These include McLean's original homestead and a massive stone wool-shed, built about 1880, which was capable of holding up to 1,500 sheep.

Wanaka

🅰B6 ℹ100 Ardmore St; www.lakewanaka.co.nz

Located at the southern end of the lake, Wanaka is one of the country's favourite holiday spots. The willow-lined shores and bays of Lake Wanaka are popular in summer for boating, fishing and water-skiing, while in winter skiers and snowboarders flock to the local ski areas. Wanaka is home to New Zealand's famed helicopter skiing operations, with ski touring and summer hiking in the nearby Mount Aspiring National Park (p258).

HEAD FOR THE HIGHEST HEIGHTS

Wanaka's dramatic landscape can be experienced through a host of awesome adventure activities. Scale the world's highest waterfall with Wild Wire Wanaka's via ferrata course (www.wildwire.co.nz) or take to the skies in a light aircraft on an utterly exhilarating flying lesson (www.learntoflynz.com).

Aside from the area's natural features, there is plenty to visit and see around the town. **Warbirds and Wheels**, located at Wanaka Airport, combines classic cars with a variety of World War II fighter aircraft, such as a Hawker Hurricane, Tiger Moth, Vampire, Chipmunk, a replica of an SE5A, and rare Russian Polikarpovs. Illustrated displays explain the role of New Zealand fighter pilots and crews in several theatres of war. Visitors can also see aircraft being restored in the maintenance hangar. "Warbirds Over Wanaka", a major biennial airshow involving military aircraft, is held every second Easter in even-numbered years. It features aircraft from New Zealand as well as overseas in acrobatic displays and mock battles. Wanaka's open skies and alpine scenery provide an amazing backdrop.

Next to Wanaka Airport is the **National Transport & Toy Museum**. Its large private collection of more than 13,000 items includes memorabilia, such as toys and models, as well as military vehicles and aircraft. A special exhibit is a

huge Russian Antonov AN-2, the world's largest single engine biplane.

Stuart Landsborough's Puzzling World is based around "The Great Maze", 1.5 km (1 mile) of three-dimensional wooden passages and under- and over-bridges. Other attractions include the incredible Illusion Rooms, a Hologram Hall, the bizarre Tumbling Towers/Tilted House, and the Puzzle Centre and Café where you can take a break and try to solve one of the many challenging puzzles on display.

Like many other parts of Central Otago, Wanaka's climate is proving ideal for grape growing. **Rippon Vineyard**, established in 1974 just 4 km (2.5 miles) from the centre of town, is one of the pioneering growers and wine-makers of the region. The vineyard produces wines from a number of grape varieties.

Warbirds and Wheels

⊗ 🏛 🏠 Wanaka Airport ⏰ 8am–4pm daily 🌐 warbirdsandwheels.com

📷 PICTURE PERFECT
Powder Blue Wanaka Lake

Wander towards Lake Wanaka, bordering the north of the town. From here you can snap stunning shots of the town's famous lonely willow tree, reflected in the lake's shimmering blue depths and encircled by snowy peaks.

National Transport & Toy Museum

⊗ 🔄 🏛 🏠 891 Wanaka-Luggate Hwy ⏰ 8:30am–5pm daily 🌐 nttmuseumwanaka.co.nz

Stuart Landsborough's Puzzling World

⊗ 🔄 🔄 🏛 🏠 State Hwy 6 ⏰ 8:30am–5:30pm daily 🌐 puzzlingworld.com

Rippon Vineyard

⊗ 🏛 🏠 242 Mt Aspiring Rd ⏰ 11am–5pm daily 🚫 May–June, 25 Dec 🌐 rippon.co.nz

→

Lake Wanaka's lone willow tree, set against Mount Aspiring National Park

EAT

Fleurs Place

Perched on the edge of the Moeraki Bay, with stunning sea views, this place serves up some of the best fresh seafood on the South Island.

 C7 169 Haven St, Moeraki fleurs place.com

$$$

Haast

B6 State Hwy 6 & Haast-Jackson Bay Rd; www.westcoast.co.nz

A tiny community on the coast where the broad Haast River meets the sea, Haast is little more than a stopover and supply point for people travelling between the West Coast and the southern lakes, although it does offer good surf and river fishing. The visitor centre provides information on walks and tracks in the area, as well as maps, souvenirs and visitor publications. The staff can also advise on track and weather conditions in this high rainfall

area. Fill up with fuel here before driving over the pass to Wanaka.

The road south to the fishing village of Jackson Bay provides a number of walking and sightseeing opportunities, such as the Hapuka Estuary Walk, the Cascade Viewpoint and the Smoothwater Bay track at Jackson Bay itself. The Wharekai Te Kau Walk leads to the Okahu Wildlife Refuge.

There are several places of interest north of Haast, such as the Dune Lake Walk through dense coastal forest stunted by wind at Ship Creek, and the stunning Knights Point viewpoint.

Further on, past Lake Moeraki, the Monro Beach Walk passes through luxuriant coastal forest to a remote beach where (from July to December) Fiordland crested penguins are sometimes seen. The road carries on to trout-filled Lake Paringa where a 15-minute walk passes through native trees such as silver beech, rimu and kahikatea.

Moeraki Boulders Scenic Reserve

C7

The Moeraki Boulders, 78 km (49 miles) north of Dunedin on State Highway 1, have long been the subject of legend and curiosity. Almost perfectly spherical, with a circumference of up to 4 m (13 ft), the grey boulders lie scattered along a 50-m (164-ft) stretch of the beach. They were formed on the sea bed about 60 million years ago as lime salts gradually accumulated around a hard core. Māori legend claims that the boulders were the food baskets or Te Kaihinaki of

←

Following the river path through rainforest near Ship Creek, Haast

→

Mysterious spherical boulders lying on the beach at Moeraki

the Araiteuru canoe, one of the great ancestral canoes that brought Māori to New Zealand from Hawaiki. The canoe was wrecked while on a greenstone gathering trip. It is said that the kumara on board became rough rocks, the food baskets became smooth boulders and the wreck turned into a reef.

It is not unusual to see small black-and-white Hector's dolphins playing in the surf near the boulders. A nearby café and restaurant service the flow of visitors.

The tiny, picturesque fishing village of Moeraki, a former whaling station established in 1836, is on the opposite side of the bay from the reserve.

Arrowtown

B6 49 Buckingham St (in museum); www.arrow town.com

Nestled at the foot of rugged hills 21 km (13 miles) from Queenstown (p242), Arrowtown is the most picturesque and best preserved gold-mining town in the area. In 1862, a small band of local miners,

a good example of vineyards in the area. Gibbston's wine is stored in a cool underground cave, and cellar and vineyard tours, along with wine tastings, are available.

Chinese Village
🏠 2 Buckingham St 📞 (03) 442 1824 🕐 9am–5pm daily

Lakes District Museum and Art Gallery
♿ 🅿️ 🅱️ 🏠 49 Buckingham St 🕐 8:30am–5pm daily
🌐 museumqueenstown.com

Gibbston Valley Winery
♿ 🅿️ 🍽️ 🅱️ 🏠 1820 State Hwy 6 🕐 10am–5pm daily
📅 Most public hols
🌐 gibbstonvalley.com

including William Fox and John O'Callaghan, discovered gold in the Fox River and within weeks they had recovered a staggering 113 kg (250 lb) of the precious metal. Arrowtown's population peaked at more than 7,000 and is one of the few boom towns not to have become a ghost town or been overrun by more modern development. The main street, partly lined with deciduous trees, has many old colonial shops and buildings at one end and, at the other, tiny miners' stone cottages dating back to the 1860s and 1870s.

Chinese miners played a big part in Arrowtown's history after 1865, when they were invited to fill the vacuum created by European miners who had left for the West Coast gold rush. Their legacy is Arrowtown's **Chinese Village** with its preserved and restored stone buildings, including tiny cottages and an outhouse.

The **Lakes District Museum and Art Gallery** chronicles Arrowtown and Queenstown's past, focusing on gold-miners and their innovations. It includes a display on New Zealand's first hydroelectric plant, built in 1886 in what

is now the ghost town of Bullendale. Other displays cover local geology, agriculture, sawmilling and domestic life of the gold rush period. The museum doubles as the town's visitor centre.

Near to Arrowtown is the much-photographed Lake Hayes, which is at its best in autumn. The back road from Arrowtown to Queenstown passes the access road to Coronet Peak, which heads 7 km (4 miles) up to great views from the ski area. **Gibbston Valley Winery** is

 GREAT VIEW
Tobins Track

Head up Tobins Track, the short but steep riverside footpath which runs along the east edge of Arrowtown, starting from the bottom of Ford Street. You may break a sweat, but the view at the top is well worth it: a 360-degree vista of the Wakatipu Basin, Arrowtown's geometric streets and the snowy peaks over Queenstown.

↑ A stunning autumn scene of a miner's cottage concealed among the trees near Arrowtown

The Moeraki Boulders, scattered across Koekohe Beach

⓯
Glenorchy

🅰B6 🛈 Cnr Mull & Oban sts; www.glenorchy-nz.com

Glenorchy is a small township nestled on the northern shores of Lake Wakatipu, 44 km (27 miles) and a spectacular 45-minute drive from Queenstown. The town stands in the shadow of towering snowcapped peaks with names such as Mount Chaos and Mount Head, which rise steeply above the Rees and Dart river valleys.

The town is the transit point for hikers entering the valleys, which are part of the Mount Aspiring National Park (p258), and among New Zealand's Great Walks, the country's ten prestigious premier walking tracks (p32). For the serious hiker, there is a 77-km (48-mile) loop track that connects both valleys via the 1,447-m (4,747-ft) Rees Saddle. Although the walk takes four to five days and requires proper equipment, it is also possible to enjoy a few hours' return walk up either valley.

HIDDEN GEM
Moonshine Museum

In the late 19th century, whiskey was produced (illegally) all over the country. Hokonui moonshine is the most famous and enduring, and is still made today. Buy it at the Moonshine Museum (www.hokonui whiskey.com).

⓰
Gore

🅰B7 🚌 🛈 Cnr Hokonui Drive & Norfolk St; www. gorenz.com

Lying 66 km (41 miles) north of Invercargill (p268), Gore has varied claims to fame: brown trout in the Mataura River and its tributaries (symbolized by a large trout statue in the middle of the town), sheep (the town is surrounded by fertile farmlands and thrives as an agricultural service town), and a reputation as the country music capital of New Zealand (fans come each May for the New Zealand Gold Guitar Awards).

Learn more about the local area at the Gore Visitor Centre, in the Hokonui Heritage Centre. The **Eastern Southland Art Gallery** features major works by New Zealand artists.

Fifteen km (9 miles) west, on State Highway 94, is the **Croydon Aviation Heritage Centre**, which has one of the world's largest collections of vintage de Havilland aircraft and offers flights to visitors.

Eastern Southland Art Gallery

🖐 🏠 14 Hokonui Dr 🕙 10am-4:30pm Mon–Fri, 1–4:30pm Sat & Sun 🕙 1 Jan, Good Fri, 25 & 26 Dec 🌐 esgallery.co.nz

Croydon Aviation Heritage Centre

🖐 🏠 1558 Waimea Hwy, Mandeville 📞 (03) 208 6046 🕙 10am–4pm daily 🕙 25 Dec

---

⓱
Cromwell

🅰B6 🛈 The Mall; www. cromwell.org.nz

Cromwell survived the gold era to become a leading fruit-growing areas. In the 1980s, an electricity generating dam built downriver created nearby Lake Dunstan, flooding much of Cromwell's quaint main street, although

← Hikers taking a rest to admire snowcapped peaks in Glenorchy

several of the more notable buildings were relocated stone by stone to a new site. Cromwell now makes its living from farming, horticulture, viticulture and tourism.

Gold-mining relics in the area include Bendigo, a ghost town 4 km (2 miles) off State Highway 8. By 1866 Bendigo was all but deserted until a rich gold-bearing quartz reef was found, and mined for more than 50 years. The **Goldfields Mining Centre**, just outside Cromwell, offers visitors working exhibitions of gold-mining techniques.

Goldfields Mining Centre
⊘⊛⊜⊕ ⌂Kawarau Gorge, State Hwy 6 ⏰9am–5pm daily 🔤goldfields mining.co.nz

↑ An old steam engine still running at the former railhead terminal of Kingston

⑱
Bluff

🅰B7 🚌Gore St 🚢Stewart Island Wharf 🛈bluff.co.nz

Bluff is the southernmost export port of the country and the departure point for ferries to Stewart Island (p270). It is also the base for fishing fleets that cruise the coasts for fish, crayfish and rock lobsters as well as the unique "Bluff oysters", harvested from March to the end of August.

Bluff has a long history of human occupation, with Māori settlement dating back to the 13th century. The town takes its name from the 265-m-(870-ft-) high Bluff Hill that overlooks Foveaux Strait towards Stewart Island, 32 km (20 miles) away. Beneath the hill is Stirling Point, where there is a much photographed international signpost. Many walks, including the Foveaux Walkway and the Glory Track, pass through native forest. A 45-minute climb up the hill gives panoramic views of the Foveaux Strait and inland areas.

The **Bluff Maritime Museum** traces the history of whaling, oyster harvesting, and the development of the port and the Stewart Island ferry.

Bluff Maritime Museum
⊘⊛⊕ ⌂241 Foreshore Rd 📞(03) 212 7534 ⏰10am–4:30pm daily 🚫Good Fri, Easter Sun, 25 Dec

⑲
Kingston

🅰B6 🅿

For a long time the settlement of Kingston served as a railhead and steamer terminal for travellers heading towards Lake Wakatipu from the south. Now a small town, Kingston is still a lovely stop for visitors, with its beautiful lakeside scenery, picnic spots and cafés.

To the south of Kingston, on State Highway 6, is Lumsden, well known for the trout-filled rivers that cross the countryside surrounding the town. Just before Lumsden, State Highway 94 branches west to Manapouri, Fiordland National Park and Te Anau, and east to the farming area of Gore.

GOLD RUSH

The Otago gold rush began in 1861 with the discovery of gold in Gabriel's Gully. A tent town sprang up and prospectors began to push further inland. Finds in Dunstan and Alexandra followed in 1862, and then the Wakatipu region soon after. Miners braved hot summers, harsh winters and starvation in search of a fortune. In the late 1860s, focus shifted to the West Coast. Gold-mining continued well into the 1900s and the development of modern methods has led to large-scale mining.

← Signpost at Stirling Point, Bluff

A DRIVING TOUR
THE CATLINS

Length 215 km (130 miles) **Stopping-off points** Waipapa Point, Cathedral Caves, Nugget Point Lighthouse
Terrain Paved roads on clifftops

Natural curiosities and beauty combine to make this southeastern corner of the South Island a scenic treasure. Fossilized trees, beautiful waterfalls, golden beaches, high cliffs and secret caves are all part of a unique mix of attractions in this area. A varied coastline of cliffs and surf beaches provides a home to a wide range of wildlife, from rare Hector's dolphins to penguins. The area is made all the more spectacular by the ancient forests which reach almost to the sea.

A picturesque spot, **Waipapa Point** is the site of New Zealand's worst shipping disaster, when the SS Tararua ran aground on a hidden reef in 1881, with the loss of 131 lives.

At **Curio Bay**, the fossilized remains of a 160 million-year-old forest from the Jurassic period can be seen on a rock platform at low tide.

← The lighthouse at Waipapa Point overlooking the site of the SS Tararua shipwreck

The Tautuku River, cascading at the magnificent McLean Falls

Balclutha
FINISH

Clutha River

Romahapa

Molyneux Bay

Kaka Point

Campbell Point

OTAGO

Owaka River

Nugget Point

Owaka

Catlins Lake

Ratanui

Catlins Head

Jack's Blowhole

Tahakapa River

Parakaunui Falls
Parakaunui

Maclennan

White Head

Papaltowai

Tautuku River

Tahakapa Bay

Iruhuka

McLean Falls

Chaslands

Tautuku

Lake Wilkie

Cathedral Caves

Waikawa River

Waikawa

Porpoise Bay

Brothers Point

A 10-minute walk through the forest leads to a viewing platform overlooking attractive **Purakaunui Falls**.

Only a short walk from the road, **Lake Wilkie** *is nestled in a forest with large native trees.*

At **Jack's Blowhole**, *sea water sprays out of the 60-m (197-ft) deep blowhole.*

The lighthouse at **Nugget Point**, *built in 1869, overlooks a series of wave-like pinnacles. The area is home to seals, sea lions, gannets, shags and penguins.*

P a c i f i c

O c e a n

A 30-minute walk leads to impressive **McLean Falls**, *which drops 22 m (72 ft).*

Cathedral Caves *is only accessible at low tide. It can be reached after a 40-minute walk along a beach.*

Little black and white Hector's dolphins are often seen playing in the surf at **Porpoise Bay** *as the waves break along this long, curving beach.*

0 kilometres   10

0 miles   10

N

281

NEED TO KNOW

On the road in Waitangi, Northland

BEFORE
YOU GO

Forward planning is essential to any successful trip. Be prepared for all eventualities by considering the following points before you travel.

AT A GLANCE

CURRENCY
New Zealand Dollar (NZD)

AVERAGE DAILY SPEND

SAVE	SPEND	SPLURGE
$125	$250	$500+

BOTTLED WATER	COFFEE	BEER	DINNER FOR TWO
$2.50	$5	$10	$90

ESSENTIAL MĀORI PHRASES

Hello	Kia ora (informal)
Welcome	Haere mai (more formal)
Goodbye	Ka kite (informal)
New Zealand	Aotearoa

CLIMATE
Temperatures average 20/12°C (68/54°F) in summer (Dec–Feb) and 12/6°C (54/43°F) in winter (Jun–Aug).

ELECTRICITY SUPPLY

Power sockets are type I with three angled pins. Standard voltage is 230/240v.

Passports and Visas

Visa free travel for up to three months is permitted for citizens of the EU, US and Canada; for up to six months for UK citizens; and indefinitely for Australian citizens subject to character requirements. For those planning to stay longer or arriving from other countries, check **Immigration New Zealand** or consult your local New Zealand embassy.
Immigration New Zealand
W immigration.govt.nz

Travel Safety Advice

Visitors can get up-to-date travel safety information from the **UK Foreign and Commonwealth Office**, the **US State Department** and the **Australian Department of Foreign Affairs and Trade**.
Australia
W smartraveller.gov.au
UK
W gov.uk/foreign-travel-advice
US
W travel.state.gov

Customs Information

Strict rules with penalties apply for bringing in undeclared plant, animal or food products. If in doubt, declare it. An individual is permitted to carry the following for personal use:
Tobacco products 50 cigarettes; or 50g of either cigars or smoking tobacco.
Alcohol 4.5 litres of wine or beer; or 3 bottles of spirits or liqueur up to 1.125 litres.
Cash If you plan to enter or leave with NZ$10,000 or more in cash (or the equivalent in other currencies) you must declare it.
Prescription medicine must be declared in its original packaging along with the prescription.

Insurance

It is wise to take out an insurance policy covering theft, loss of belongings, medical problems, cancellations and delays.

Reciprocal health agreements exist for citizens of the UK along with citizens or residents of Australia. Neither agreement provides full medical coverage and benefits are for temporary visitors only.

Ministry of Health
 health.govt.nz

Vaccinations

No inoculations are needed for New Zealand.

Money

Mastercard and Visa are accepted in most shops and restaurants. Contactless payments becoming more widely accepted except on public transport. ATMs are widely available in New Zealand. Handling fees usually apply on international credit and debit cards so check carefully before withdrawing cash.

Booking Accommodation

New Zealand offers a range of accommodation from luxury boutique lodges, through B&Bs and holiday houses, to hostels and hotels. Rooms fill up quickly in the summer months (from December to February) so booking in advance is advisable. Discounts can be picked up outside the peak months. **Tourism New Zealand** lists accommodation to suit any budget.

Tourism New Zealand
 newzealand.com

Travellers with Specific Needs

Travellers with disabilities are generally well catered for in New Zealand. Most tourist sites have wheelchair facilities. Ramps, lifts and adapted toilets are common around towns and at most hotels. However, public transport is not always mobility-friendly, and most towns don't yet have many wheelchair accessible taxis. Guide dogs require relevant documentation and at least ten days quarantine time after arrival, unless visiting from Australia.

Be.Accessible offers support and travel information to all disabled visitors. **Freedom Mobility** specializes in disability-friendly rental vehicles. **Accessible Kiwi Tours** offers tour packages for both mature travellers and those with specific needs.

Accessible Kiwi Tours
 toursnz.com
Be.Accessible
 beaccessible.org.nz
Freedom Mobility
 freedommobility.co.nz

Language

English is the main language in New Zealand, but *te reo* Māori also enjoys official status too. The main anomaly of the Māori language is the pronunciation of the letters Wh, which sound like an English "ph".

Closures

Winter Shops, cafés and tourism retailers in smaller towns often close in winter or have reduced trading days.

Public holidays Shops and museums close by law on Good Friday, Easter Sunday, Christmas and ANZAC day.

PUBLIC HOLIDAYS

1–2 Jan	New Year's
Late Jan	Anniversary Day (Wellington, Auckland and Northland)
Early Feb	Anniversary Day (Buller and Nelson)
6 Feb	Waitangi Day
Early Mar	Anniversary Day (Taranaki)
Late Mar	Anniversary Day (Otago)
Mar/Apr	Good Friday
Mar/Apr	Easter Monday
Late Apr	Anniversary Day (Southland)
25 Apr	ANZAC Day
3 Jun	Queen's Birthday
Late Sep	Anniversary Day (Canterbury South)
Late Oct	Anniversary Day (Hawke's Bay)
28 Oct	Labour Day
Early Nov	Anniversary Day (Marlborough)
Mid Nov	Anniversary Day (Canterbury)
Early Dec	Anniversary Day (Chatham Islands and Westland)
25 Dec	Christmas Day
26 Dec	Boxing Day

GETTING AROUND

Whether you are visiting the cities or heading to the countryside for a rural retreat, discover how best to reach your destination and travel like a pro.

AT A GLANCE

PUBLIC TRANSPORT COSTS

AUCKLAND

$18

Day Pass
Bus, train, most ferries

WELLINGTON

$10

Day Pass
Bus and train

CHRISTCHURCH

$5.50

Per trip
Bus (one free transfer)

SPEED LIMIT

MOTORWAY OR STATE HIGHWAY

100 km/h (60 mph)

URBAN AREAS

50 km/h (30 mph)

SECONDARY ROAD

100 km/h (60 mph)

SCHOOL ZONES (WHEN ACTIVE)

40 km/h (25 mph)

Arriving by Air

Almost all visitors arrive in New Zealand by air. Auckland is the busiest port of entry, followed by Christchurch then Wellington. Some international flights also arrive into Dunedin and Queenstown. Once in New Zealand, air-travel is the quickest and most convenient way to get around. The domestic air network links 26 towns and cities across the two islands and flights across the country are fairly affordable. **Air New Zealand** and **Jetstar** dominate this domestic network; both also offers international flights to a number of destinations. One of the most popular routes for visitors is to fly between Auckland and Queenstown (or vice versa) and rent a car or campervan for the reverse journey.

Air New Zealand
w airnewzealand.co.uk
Jetstar
w jetstar.com

Train Travel

New Zealand's diminishing rail network is operated by a private company, **KiwiRail**, and connects the major cities and a handful of provincial towns only. It's a rather slow way to get around and is used mostly by visitors for its visual appeal. The most stunning of the three routes is the **TranzAlpine**, running daily between Christchurch and Greymouth, cutting dramatically through the Southern Alps via Arthur's Pass and the Otira viaduct (p218). Other routes include the **CoastalPacific**, also on the South Island, connecting Picton and Christchurch; and the three-times weekly **NorthernExplorer** linking Auckland and Wellington in 11 hours.

CoastalPacific
w greatjourneysofnz.co.nz/coastal-pacific
KiwiRail
w kiwirail.co.nz
NorthernExplorer
w greatjourneysofnz.co.nz/northern-explorer
TranzAlpine
w greatjourneysofnz.co.nz/tranzalpine

Airport	Distance to city	Taxi fare	Public transport	Journey time
Auckland	20 km (12.5 miles)	$65	Skybus ($19)	35 mins
Wellington	6 km (3.7 miles)	$30	Airport Flyer ($12)	15 mins
Christchurch	11 km (6.8 miles)	$50	Metro Bus ($8.50)	20 mins
Queenstown	8 km (5 miles)	$45	Orbus ($8)	15 mins

JOURNEY PLANNER

This map plots the main driving routes around New Zealand. Times given reflect the fastest and most direct routes available. The AA website route planner is a great tool for calculating road routes and distances

AA

w aa.co.nz

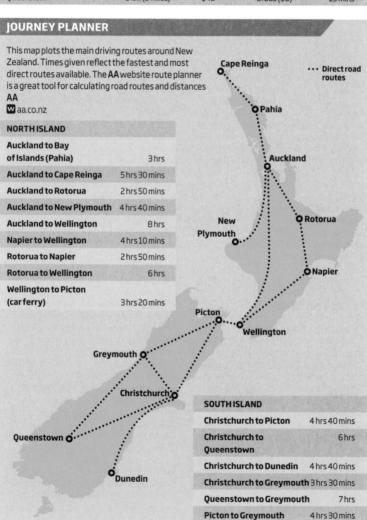

••• Direct road routes

NORTH ISLAND

Auckland to Bay of Islands (Pahia)	3 hrs
Auckland to Cape Reinga	5 hrs 30 mins
Auckland to Rotorua	2 hrs 50 mins
Auckland to New Plymouth	4 hrs 40 mins
Auckland to Wellington	8 hrs
Napier to Wellington	4 hrs 10 mins
Rotorua to Napier	2 hrs 50 mins
Rotorua to Wellington	6 hrs
Wellington to Picton (car ferry)	3 hrs 20 mins

SOUTH ISLAND

Christchurch to Picton	4 hrs 40 mins
Christchurch to Queenstown	6 hrs
Christchurch to Dunedin	4 hrs 40 mins
Christchurch to Greymouth	3 hrs 30 mins
Queenstown to Greymouth	7 hrs
Picton to Greymouth	4 hrs 30 mins

Inter-Island Ferries

The inter-island ferry service connecting the North Island with the South Island travels between Wellington and Picton. The journey takes just over three hours one way. **Bluebridge Cook Strait Ferry** and **Interislander** ferries each travel four to six times daily and carry passengers from around $60 for a seat as well as transporting cars and freight. The trip is one of the most scenic cruises in the world, offering stunning views, but the seas can be choppy.

Bluebridge Cook Strait Ferry
[w] bluebridge.co.nz
Interislander
[w] interislander.co.nz

Long-Distance Bus Travel

Coach travel is a safe, efficient and popular means of transport. Tickets can be purchased as either scheduled one-way trips or as a travel pass with unlimited travel over a set period of time. The main scheduled bus operator is Intercity linking the majority of towns and cities on both North and South Islands. Tourism-focused bus companies **Stray** and **Kiwi Experience** offer a flexible travel pass enabling hop-on hop-off options. Organized coach tours are plentiful, from the adventure-orientated **Haka Tours** to the more formal **Kirra Tours**. These guided options generally include accommodation and meals.

Haka Tours
[w] hakatours.com
Kirra Tours
[w] kirratours.co.nz
Kiwi Experience
[w] kiwiexperience.com
Stray
[w] straytravel.com

Public Transport

In most cities and towns bus services suffice as the only means of public transport. Metro trains can be found in Auckland and Wellington. Ferries operate extensively around Auckland harbour and to a lesser degree in Wellington, Christchurch and on Queenstown Lake. Public transport is managed regionally and independently through council districts. Generally, single journey bus tickets can be purchased with cash from the bus driver. Travel cards are available in the larger cities and offer good discounts over cash fares but usually cost $10 to set-up. Each city has its own card system and these are not transferable.

A single bus journey within Auckland's zone 1 costs $3.50 as a cash fare. The same fare using Auckland's Ad Hop card costs $1.75; an All Day Pass costs $18 and enables travel on any bus or train plus most ferries. In Wellington, a cash fare for travel within zone 1 costs $2.50 and a day pass starts from $10 – this does not include travel on ferries. The city's Wellington's Snapper card offering savings of 25 per cent. In Queenstown, a single cash fare costs $5 and a Go Card fare costs only $2.

Taxis

Taxis are readily available in all towns and cities, operated by private companies and licensed by the New Zealand Transport Association (NZTA). Taxi ranks are found at all airports, in roadside bays around town centres and near shopping malls but are rarely hailed down on the street. Fares can be negotiated but are generally metered by default at $3 per kilometer plus $3.50 flag-fall. Throughout New Zealand, taxi drivers cannot refuse you as a passenger just because you want to go a short distance.

Auckland Co-op Taxis can be found in Auckland along with **Green Cabs**, which also operates in Christchurch, Dunedin, Queenstown and Wellington although **Wellington Combined Taxis** were New Zealand's first CarbonZero certified taxi company.

Uber operates in Auckland, Hamilton, Tauranga, Wellington, Christchurch, Dunedin and Queenstown.

Green Cabs
[w] greencabs.co.nz (to download the app)
Auckland Co-op Taxis
[w] cooptaxi.co.nz
Wellington Combined Taxis
[w] taxis.co.nz

Driving

The quality of New Zealand's roads is excellent. However, there are only a few motorways, and only a painted centre line separates opposing traffic on most roads, with winding stretches common. Many roads also have steep inclines over mountain ranges making journey times much slower than planned.

Check road conditions with the **Department of Conservation** or **AA** before travelling on roads in mountainous and inland areas of the South Island.

AA
[w] aa.co.nz
Department of Conservation
[w] doc.govt.nz

Car Rental

Rental cars are available in all cities and airports: companies like **Avis**, **Budget** and **Hertz** have nationwide networks. Smaller local companies like Ace or Apex may be cheaper and offer greater flexibility. One-way rentals are common, especially heading north to south. Discounted rates are often given for relocation although. Check with your provider if they allow their cars to be taken on the ferry as not all rental companies permit this.

For motorbike hire, try Christchurch-based **South Pacific Motorcycle Tours**. **New Zealand Motorcycle Rentals** has bases in both Christchurch and Auckland.

Avis
w avis.co.nz
Budget
w budget.co.nz
Hertz
w hertz.co.nz
New Zealand Motorcycle Rentals
w nzbike.com
South Pacific Motorcycle Tours
w motorbiketours.co.nz

Parking

Parking in New Zealand poses few problems other than occasional theft when parking in remote car parks. In most town centres there is a combination of free and metered parking, and car parks. Cars must park facing the same direction as the flow of traffic.

Rules of the Road

New Zealanders drive on the left-hand side of the road. Holders of a current driving licence can drive in New Zealand for up to 12 months. Foreign licences must have an authorized English translation if they are not in English.

If you do not hold a driving licence, you will need an International Driving Permit. All drivers must carry their licence when driving. A yellow line down the centre of the road means it is illegal to overtake.

Drink-driving laws are strictly enforced in New Zealand. A driver may be required to give a breath test at any time. The legal blood alcohol level is 50 milligrams of alcohol per 100 millilitres of blood for drivers 20 and over. There is zero-tolerance for drivers under 20.

It is compulsory for the driver and passengers to wear a seat belt, while children under seven years must use an approved car seat. It is illegal to use a handheld mobile phone while driving. Traffic accidents involving injury must be reported to the police within 24 hours.

Campervans and Freedom Camping

Self-drive holidays are hugely popular in New Zealand and renting a campervan is a great way of experiencing the great outdoors. As a minimum, campervans have a refrigerator and gas cooker, plus somewhere to sleep.

The more elaborate have a shower, toilet, microwave, foldaway beds and remote-control blinds.

Sleeping overnight parked in a public road or car park is not permitted unless stated otherwise. Some councils allow overnight stays in designated car parks, often beside beaches, which is known in New Zealand as freedom camping; although campervans entitled to this freedom must have self-contained composting toilets. Check the local authority council websites for detailed information about freedom camping as each council has its own bylaws. Otherwise, fee paying camping grounds can be found all around the country.

One-way drop off fees and high insurance costs add to the rental cost as does travelling in the peak summer months when rentals book out well in advance.

Maui Rentals and budget operator **Jucy** have depots in Auckland, Wellington, Christchurch and Queenstown. **Venture RV** offers a more personalized service from Auckland only.

Jucy
w jucy.co.nz
Maui Rentals
w maui-rentals.com/nz
Venture RV
w venturerv.co.nz

Cycling

Cycling is a great way to get around Auckland, with plenty of protected cycle lanes and shared paths (though you'll need to contend with road traffic when travelling around the central business district). **Auckland Transport** has a cycle route map, making cyclists aware of crash hotspots and indicating the location of bike lockers and parking, cycle-friendly cafés and cycle repair shops.

Hilly Wellington has heaps of mountain bike trails, including Mount Victoria and the Polhill Reserve, both just a few minutes away from the central business district. Central Christchurch is flat, compact and ideal for cycling: **Cycle Hire Christchurch** caters to all visitors on two wheels, from experienced mountain-bikers to those wishing for more sedate city trails.

If you're looking for longer cycle routes in rural locations head to **New Zealand Cycle Trail** or hire bikes from **Natural High** based in Auckland and Christchurch.

Auckland Transport
w at.govt.nz
Cycle Hire Christchurch
w cyclehire-tours.co.nz
Natural High
w naturalhigh.co.nz
New Zealand Cycle Trail
w mudcycles.co.nz

PRACTICAL
INFORMATION

A little local know-how goes a long way in New Zealand. Here you will find all the essential advice and information you will need during your stay.

EMERGENCY NUMBERS

GENERAL EMERGENCY

111

EARTHQUAKE

getthru.govt.nz

TIME ZONE
NZST/NZDT. New Zealand Daylight Time (NZDT) is +1 hr and runs from last Sun in Sep to first Sun in Apr. Chatham Islands (CHAST/CHADT) is NZST/NZDT +45 mins

---

TAP WATER
Unless stated otherwise, tap water in New Zealand is safe to drink.

TIPPING
Tipping in restaurants and hotels is not obligatory, nor expected. Many New Zealanders do not tip taxi drivers, bartenders and porters, although in large cities it is becoming more common to reward good service in a restaurant (about 10 per cent of the bill).

Personal Security

There are few areas in New Zealand that are unsuitable for tourists to visit. However, use common sense to ensure your personal safety. Hitchhiking is not recommended.

If you have anything stolen, report the crime within 24 hours to the nearest police station and take ID with you. Get a copy of the crime report to make an insurance claim.

Contact your embassy if you have your passport stolen, in the event of a serious crime or accident.

Awareness in the Wilderness

Before hiking in the wilderness, let someone know your plans. New Zealand's weather can turn very quickly so be prepared, take precautions, and always have a medical kit and plenty of water with you.

Many hikes include river crossings and water levels can rise rapidly after heavy rain. Don't attempt to wade rivers until the water recedes. The **Department of Conservation** is a useful source of information about national parks.

Hyperthermia is a common risk so always pack adequate clothing. Mobile phone coverage is often limited or non-existent in remote areas. If concerned, ask the local **Department of Conversation** where to rent a Personal Locator Beacon in case of an emergency .
Department of Conservation
W doc.govt.nz
New Zealand Mountain Safety Council
W mountainsafety.org.nz

Health

New Zealand has an extensive network of pharmacies, which offer over-the-counter remedies and prescription drugs. Qualified pharmacists provide free advice but a doctor must write out prescriptions. All major towns have pharmacies that open 9am–5:30pm daily and later on Thursday and Friday.

Urgent medical treatment, including emergency dental care, can be received at hospital A&E

departments or at 24-hour walk-in GP surgeries. For Australian and UK citizens, medical treatment is partly free under government reciprocal agreements. For all other citizens, the cost of all medical treatment is the patient's responsibility so it is important to arrange comprehensive medical insurance before travelling.

Smoking, Alcohol and Drugs

Smoking, including the use of e-cigarettes, is banned in cafés, bars, restaurants, shops and on public transport.

Drinking in public places is permitted unless specifically prohibited. Any person over the age of 18 years may buy and consume alcohol from a licensed premise. Children under 18 years may consume alcohol in a restaurant if accompanied by their legal parent or guardian.

The blood alcohol limit for drivers over the age of 20 is 80mg of alcohol per 100ml of blood (0.08), to 50mg (0.05), equivalent to a small beer or glass of wine. The limit for drivers under the age of 20 is zero.

The use or possession of all class A, B and C drugs is prohibited; laws are strictly enforced.

ID

There is no requirement for visitors to carry ID, but if one is requested by police, or for proof of age, a valid driving licence or passport should be shown.

Marae Customs

Marae are the sacred spaces where the rituals of Māori life are performed. Each family, sub-tribe and tribe has its own marae. Visitors are welcome to stop and look at these marae from the outside, but can only step inside when given permission by one of its members. For tourists this is usually as part of an organized tour group. Never enter a marae during the welcoming ceremony. Shoes should always be removed before entering any wharenui (meeting house).

Mobile Phones and Wi-Fi

Broadband internet coverage extends to most parts of New Zealand, but reception in remote areas can be unreliable.

Post

New Zealand Post operates the country's efficient postal service. **PostShop** branches are generally open from 9am–5pm Mon–Sat. Stamps can be bought at most newsagents and convenience stores. International airmail takes four to ten days to reach most countries.
Postshop
W nzpost.co.nz

Taxes and Refunds

Goods and Services Tax (GST) is charged on most goods and services in New Zealand at a rate of 15 per cent. With the exception of some business hotels, GST is always included in the quoted price..

Discount Cards

Commercial tour companies sell discount deals, such as **Discover Auckland Pass** and **Queenstown Combos,** for most major tourist destinations in New Zealand. The latest discount deals are published in the **Arrival** magazine available for free at all international airports.
Arrival
W arrivalmagazine.co.nz
Discover Auckland Pass
W discoveraucklandpass.co.nz
Queenstown Combos
W combos.co.nz

WEBSITES AND APPS

100% Pure New Zealand
W newzealand.com
   The country's official tourism website
Department of Conservation
W doc.govt.nz
   Great resource for national parks which includes downloadable maps
Hiking New Zealand
W hikingnewzealand.com
   Long-established agent focusing on adventure tours on paths less trodden
New Zealand Self Drive Tours
W newzealandselfdrivetours.co.nz
   Handy for itinerary samples

INDEX

Page numbers in **bold** refer to main entries

Index

ACKNOWLEDGMENTS

The publisher would like to thank the following for their kind permission to reproduce their photographs:

Key: a-above; b-below/bottom; c-centre; f-far; l-left; r-right; t-top

123RF.com:
mohd hairul fiza musa 11t; Rafael Ben-Ari 22cr, 109cr.

4Corners:
Michael Breitung 26-7t; Justin Foulkes 22crb, 71bl, 282-3; Maurizio Rellini 222clb; Massimo Ripani 84b; Francesco Tremolada 218tl; Matt Williams-Ellis 33c, 123clb.

Alamy Stock Photo:
130-1b; AA World Travel Library 131tr, 194b; age fotostock / Colin Monteath 123bc, 258-9b; Alan King engraving 56cb; All Canada Photos / Ron Erwin 279tr; Fabian Andriessen 200-1t; Rafael Ben Ari 40br, 71cl; Rob Arnold 195tr; ASK Images 54cra; Andrew Bain 272bc; Robert Bird 49crb; Russ Bishop 28bl; Gary Blake 105bl; Mark Boulton 173bl; Cephas Picture Library / Jeffery Drewitz 146bl, 223, 259tr, / Mick Rock 202bl; David Crane 253bl; Tim Cuff 8cl, 183crb, 231bl; Park Dale 72bl; Danita Delimont 67br, 256-7t, / Walter Bibikow 85tl, / Lee Foster 10-11b, 205cra; Danita Delimont Creative 183br; Shaun Davey 232-3t; David Tipling Photo Library 236bl; John Dick 130crb; dpa picture alliance 129br, 213tr; John Elk III 149tr; Greg Balfour Evans 58tl, 96t, 139br, 184-5t, 186-7b, 212b, 228tr, 236-7b, 267tl, 270-1t; eye35 74-5t, 120crb; eye35.pix 126bl, 236tr; Constanza Flores 249cra; FLPA 70br; FOR ALAN 55tr; Galaxiid 278b; Robin Galloway 266clb; Thomas Hagenau 20bl; Urmas Haljaste 250-1b; Hemis 66tl, / Franck Guiziou 108cl; Hemis.fr / BIBIKOW Walter 80t, / GUIZIOU Franck 77t, 106b; Julia Hiebaum / BMD Shark Mural, 2013 18tl, 150-1; History and Art Collection 83c; Horizon 86-7t; Dave G. Houser 117tr; imageBROKER 202-3t, 219cb, / Gerhard Zwerger-Schoner 167cra, 265cra, / Moritz Wolf 242-3t, 248-9b, 254bl, 254-5t, 272-3t, 274bl; incamerastock / ICP 157tc; jejim120 265t; Mark A. Johnson 142tr, 176bl; Marion Kaplan 59cb; paul kennedy 70-1t; Joana Kruse 10clb, 257clb; frans lemmens 54crb; Ben Lewis 115br, 255tr; Karel Lorier 55tl; Vincent Lowe 201b; Dennis MacDonald 88bl; Geoff Marshall 175b; Lennart Maschmeyer 41br; mauritius images GmbH 67bc, / ClickAlps 242bl, / Raimund Linke 142-3b, / Walter Bibikow 82tr, 146br, 170-1t; Chris McLennan 37bl, 51b, 115crb; MJ Photography 103b; Theo Moye 127tl; Nathaniel Noir 71cr; Michele Oenbrink 39cla; PACIFIC PRESS 55cr; PBimages 109tl; Daniel Poloha 79b; Lionela Rob 78tl; robertharding 31tr, 217, / Ian Trower 76b, / Jochen Schlenker 275br; Rolf Hicker Photography 80bl, 196b; Krista Rossow 46-7t; Boaz Rottem 20t; Nick Servian 156t; David Shield 141bc; simon margetson travel 188cl; Andy Spain-VIEW 168bl; Jon Sparks 36bl, 76cr; Stockimo / Mathieu B.Morin 47br; Stephen Sykes 75b; Markus Thomenius 167tr; David Tomlinson 48-9t, 204bl; Travel Pictures 24bl, / Dallas and John Heaton 145br; travellinglight 73b, 130tl, 132b, 138t, 144b, 159tr, 216br, 233bc, 262-3t; Reinhold Tscherwitschke 279bc; Uber Bilder 57tl; Zig Urbanski 225tl; David Wall 133tl, 147br, 174tl, 182-3t, 247b, 252-3t, 260br, 260-1t, 264bl, 268br, 268-9t; Greg Ward 247c; Gary Webber 192-3b; Westend61 GmbH / Gaby Wojciech 141tl, / Stefan Schurr 128-9t; Wildscotphotos 172cra; WS Collection 231cr; Robert Wyatt 55clb, 99t; Xinhua Photo / Guo Lei 54clb; ZUMA Press, Inc 129cl.

Anahata Yoga Retreat New Zealand:
50-1t.

ATEED & Matakana Village Farmers' Market:
47c.

Auckland War Memorial Museum - Tāmaki Paenga Hira:
67clb.

AWL Images:
Walter Bibikow 262b; Danita Delimont Stock 22bl, 37cr, 66-7t; Doug Pearson 116t, 230bl; Francesco Vaninetti 38b; Gerhard Zwerger-Schoner 72-3t.

BC Photography:
40-1t, 41cl.

Bridgeman Images:
Alexander Turnbull Library, Wellington, New Zealand 57tr; Look and Learn 56br, 57cla; Mark and Carolyn Blackburn Collection of Polynesian Art 57clb; National Army Museum, London 56t; Ken Welsh 57br.

Courtesy of Auckland Art Gallery Toi o Tāmaki:
68-9b, 69tl, 69tr, 69cra.

Depositphotos Inc:
mvaligursky 224b.

Dorling Kindersley:
Gerald Lopez 107br.

Dreamstime.com:
Annaorl 189tr; Rafael Ben Ari 11crb, 28cr, 89tl, 134tl; Lukas Bischoff 115clb; Bobhilscher 11br; Cbork7 32br; Henner Damke 28crb; Deyan Denchev 215tr; Elen33 4; Hellen8 246t; Junofish 116bl; Radek Křenek 193tl; Keng Po Leung 273br; Bundit Minramun 13br; Christian Mueringer 215cra; Mohd Nadly Aizat Mohd Nudri 164t; Julian Peters 280bl; Roussien 183bl; Rudi1976 16, 62-3; Rusel1981 19bl, 214bl, 238-9; Petr Švec 10ca, 193br, 231t; Jordan Tan 167tl; Tpeskin 259cla; Travelling-light 154t, 215ca; Rudmer Zwerver 191cr.

Getty Images:
500Px Plus / Philip Armitage 103tr; AFP / Michael Bradley 54cla; Anadolu Agency / Rasit Aydogan 58-9t; Apexphotos 274-5t; Anthony Au-Yeung 52-3t; Boy_Anupong 43crb; Jesper Bülow 19t, 24crb, 206-7; David Cannon 53b; chrisadam 198-9; Matteo Colombo 6-7, 18br, 49cla, 119tl, 122, 178-9; Corbis / Tim Clayton 102t; DEA / BIBLIOTECA AMBROSIANA 58clb; Danita Delimont 184cr; EyeEm / Anneloes Beekman 36-7t, / George Clifford 26-7ca, / Laetizia Haessig 12t; Fairfax Media 59br; Simon Fergusson 234bl; Anna Gorin 172tr; Hagen Hopkins 123cra; IWM 58br; Jessica Page Photo 189cra; Kerry Kissane 229b; Reyaz Limalia 197cr; Dianne Manson 54cl; MB Photography / Moment Open 176-7t; Verity E. Milligan 197t; Doug Pearson 33br, 60-1; Douglas Pearson 22t; Hannah Peters 59cr; Marco Simoni 35cla; Stocktrek Images / Richard Roscoe 119br; Tim Clayton - Corbis 140b; ullstein bild Dtl. 58cla.

iStockphoto.com:
alex_tok 235cla; apsimo1 98tr; arielmaor 190br; AsianDream 12-3b; chameleonseye 26cla; ChristianB 188-9b; dbabbage 253bc; dchadwick 193cra; denizunlusu 17t, 39br, 81br, 82-3b, 90-1, 97cl, 98b;

Main Contributers Rachel Mills, Paul Whitfield,
Gerard Hindmarsh, Ian Osborn, Doug Sager,
Helen Corrigan, Roef Hopman, Gerard Hutching,
Rebecca Macfie, Geoff Mercer, Simon Noble,
Peter Smith, Michael Ward, Mark Wright

Senior Editor Ankita Awasthi Tröger

Senior Designer Owen Bennett

Project Editor Lucy Sienkowska

Project Art Editors Dan Bailey,
Stuti Tiwari Bhatia, Bharti Karakoti,
Ankita Sharma, Hansa Babra, Rashika Kachroo,
Kanika Kalra, Priyanka Thakur

Factchecker Doug Sager

Editors Louise Abbott, Rebecca Flynn,
Rachel Laidler, Lucy Sara-Kelly,
Jackie Staddon, Lauren Whybrow

Proofreader Ben Davies

Indexer Hilary Bird

Senior Picture Researcher Ellen Root

Picture Research Sumita Khatwani,
Harriet Whitaker

Illustrators Yeap Kok Chien,
Tan Hong Yew, Denis Chai Kah Yune

Senior Cartographic Editor James Macdonald

Cartography Subhashree Bharati,
Simonetta Giori, Reetu Pandey

Jacket Designers Bess Daly,
Maxine Pedliham

Jacket Picture Research Susie Watters

Senior DTP Designer Jason Little

DTP Neeraj Bhatia, George Nimmo,
Azeem Siddiqui

Senior Producer Stephanie McConnell

Managing Editor Hollie Teague

Art Director Maxine Pedliham

Publishing Director Georgina Dee

MIX
Paper from
responsible sources
FSC
www.fsc.org FSC™ C018179

**The information in this
DK Eyewitness Travel Guide is checked regularly.**
Every effort has been made to ensure that this book
is as up-to-date as possible at the time of going to
press. Some details, however, such as telephone
numbers, opening hours, prices, gallery hanging
arrangements and travel information, are liable to
change. The publishers cannot accept responsibility
for any consequences arising from the use of this
book, nor for any material on third party websites,
and cannot guarantee that any website address
in this book will be a suitable source of travel
information. We value the views and suggestions
of our readers very highly. Please write to: Publisher,
DK Eyewitness Travel Guides, Dorling Kindersley,
80 Strand, London, WC2R 0RL, UK, or email:
travelguides@dk.com

First edition 2001

Published in Great Britain by Dorling Kindersley Limited,
80 Strand, London, WC2R 0RL

Published in the United States by DK Publishing,
1450 Broadway, Suite 801, New York, NY 10018

Copyright © 2001, 2019 Dorling Kindersley Limited
A Penguin Random House Company
19 20 21 22 10 9 8 7 6 5 4 3 2 1

A CIP catalog record for this book
is available from the British Library.

A catalog record for this book is available
from the Library of Congress.

ISSN: 1542 1554
ISBN: 978 0 2413 6541 0

Printed and bound in China.

www.dk.com